Hoyt Street

Hoyt Street

MEMORIES OF A CHICANA CHILDHOOD

Mary Helen Ponce

Anchor Books
Doubleday
New York London Toronto Sydney Auckland

AN ANCHOR BOOK

PUBLISHED BY DOUBLEDAY

a division of Bantam Doubleday Dell Publishing Group, Inc.

1540 Broadway, New York, New York 10036

ANCHOR BOOKS, DOUBLEDAY, and the portrayal of an anchor
are trademarks of Doubleday, a division of Bantam Doubleday
Dell Publishing Group, Inc.

Hoyt Street was originally published in hardcover by the
University of New Mexico Press in 1993.
The Anchor Books edition is published by arrangement with the
University of New Mexico Press.

Some names have been changed in this book to protect
the privacy of individuals.

Library of Congress Cataloging-in-Publication Data
Ponce, Mary Helen.
Hoyt Street : memories of a Chicana childhood / Mary Helen Ponce.
p. cm.
1. Ponce, Mary Helen—Homes and haunts—California—Los Angeles.
2. Mexican Americans—California—Los Angeles—Social life and customs.
3. Mexican American women—California—Los Angeles—Biography.
4. Women novelists, American—20th century—Biography.
5. Pacoima (Los Angeles, Calif.)—Biography.   6. Ponce, Mary Helen—
Biography—Youth.   I. Title.
PS3566.0586Z467   1995
813'.54—dc20
[B]   94-36505
CIP

ISBN 0-385-47547-0
Copyright © 1993 by the University of New Mexico Press

1   3   5   7   9   10   8   6   4   2

Dedicatoria

To the memory of my parents:
Tranquilino R. Ponce and Vicenta Solís,
whose love and care nurtured and sustained me
and whose ethics continue to mold my life.

For my brothers and sisters whom I love very much.

For my children Joseph, Ana, Mark, and Ralph:
That thou mayest walk in the way of
good men, and keep the paths of
the righteous. Proverbs 2:20

Contents

Note from the Author

The memory is a mysterious—and powerful—thing. It forgets what we want most to remember, and retains what we often wish to forget. We take from it what we need.

Hoyt Street: An Autobiography began as a research paper for a folklore seminar. As an anthropology/Chicano studies major at California State University Northridge (1974–1980), I compared Easter observances in three generations: grandparents, parents, and my own immediate family. In the process of recollecting specifics about Holy Week, about what we did, what we ate, I began to recall other events—the *fun* things that took place in our town of Pacoima, California: el circo, las jamaicas, las misiones, las vistas. Each one was a potential cuento.

My original plan once I decided this collection of stories could be a book was to write anecdotes of Mexican-American culture in general, but I found myself writing of family and friends. Of Pacoima. I later realized I was writing a social history of sorts.

"Why write of Pacoima?" people frequently asked. "That place [they never referred to it as a town] is infested with gangs and drugs." I have no set answer, only that I had a very happy childhood. So I persisted to write of what a friend calls my "Macondo," a reference to Gabriel García Márquez's mythical town.

This work was written de memoria. I thought of researching Pacoima history, the founding of the town, origins of street names, and so forth, but decided against it. Often my siblings corrected a fact or two, but for the most part, I wrote what I remember. The end result is an autobiography, or life story, but also a communal history.

Although not all the events stand out as clear as, for example, el ofrecimiento de las flores, each experience recounted here actually happened. Names, characteristics, and physical descriptions of people have changed to avoid embarrassing or hurting anyone. In 1988 I sent "Father Mueller" a copy of "Holy Week." He then called to say how delighted he was to know I was writing a book. He wanted me to use his real name, but I declined.

For those who wonder why I feel *my* life story merits discussion, let alone publication, let me say that Mexican-Americans need to tell their side of the story in order to put to rest negative stereotypes. The majority of Mejicanos who lived in Pacoima during the 1920s to the 1950s (when some homes were torn down to build the "projects") were hard-working, decent, and honorable. It is for them that I write.

I hope that this work will encourage other Mexican-Americans/Chicanos to write their historias. It is through the common experience that we learn about a society.

Finally, to my editor Andrea Otañez, who saw the value of this work, un abrazo.

November 15, 1992
Santa Barbara, California

INNOCENCE

13011 Hoyt Street

The town of Pacoima lay to the northeast of Los Angeles, about three miles south of the city of San Fernando. The blue-grey San Gabriel Mountains rose toward the east; toward the west other small towns dotted the area. Farther west lay the blue Pacific and the rest of the world. The barrio, as I knew it, extended from San Fernando Road to Glenoaks Boulevard on the east and from Filmore and Pierce streets on the north. We lived in the shadow of Los Angeles, twenty odd miles to the south.

Most of the townspeople were Mexican immigrants, as were my parents, who had moved to Pacoima in the 1920s. Across the tracks lived the white folks, many of them Okies. There were few blacks in the area up until the early fifties, when the Joe Louis housing tract near Glenoaks Boulevard allowed black ex-GIs to buy there.

Many men in the barrio worked in agriculture, en el fil, weeding, pruning, or watering various crops. Others worked as troqueros, as did Rocky, my father's compadre, who each fall drove workers in his truck to the walnut orchards of Camarillo. Men who owned their own trucks worked for themselves. They lugged fertilizer from poultry farms to nearby ranches or trucked produce into Los Angeles. Still others took the bus to the union hall in San Fernando, where they hired out as "casual laborers" or found work in the packinghouse in that same town. A neighbor, el Señor Flores, owned a flower nursery; Don Jesús, a kind, rotund man, had his own grocery store. For the most part men either hired out as unskilled laborers or worked for themselves, as did my father, who sold used wood from our backyard.

Pacoima streets were unpaved, full of holes and rocks. During a rain the rich, brown mud clung to our shoes. Van Nuys Boulevard, the main street, was paved and lit with lamps that burned till late at night; that was where most stores and businesses were located. The boulevard cut through the middle of the barrio, then continued west to Van Nuys, North Hollywood, and other towns.

San Fernando Road, which ran north and south, was the main artery to Los Angeles; it connected Pacoima with Roscoe (later renamed Sun Valley), Burbank, and Glendale, then curved west to the Hill Street overpass that led to downtown Los Angeles, called "Elay" or "Los" by the locals. To the north this highway went over the mountains to become Highway 99. It cut through the town of Gorman, a truckers' stop with a huge restaurant and one motel, and on to the "Grapevine," a long, lonely section constantly filled with huge trucks. Once past the highest mountain peak, the road no longer curved but shot into the fertile San Joaquin Valley in an endless straight line.

The barrio was laid out like a huge square. The streets ran up and down with nary a curve or dead end. Streets that ran north and south started at Filmore Street and came to a screeching halt en la Pierce, where the Pacoima airport, known as Whiteman Airport, stood. The airstrip was more like a weed-infested field with cracked pavement. Small shedlike buildings stood at one end. At one time this area was an empty space where students playing hookey from school would hide out. During Easter vacation and in the summer, kids used the unpaved road along the airport as a shortcut to the nearby hills that dipped and rolled toward Hansen Dam. In spring they came alive with scrub bushes and other plants, none of which grew very tall. From the highest peak you could see Guardian Angel Church and the Pacoima General Store, the two tallest buildings in town. When later a chain link fence and gates with padlocks went up, hiking to the Pacoima hills became less fun.

Homes in Pacas, as we called Pacoima, were modest, ranging from a one-room shack where people slept in the "front room," to the more elegant homes such as Rocky's, which boasted an ample living room, a bathroom with tile and chrome faucets, and a separate bedroom for each child. On our street, and in the immediate neighborhood, houses were one story high except for that of the Torres family; theirs had upstairs bedrooms with tall windows. In the next block was the quasi-Victorian structure belonging to Doña Mercedes. It sat back from the street, as if ashamed to be seen next to older, shabbier homes.

On Hoyt Street the houses were neither fancy nor ugly, but like the houses of poor folks everywhere. While some were constructed of stucco, the majority were of wood, madera. Wood was plentiful and cheaper than cement, so wood it was. The houses, while not uniform, had some similarities: a window on each side and a door smack in the middle. Others appeared lopsided because of the many additions tacked on as a family grew. Still others were of different types of wood bought for price and not appearance. From afar it was easy to spot the short boards nailed next to the smooth planks of polished wood bought at the lumberyard. People were innovative, too, and sometimes built houses of rock and cement.

On Filmore Street sat two stone houses made of the white and gray rocks that filled the Pacoima Wash, a small stream to the east. The sturdy-looking homes, so unlike any others in the barrio, were fascinating. Unlike Rapunzel's castle, they were not surrounded by trees, nor did they have a large tower. Still they were quaint, like the stone huts in the dark German forests where Hansel and Gretel lived. Along the front were large windows embedded in the round stones, with a wooden door in the middle. One rock house even had a fireplace, an anomaly in our town, where few homes even had a spacious living room.

Not all homes had electricity or indoor plumbing. Many casitas on Hoyt Street still had an outhouse somewhere in the back, hidden behind a nopalera or standing blatantly in the middle of the yard. Once the electrical lines reached Van Nuys Boulevard, and local residents were allowed to connect, my father was among the first to do so. After he wired our house, he did that of Doña Luisa, our adopted grandmother, who lived next door. She, like others in our town, continued to use la lámpara de petroleo, which had a long wick and gave only a faint light. She felt that electricity was terribly expensive, and insisted that every time el foco was turned on, it cost a penny! Each time I yanked the string hanging from the light bulb on the ceiling, Doña Luisa pursed her thin lips and reminded me I was wasting electricity—and pennies. She then lit the kerosene lamp and set it next to the trunk alongside her bed.

Mejicanos in our town took pride in their homes and, when money allowed, repaired a dilapidated roof or painted their casitas a bright color. They took special pride in having a yard full of plants and flowers, and these grew well in the rich California soil. La familia Santos had a pretty front yard with bright red geraniums growing in old cans and fruit trees along the side. Like other women in our street, each morning Mrs. Santos raked the front yard, sprinkled water on it to keep the dust down, then trimmed her geraniums. In the Lopez family's yarda was a birdbath made of crude cement, rocks, and pipes. It was pretty and the pride of Mr. Lopez, who had designed and made it himself. People said he was un artista. Each day the birdbath was filled with clean water for the many birds that congregated there. In other gardens, bird cages bought at the five and dime in San Fernando hung from the various trees. Still other casitas sported a porch swing where, on warm summer evenings, adults gossiped or told stories of la llorona to pesky children, the soft Spanish words drifting down Hoyt Street and dissolving into the night. While the homes on our street were different in color, shape, and size, they had one thing in common: each had a junk pile somewhere in the back yard.

El yonque was important for folks who were short on money but full of ingenuity. The junk pile held the necessary parts to wire a car together or replace rusted pipes, and it helped keep folks from spending hard-earned cash at the hardware store in town. The Morenos had not one but several junk piles in their huge yard. On one side la Señora Moreno grew flowers and vegetables. On the other were two piles of junk that included automobile parts: engines, carburetors, dented fenders, old batteries, and flat tires. Except for la familia Soto, whose backyard held only a crude table and benches and a row of apricot trees, the junk pile was an accepted part of a Mexican household.

My father, too, clung to junk, a thing that bothered my mother, who functioned best in a clean and orderly household. The yonque, or clutter as I thought of it, was of value to my father as it was to other pobres. Pipes, rusty tin tubs, old tires, wood, wire, and car radios lay scattered here and there. My father was certain that at some point, good use could be made of the stuff. Neighbors and friends would come by for a piece of pipe, a strip of tar paper, or some two-by-fours, all from the junk pile and all freely given to someone in need.

People in Pacoima, I often thought, needed more space than did those in upwardly mobile San Fernando, where homes had sidewalks and paved streets, but sat close together, as if afraid to breathe too much of their neighbor's air. On Hoyt Street most residents had once lived in Mexican ranchitos and had a greater need for land. In the large double lots, they planted fruit trees, vegetable and flower gardens, and assorted hierbas that also grew in Mexico. The Garcias had a nopalera, a wall of prickly pear cactus in the back that served two purposes: it was a fence that kept out errant dogs and kids, and it also provided food. The succulent cactus, nopalitos, were popular during Lent along with deep-fried camarones, shrimp; the prickly pear fruits, or tunas, fell off when ripe and were quickly gobbled up.

We lived at 13011 Hoyt Street, a block from church and the Pacoima General Store (called la tienda blanca), and two blocks from Pacoima Elementary School. Our house sat in the middle of a double lot. The front door, which was rarely used, faced Hoyt Street. The back gate led to the alley and an open field, el llano, which faced Van Nuys Boulevard. To our right lived Doña Luisa. Next to her, in a house that extended the length of the lot, lived the Morenos. To our left was a roomy yellow house with a big garage, occupied on and off by different families. I remember best the Montalvos, a handsome family with light hair and eyes; their daughter Margarita was close to my age.

Our house was built by my father when he and my mother and their three older children moved from Ventura to the San Fernando Valley, sometime in the 1920s. Originally our house had three rooms: a kitchen and two bedrooms. The large kitchen extended the length of the house. Later, as his family grew, my father added on to the house, with some interesting results—our kitchen had a window that opened into the living room! The kitchen floor was covered with dark green linoleum. On one wall was el trastero, the pantry, where flour, sugar, and beans were stored. On the other wall were two large cabinets in which sat assorted dishes and the blue-willow plates that came in a soap box and were used for company. A double sink faced the west wall, and in one corner was the white gas stove with a big griddle. A large window hung with dotted-swiss curtains trimmed in rickrack faced the driveway and framed a huge eucalyptus tree. In the summer my sisters moved the kitchen table next to the window; from there we looked out at the wild birds in the tree branches. In the summer too, my sisters served our dinner outdoors on the cement patio with the roof of palm fronds that my father had also built.

My first memories are of the kitchen with the window, the small room where my parents slept, and the large living room with a bed where my sisters slept. Nora, the eldest of the bunch, was said to have "good taste." She kept after my father until he put up a wall to separate their bed from the living room. Although the bed against the wall was covered with a pretty bedspread bought at J.C. Penney, Nora did not care to have her friends see a bed en la sala. That was much too ranchero, too low class for her taste. She never could do anything about the kitchen window in the living room, though.

As we grew older, my father built los cuartitos. The men's rooms, as we called them, were separate from the main house, with windows that looked out on the front and back yards, and had room for several beds. My two older brothers slept there. Later, when my mother had her own bedroom, my father too slept there. Josey, the youngest, slept in my mother's room. From the age of three, I slept with Doña Luisa. Later my uncles, who emigrated as braceros, also slept in the men's rooms. As was the custom, they first stayed with a close relative, in this case my father. Much later their sons laid claim to the beds used earlier by their fathers.

My friends found it strange that my father slept in the cuartitos and my mother in her room; I thought it perfectly natural, until I grew older and learned otherwise. After my mother gave birth to my younger brother, Josey (at age forty or so), she decided that in order not to have more children, she and my father should sleep apart. She often said (a bit smugly, I thought) that *her* mother's children were born three years apart, and that when my grandmother turned forty (after giving birth to thirteen children) she and my grandfather slept apart. This ended the possibility of continual pregnancies, considered muy ranchero even out on the ranch. On our street women often grew sick and worn out from having children year after year; they would die, leaving behind large, motherless families. Having separate beds was, for most couples, the prudent thing to do. No one else thought otherwise, except perhaps my father.

I often think my father agreed to sleep in the men's rooms because by the time my mother was forty, she had already given birth to eleven children and was often sick. She never recovered from the death of Rosalie, her firstborn, who died when I was an infant, nor from that of Socorro, who died in Ventura. The death of Rito, my older brother, depressed her more. Still my father, a healthy man in his forties, often sneaked into my mother's bedroom. I once saw him near her bed. I heard him say the word "tetas," but did not understand this Spanish word. When I lingered to talk with my mother, he quickly left the room. My mother, who was taking her afternoon nap, appeared relieved.

By the time I was in school, my father had remodeled our house more than once. He drew up a simple plan, then hired two carpenters to help him build the new additions. Down came the embarrassing kitchen window and up went a bedroom. The old front room became two bedrooms and a hall. A sunny living room with large, pretty windows that looked out on the lawn and picket fence was added with money earned en la nuez, when our family harvested walnuts in Camarillo. A maroon sofa and stuffed chair sat against one wall. Two scatter rugs lay on the living-room floor. Later we had a coffee table, lamps, and a small bookcase. We were not allowed in la sala, but sneaked in there anyway, being careful not to slide on the rugs. The front door led to a half-porch that faced the street; this was swept clean each morning. Last of all, our house, formerly a sick green, was painted a creamy white. Sometimes, though, I thought I detected the slimy green trying to seep through.

As our house grew, so did our extended family of relatives who arrived from Mexico to find work. Andrés, a handsome cousin with blue-green eyes, and José, or Joe as he was soon called, stayed with us. Still later two brothers, also cousins, moved into the men's rooms. When they first came they spoke only Spanish and would answer "what?" to any and all questions; we nicknamed them "Los Whats." Although they learned to speak English within a year, we still called them "Los Whats."

The kitchen was the heart of our home, the place where my mother cooked, ironed, and bathed her many children. Everyone congregated there to eat, and when relatives visited, they sat there as my mother bustled around the stove. A huge wooden table built by my father dominated the room. Against the wall sat a large bench where we, the youngest children, sat to eat. In our family it was the custom to wait until everyone finished eating before leaving the table. Josey and I were forced to sit while our elders finished supper. Often we tired of the wait (our father chewed so slow) and taking care not to pass within reach of our older sister Trina's foot, we slid from the bench. But Trina was quick and often sent us flying with a swift kick.

"Trina kicked me."

"Liar."

"Owwwwwwww!"

Josey and I would come out wailing and rubbing a bruised elbow; we often bumped heads too! In her moderate voice my mother would caution us not to fight. My father would say nothing, merely fixing us with a stare that ended all arguments.

In our backyard grew an abundance of trees: pepper, eucalyptus, walnut, and a small fig tree, called la higuera, that never gave fruit. The two eucalyptus trees grew next to the garage and were the tallest trees in the yard. They had come with the property; my father built around them. Their branches appeared to reach to the sky and were much too high for us to climb. They gave some shade and in fall shed fragrant gray leaves. One year my father put one of the branches to good use; he hung a thick rope with a tire on it to make a swing. Later he built a wooden seat from pieces of lumber from the wood pile. The seat was wide enough for two, and only we youngest kids got to swing in it. The rest were too old—and heavy. On summer days Josey and I climbed on the swing, kicked to get going, pumped hard, then drifted to and fro. It was fun to lean back and gaze at the blue California sky between the branches.

In the front yard, to the left of the driveway, grew los pirules. The two pepper trees grew close together and were my favorite trees. My father, who had good instincts about what made us children happy, nailed a wide board across the two trees to make a bench. My friends and I sat there all the time, because it was close to the street. Later mi papá fastened wide boards across the branches to make something similar to a tree house. It was here, among the pungent branches thick with red berries, that Josey and I would whisper to each other, while below us Doña Luisa, who helped our mother with our care, pretended not to know where we had disappeared to.

From the treehouse Josey and I had fun throwing rocks at cars and dogs. First we stashed small pebbles on the boards, then we picked a target. As a car went past, we aimed for the rear fender. When we heard a *ping,* we scampered to the top branches, afraid the driver might spot us and turn around. On hot summer days we sat atop the boards, playing until a car came by. We planted our feet, let fly with the rocks, then disappeared inside the trees.

Facing the street was a garden with rambling roses and yellow and white daisies. In spring and summer, Shasta daisies, called margaritas, bloomed next to healthy weeds. In the middle of the lawn, toward the right, grew an orange tree with glossy green leaves; in the summer the intoxicating, sweet smell of orange blossoms attracted hordes of bees, but it never gave oranges. Near the front porch was una rosa de castilla, a bush of roses with velvet petals and huge thorns. A wisteria vine grew alongside my mother's bedroom window; its branches, like tentacles, reached to the corner, where they met the rambling roses growing on the opposite wall.

To the right of the front yard, facing Doña Luisa's house, my father planted a variety of trees. First came the willow tree bought home by my brother Norbert. It was beautiful and exotic but soon died, leaving a huge hole that was filled by a stumpy palm tree that gave little shade. I hated this tree, although I knew palm trees did well in California.

Close to Doña Luisa's yard, my father planted tomatoes and chiles. Later either he or my mother planted sweet peas, called chícharos, with glossy leaves similar to those of tomato vines. The flowers were a bright pink, delicate, but when cut, never lasted long. At one time my father planted peanuts given him by my Uncle Nasario, but like the willow tree, they too died. I was not surprized, because Uncle Nasario, a handsome, pompous man, claimed only he knew how to cultivate peanuts.

Toward the rear of the house, near Doña Luisa's property, were the clotheslines that separated our two yards. These were in addition to those facing the alley, which because of the eucalyptus trees were always in the shade. Near the cement pole that held the lines grew a thick-trunked walnut tree where I hid out when in trouble. Next to it stood the solitary fig tree with a large white trunk and round holes that resembled eyes. When at night I went to the outhouse, I avoided looking at that tree.

Beneath the walnut tree and next to the fig tree were the stacks of used lumber my father sold to make a living. Josey and I liked to play atop the wood. It was an easy climb to the top of the boards but another thing to get safely down the woodpile, because the wood shifted under our weight. More than once Josey and I got our feet caught between the boards and our knees scratched by nails; however, no one thought of rushing us to a doctor for a shot. Either our parents did not know the dangers of a rusty nail, or they could not afford the doctor. My mother or Doña Luisa would put alcohol on cuts; we would put mud, lodo, on all insect bites. Somehow we survived.

In the back, next to the eucalyptus trees, was the garage. Here my father and older brothers Berney and Norbert piled old bike and automobile tires; rubbery tubes hung along the walls. On a shelf sat coffee cans chock full of nails, nuts, and bolts. Below this was a vise and assorted pliers and ball peen hammers. A lone light bulb hung from the middle of the ceiling. Near the door was the leather punching bag with which Berney and Norbert worked out. Each evening Norbert, the huskier of the two, used both the punching bag and barbells, following the instructions sent him by Charles Atlas, who guaranteed that Norbert need not be a ninety-nine-pound weakling. Norbert knew that if he exercized each day he would become muscular. Once finished with the barbells and weights, Norbert went another round with the punching bag. I liked to watch him work out, amazed at the perfect rhythm of the punches: *ba boom, boom, boom. Ba boom, boom, boom.* Norbert danced on his feet, moving around the punching bag with ease, leaning in and out with each punch. *Boom, ba-boom, boom, boom.* He rarely varied from this pattern. He once offered to teach me how to hit a "right to the jaw," just like Joe Louis, but I was too clumsy. He grew bored with my efforts and politely told me to go back to my dolls.

In the back, near the alley, was the outhouse made of old, old wood with a rickety door and two seats, or holes. I hated to use it, scared stiff of falling into the bigger hole. I refused to use Doña Luisa's

outhouse, as it was too close to the alley, and was relieved when my
father, who wanted the best for his family, built our first bathroom.
He left the outhouse for emergencies. Although I had to wait my turn
for the bathroom, I refused to use el excuzado after that.

My father had a thing about fences. We had many different ones!
One year I counted eight different fences on our property. A picket
fence on cement faced Hoyt Street. The wall facing the Montalvos'
was made of chicken wire, and cement slabs on a cement founda-
tion. Alongside the men's rooms was a wooden fence that connected
with the garage. The back fence next to the alley was made of wood
overgrown with cactus. The side fence behind which the goats and
chickens were kept was part of the cactus wall. No fence was to
be found between Doña Luisa's house and ours, only my mother's
flowers and my father's chiles and tomatoes. Doña Luisa, though
not a blood relative, was considered family; *entre familia* there was
no need for fences.

My father's pride and joy was the white picket fence. It faced
Hoyt Street and was his original design, or so he liked to think. The
wooden spikes were set in cement; the bottom half was of wood and
cement slabs set in concrete. Each picket was exactly the same size;
each was nailed to a thin crosspiece. When finished it was sanded
and then painted white. We were not allowed to hang onto this fence,
which was the only one of its kind on our street. I hated el cerco that
faced the Montalvos; it looked like a huge cement wall and was out
of place next to the pretty picket fence. But this too was my father's
original design.

On the summer day on which he poured the concrete for this wall,
my father allowed Josey and me to scratch our names on the still-
wet cement. Josey, acting like the brat he was, insisted on putting his
handprint on the cement too! When I tried to do the same he pushed
me; I fell on the cement, and left two knee holes on the smooth finish! My father became angry, but just for a minute. After that he no
longer let Josey and me help him but told us to go play on the tree
swing. For years I could still make out the names on the wall. Josey.
Mary Helen. June, 1945.

While studying the many fences I often thought that perhaps my
father's family had not owned property in Mexico. It was important
for him to fence, to secure the right of ownership. Or perhaps, un-

known to us, my father was an artist who liked to express himself in works of cement, wire, and wood. Probably he liked to keep busy. Like most men of his generation, my father hated to be de oquis, with nothing to do.

Josey and I were always alert for the sound of cement being mixed in the big wheelbarrow. This meant a new wall would soon go up at 13011 Hoyt Street, where we might record our names for posterity.

La Familia

What I most remember about my family was how different yet alike we all were. We ranged from tall to short, dark to light. And although I had no way of knowing what my first three siblings, Rosalía, Socorro, and Rito, had really looked like, I had four sisters and three brothers whom in some way I resembled.

Unlike those of our friends who looked Spanish, with light hair and green eyes, we looked like what we were: Mejicanos, with the coloring found among most people in Mexico. Yet our skin tones ranged from Nora's pale ivory to Ronnie's light olive and on down to Joey's dark olive. My skin was in between that of Ronnie and Elizabet: a medium olive with a yellow tinge.

Our eyes were mostly dark but all shaped differently. Nora's brown eyes were set far apart; in between was a pretty nose. Berney's hazel-green eyes turned a dark brown when he was angry. Elizabet had friendly brown eyes that twinkled when she smiled, which was often. Ronnie's eyes were a chocolate-brown rimmed in black and fringed with thick eyelashes. Trina's wide brown eyes were framed by black eyebrows that resembled birds' wings. My own eyes were neither as wide as Trina's nor as brown as Ronnie's. Josey had huge brown eyes that quickly filled with tears when he did not get his way.

We were tall, short, and in between. Nora, the eldest, was also the tallest of the girls. Elizabet and Ronnie were short-waisted (like our mother) and somewhat petite. Berney was tall and slender; Norbert was of medium height, with a muscular torso. Trina was tall and thin; I was tall and hefty. Josey was perfect.

Our handwriting was so similar! Berney, Norbert, and Josey all wrote the same squiggly letters, except that Norbert never misspelled a word. Nora's script was round, flowing, and graceful. Elizabet wrote in a delicate scrawl that was so like Nora's, except her *L*'s weren't as round. Ronnie wrote almost like Elizabet and Nora, so that it was difficult for me to tell their notes apart. Trina's letters slanted to the right in graceful, round loops. Her *P* was fat, with a fancy cirlicue at the beginning; she dotted her *i*'s with a round, fat mark.

I learned to write using the Palmer method and slanted my letters to the right. Often they dropped off the page. I printed in block letters, but that took too long. Reluctantly I returned to cursive writing, intent on developing a distinctive style. But when I wasn't concentrating, I wrote just like my sisters.

Not only did the women in my family write alike, we all spoke in the same moderate voice. Just as my parents rarely raised their voices, I only learned to shout at Josey. Nora, a bit remote, never chatted, but talked only when she had to. Elizabet spoke in clear, concise paragraphs, while Berney would mumble his responses. Ronnie's voice was high and soft, like a dove cooing. She also whistled, a thing that irritated my brothers, who felt that only boys should know cómo chiflar. Norbert sounded like a grown-up man when he talked. Trina and I inherited the same voice; we often even confused our parents. Josey whined like the spoiled brat he was; but his voice would rise to a deafening pitch when I rode his bike without permission.

We inherited straight teeth and small mouths. My father's teeth were tiny and straight, like a baby's milk teeth. Berney's teeth were larger than those of my father. Nora, Elizabet, and Ronnie had identical teeth and smiles. Norbert had large teeth, strong and white. Trina had bigger teeth than I did; her mouth was also wider. Josey and I had similar teeth. His mouth, I often thought, was more like that of a petulant girl's.

We were so alike, so different.

I was the tenth of eleven live children born to Tranquilino Ponce and Vicenta Solís. My mother miscarried twins, said to be boys, among her first five children. Of the first three—Rosalia, Socorro-the-First, and Rito—I only knew Rito, who died before I started school. And although my parents appeared not to dwell on their loss, they would allude now and then to their first years in this country and to the children they had lost. I thought of my first three siblings as *Them*.

Rosalía, or Rosalie as she was called in this country, was born in Mexico. My father, who came to this country at seventeen to join his older brothers, Felix and Gabriel, found work in the limoneras in Ventura. He saved his money and returned to Mexico. At twenty-two he married my mother, then twenty. They lived in Barretos, a ranch near León, Guanajuato, until about 1915, when my father decided to emigrate to this country for good. Once all their papers were in order, and with money sent them by my uncles in California, they left with Rosalía, their infant daughter. My mother often spoke of the trip and of having to throw dirty diapers out the train windows because there was no place to put them. She hated to do it, something she felt was muy ranchero. She waited until night fell, then threw the diapers out into the Arizona desert.

In a photograph taken when she was about thirteen, Rosalie looks tall for her age, tall and strong. Her hair is neither curly nor fashionable, but pulled back. She is wearing a plain cotton dress and dark shoes. I found it difficult to believe Rosalie was my sister, because she was so homely! She looked old for her age and terribly serious. I would stare and stare at the photo, trying to find a resemblance. I detected my mother's nose (hers too was flat, chata), but the eyes were different. I later learned that Rosalie had resembled Don Pedro Solís, my maternal grandfather. I also heard that when my mother, pregnant with me, visited Rosalie at Olive View Sanatorium (she later died of tuberculosis), Rosalía took one look at my mother's round belly and said, "Ay, pero para qué quiere más familia?" I never heard my mother's response.

Rosalie died when I was three months old. The damp climate of las limoneras settled in her lungs. She came down with tuberculosis, a disease prevalent among Mexican immigrants, and was quarantined, first at home, in los cuartitos, the rooms my father and brothers occupied, then at a sanatarium. She died at eighteen.

María del Socorro, or Socorro-the-First as I thought of her, was born in Ventura, California. She was my parent's second child and lived but a short time. Her death was tragic and somewhat mysterious; I knew the details by heart. One day when she was about five, Socorro-the-First was playing with a boy from the labor camp. He had a box of matches and began to taunt her. The two chased each other around the camp. Suddenly he lit a match and threw it at her;

her dress caught fire. Frightened of the flames that quickly enveloped her, she ran, not toward home but into the lemon groves! By the time my mother came to her rescue, Socorro-the-First was badly burned. She died a day later.

Although the boy had a reputation for being in trouble, his parents never acknowledged his part in the incident. Mis padres forgave him and his parents, although my mother was devastated. My sister was buried in a simple plot somewhere in Ventura. Soon after that our family moved to Pacoima. When I first heard this story, I built up a hate for the boy and vowed to get him, but I never met him.

Rito, also born in Ventura, was my parent's first son; more than the others he resembled my father's family, most of whom had blue-green eyes. The one image I have of this brother, who died of tuberculosis right before World War II, is of a tall, slender man in pajamas! As a teenager sometime in the late 1930s, Rito, along with other young men from Pacoima, joined the Civilian Conservation Corps, called the CCC. He went off to dig ditches and work in the construction of roads. While there Rito caught frio; the cold settled in his lungs and developed into tuberculosis. He also spent the last years of his life at Olive View Sanatorium. Now and then he came home on a pass, but stayed alone in the cuartitos. He never ate with us; I don't remember him inside our house. Mostly he looked sad. Handsome and sad.

One day I had just finished my oatmeal and ran outside to play. Rito, then about twenty, was sitting alone in the back door of los cuartitos, in pajamas and slippers. He called me over and asked, "Why isn't your hair combed?" I put my hand to my curly hair, embarrassed at having Rito see me looking so messy. He pulled me to him, unpinned my barrette, and said, "go get a brush, and I will comb your hair." I did as he said, running past the kitchen and shouting at my startled mother, "donde 'sta el peine?" Comb in hand, I dashed outdoors again to where Rito awaited me. He sat me on his lap and began to unravel my messy hair. As he worked he spoke, his voice soft and low. "I don't like to see you with your hair in your face," he told me. "Always wash your face and comb your hair before going outdoors. Okay?"

I remember his touch, the long tapered fingers that gently separated my Shirley Temple curls, the blue-green eyes that looked into mine, the dark wavy hair that fell across his smooth white forehead. His sad look. Years later I developed a crush on actor Gilbert Roland (old even then). He reminded me of Rito, dear Rito, who by combing my messy hair had told me so much about himself.

Nora, baptized María-del-Socorro, was the eldest of our family as I knew it. She was given the same name as the sister who was burned, because it was said she looked like Socorro-the-First.

Nora had a certain air about her. Somewhat aloof and removed from the pack, she stood apart because of her height and looks. Unlike the rest of us she was not olive-skinned at all, nor did she have a flat nose. She had beautiful creamy skin and large expressive eyes. She looked "international" and was often mistaken for Italian, Greek, or French.

Nora was an intellectual, a seeker of knowledge, a buyer of books. She learned from everyone and passed everything down to us. In high school she worked after school as a mother's helper for an Irish family in San Fernando and introduced us to peanut butter. She dropped out of school to work, which she later regretted. When she was eighteen, Nora was crowned Queen of the Pacoima Sixteenth of September fiesta, which made our father, a member of el comité, very proud. She wore a white satin dress, a purple cape with a train, a rhinestone crown, and shoes bought for $2.99. She later worked as a live-in housekeeper for Helen Mack, a movie star of the thirties. There she learned about diet, hygiene, clothes, and makeup, as well as what she most tried to instill in us: good manners.

Her employer was generous; during Christmas, in addition to a bonus, she presented Nora with her old clothes: leather shoes, silk blouses, and also men's suits that fit my delighted father. One summer I was allowed to visit Nora for a week. I walked all around the pretty house and played in the garden with Miss Mack's son. All the while I pined for Josey and our pepper trees.

At the Macks' Nora acquired a taste for good hardwood furniture. She detested furniture in loud, gaudy colors, preferring muted tones that blended with everything. One piece at a time, paid for in cash, Nora bought most of what sat in our living room. The pretty hall table was brought home in my father's truck, wrapped in blankets.

I found it admirable that Nora did not spend all her hard-earned money on herself. Girls her age often spent their earnings on clothes, makeup, and ankle-strap shoes. Each Saturday they would take the bus to San Fernando to window-shop and try on the latest fashions. Nora did have pretty outfits, many of them given her by Miss Mack, and although she often missed Sunday mass, when she did attend (to please our mother) she looked lovely in print dresses and a wide picture hat with a large cabbage rose.

Nora had delicate hands. She rarely cooked but would now and then help make tortillas. She first removed her watch and bracelets, then rinsed her hands in the bathroom and pinned her hair away from her face. She made perfectly round tortillas, light and fluffy, with nary a burned edge. I liked to watch her hands as they worked the rolling pin back and forth across the masa. Even when cooking, Nora was graceful.

Elizabet followed Nora. Unlike Nora, whom I associated with *Them*, Elizabet was part of the middle bunch: those who had come after Rito and lived. She was cheerful and industrious, and just as Nora did, loved our mother deeply. She emulated her in all things, never talked back, and was always willing to do more than her share of the housework.

Elizabet was my mother's right hand, a girl who helped with both the easy and hard chores. She cooked, cleaned, ironed. Anything and everything to earn our mother's favor. Elizabet, I think, suspected that Nora (said to be the spitting image of our maternal grandmother) was my mother's favorite, su preferida, although our mother would have denied it. Stuck between Nora-the-Beauty and Berney-the-First, Elizabet spent most of her life catering to our mother.

She was a fantastic cook and liked to improvise on old tested recipes. In grammar and high school she excelled in homemaking classes and learned to make pigs-in-a-blanket, hotcakes, and bisquits for us younger kids. She made rice pudding just the way I liked it, thick with cream and eggs, with cinnamon sticks sticking out like matches. During Lent she helped toast the bread used to make capirotada, sweet bread pudding. She would cube the bread, add butter and brown sugar called piloncillo, crown this with raisins and cheese, then bake it in the oven. During Christmas she made delicious fudge. On hot summer days, Elizabet never seemed to tire of making pitchers of lemonade for her younger siblings.

She was also an expert seamstress. She knew everything about sewing: how to cut on the bias, adjust for fit, sew French seams, and add a sleeve gusset. She could turn a shirt collar and sleeve so that the material did not bunch up, followed sewing patterns to the letter, and rarely made mistakes when cutting out a dress. Best of all Elizabet knew how to make doll clothes. I thought her a genius!

Elizabet was also an excellent student. She did well in English and history, read voraciously, and acted as the family translator when necessary. She wrote letters to Mexico for our parents and explained instructions written in English to our father. In high school I once looked up Elizabet's report cards. She had earned straight A's and not a single "Unsatisfactory." She graduated with honors from San Fernando High School, the first in our family to do so.

Elizabet was a bookworm; she read far into the night. Like me she read Nora's Book of the Month Club selections and also checked out books from the library in San Fernando. While Nora stuck to the best-sellers, Elizabet liked historical novels best, books she said had something called character. It was Elizabet who bought me books each birthday and Christmas. Nora made sure I had a winter coat; Elizabet bought dolls, buggies, and books.

By the time I was twelve, I was steeped in good literature and had read *The Razor's Edge, Leave Her to Heaven,* and my favorite romance novel, *Came A Cavalier.* I rarely read *True Confessions,* although Trina and I fought over *Photoplay.* These were referred to as "garbage" by the learned Nora and studious Elizabet. From an early age I could discern good literature from trash. I never did care for comic books.

It was Elizabet who took me with her to choir practice when I was eight years old. When the choir members, citing my young age, objected to my singing with the adults, Elizabet merely smiled and stood me next to her, holding the music book down low for me to read. Later, when she no longer went to el coro, I continued on my own. In many ways Elizabet was like my second mother; she set the example for me in many things. I loved her dearly.

Elizabet was the first of her friends, all of whom aspired to something other than a job in a ceramic plant or en el fil, to land a "good" job, in an attorney's office. As a business major in high school, she had learned typing, shorthand, and accounting. During the early

1940s, girls yearned to be secretaries or telephone operators, to work in an office, and to wear high heels and white gloves. My parents were very proud of her.

No longer the disheveled teenager, Elizabet the "career girl" wore pretty clothes, fashionable hats, and white gloves. One favorite outfit was a two-piece olive-green dress. The top was polka-dotted, the skirt a swirl of neat pleats. The beige suit I remember her wearing constantly was either her favorite or all she had at the time. Always she wore white gloves, stockings with seams, and leather pumps.

As a legal secretary Elizabet often accompanied her boss to the Los Angeles county jail to take depositions. She remained at this job until World War II, when she, like others in Pacoima, went off to work in the aircraft plants, where the pay was good and women got to wear pants.

Elizabet worked on the assembly line at Lockheed Aircraft in Burbank, California. Like other Mexican-Americans on our street, she wanted to do her share in the war effort and to earn good money. She wore denim overalls and something called a snood, like a net but with bigger holes, wrapped around her dark head. On her tiny feet she wore the required safety shoes with closed toes and laces. These allowed her to work near machines; the pants let her bend over.

Nora and Elizabet both paid my mother for room and board. Elizabet still cooked, but not as much. My mother felt that she should not have to work both at the plant and at home. And then Elizabet fell from grace; she eloped with R., a handsome young man who wore a snappy uniform.

During the war everyone in town thought of eloping. Couples met in the middle of the night, then drove to Tijuana, Las Vegas, or Mexicali to get hitched, something that drove our pastor crazy. He felt that everyone should marry en la iglesia, having taken instruction and announced their marriage bans. I never got the details about Elizabet's dash to the altar, but I recall that my parents were disappointed and hurt. Up to that time, she had done no wrong. I found it terribly exciting. Almost like in the movies, except that there a girl would climb down a ladder from an upstairs window into the waiting arms of her novio, then off they went to get hitched by a judge. I was curious to know what Elizabet had worn and where they went for a honeymoon, but no one bothered to tell me. Later Elizabet did

get married en la iglesia; otherwise the whole town would say they
were living in sin. Not until her husband was discharged and they
rented a small house on Carl Street, did she have children.

I went to Elizabet's every single day! She always made me feel welcome. I liked to see and touch the things most newlyweds bought:
the new iron, shiny toaster, chrome table with matching chairs, and
the pretty flowered sheets and taffeta bedspread. Elizabet now had
a portable sewing machine on which to make curtains, tablecloths,
and pillow shams.

I never could make up my mind whom I most wanted to be like:
Elizabet or Nora. I admired Nora's cool beauty, good taste, and regal
bearing, but always felt good around Elizabet; she was always there.
When I was about ten I decided to be like both my eldest sisters, to
take bits of Elizabet and combine them with Nora's attributes.

Berney, my eldest brother, was two years younger than Elizabet.
This was hard to believe, because she appeared to defer to him. After
Rito died, Berney, still a teenager, readily assumed the authoritarian
role and privileges of el hijo mayor. He was tall, with hazel-green
eyes, a straight nose, and perfect white teeth. His black hair was
wavy, kinky almost. People said he resembled my father and that he
was almost as handsome as Rito. Unlike my father, however, Berney
was often grumpy; yet his face lit up when he smiled, his hazel eyes
crinkling at the corners. He was neither as friendly as Norbert nor as
sweet as Josey (no one was as sweet as Josey), but was a typical older
brother who liked to give orders. Being the responsible, older male
in the family made Berney serious, I often thought. He was terribly
neat and often changed tee shirts twice a day, a thing that delighted
my mother, who like others on Hoyt Street, hated for her children
to be called "dirty Mexicans." She would in fact boil our clothes for
hours. Years later I met my mother's brother, Benjamin, in Mexico
and recognized Berney's face and disposition.

Sometimes when Josey and I got into his tools, Berney would growl
and threaten to hit us; at other times he would sweetly offer to take
us to town.

"Ya wanna go?"

"Where?"

"You don't havta know."

"But . . ."

"Get in the truck and wait for me."

Josey and I, excited at the prospect of riding with our older brother, would quickly scramble into our father's flatbed truck to sit and wait. And wait. When finally we would climb down from the dusty truck, it was only to discover that Berney had taken off in his car, leaving us behind. This happened at least once a week, with Josey and me none the wiser.

Like my father, Berney was a fixer of broken things. He faithfully worked on his old jalopy, a dented Ford, called "el foringo," held together with loving care and bailing wire and washed at least once a week. He staked out a corner of the garage for himself and would stay in there for hours. Before working on his car, Berney would put on old Levis and a worn tee shirt, then borrow my father's work shoes, not wanting to smear his cordovan shoes with oil. He would sweep the area clean, then lay down pieces of cardboard to catch the oil that oozed from the car motor. Then, my father's tool box at his side, Berney would go to work. He yanked at loose wires, wound electrical tape around a torn hose, replaced spark plugs and points. Berney I often thought, could fix anything.

But Berney had one bad habit. When he was working on a car and found himself in need of rags for his oily hands, rather than getting up and hunting for rags underneath the kitchen sink, he would grab at whatever was hanging on the clothesline. This irritated my mother, who more often than not kept the lines filled with our clothes. She was forever scolding Berney, who more than once had ruined towels, pillowcases, and once a lace doily.

Ay, pero qué hiciste? my mother would ask Berney. "What have you done to my doily?"

"What doily? Ya mean this rag?"

One time I hand washed my favorite doll's dress in the kitchen sink. The pink dress of light gossamer, had lace at the bottom, tiny pearl buttons at the back, and underneath, a slip of white taffetta. I hung the dress to dry on the line, unaware that Berney was then working on his car. When I returned for the dress later, I found it streaked with oil. Berney, I suspected, had wiped the dipstick on my doll's dress, and then had hung it back on the line. I ran screaming to Doña Luisa, our next-door neighbor and adopted grandmother. Rather than show disrespect for her, Berney retreated under his car.

Whenever Berney, and later Norbert, was working on a car, my mother made sure to bring in the wash.

Berney liked to throw his weight around at home. He felt responsible for my sisters' reputations. He disapproved of the tight skirts then in vogue, and although Elizabet was older, she was too short to have much authority. Even Norbert rarely argued with the brother who had a car and could outshout him. Berney was not mean, nor did he hit us (in our house, no one was allowed to hit), but in our mother's eyes he could do no wrong. To make Berney angry was to incurr our mother's coraje. Doña Luisa called Berney "el padre"; she all but curtsied to him. Berney never talked back to our parents, although he rebelled against them when he quit high school to get a job. He was never a pachuco (what parents in Pacoima most feared), but sometimes, when my father wasn't looking, he wore draped pants that ballooned around his slender frame.

My older sisters stayed clear of Berney. Still Berney always knew where they went and with whom.

Berney came of age during the war, a time when most guys were raring to leave the barrio to "fight Japs." Many of Berney's buddies signed up with the army, navy, Seabees, and marines, choosing not only a branch of the military but also a uniform to wear. In the army, men led the charge; Seabees built airstrips and bridges; marines secured the front lines. Sailors traveled more than the others and wore snappy white hats. For Mexican-Americans with an eighth-grade education and few prospects, the war offered excitement, a steady job, and adventure.

Many of our neighbors on Hoyt Street volunteered for the draft. Friends and brothers drove to Los Angeles in beat-up cars to enlist, hoping to be assigned to the same outfit. On our street kids bragged about brothers in the service, arguing over who wore the neatest uniform. The marine dress uniform, white gloves included, won hands down.

Poor Berney. When war broke out, he was about eighteen. He too wanted to fight for his country, so he signed up with the army. During the physical his hearing was found to be defective because of a burst ear drum (the result of childhood ear infections); he was classified as 4-F. His dream of fighting in the war alongside his friends ended. In the barrio being 4-F was akin to a disgrace and somewhat suspect, because many men, especially those who feared getting shot, used any and all afflictions to evade the draft. Some fled to Mexico to live with relatives, others claimed they were the sole support of their mothers.

Berney had to endure the hard stares of those who did not know of his affliction. Wanting to contribute to the war effort, he went to work for Lockheed-Vega, the aircraft company in Burbank where Elizabet also worked.

I defended Berney to my friends. When they questioned his being at home rather than fighting, I stood tall, daring anyone to call my brother a coward. Yet he must have been very lonely, because during the war, the barrio, especially Hoyt Street, was empty of young, virile men.

My mother and Doña Luisa were perfectly content to have Berney sit out the war; they had no need to worry about his being wounded or killed. It was better to have him be alive than to have a gold star on a windowpane. My father, who understood everything, said nothing. After having lost three children, he no longer questioned fate. But I think Berney did.

Verónica, or Ronnie, followed Berney in birth order; after Elizabet moved away, she took over her side of the bed. Nora had left her job with Helen Mack and was working for Timms Aircraft; she had her own apartment.

Like Elizabet Ronnie was short, but she resembled my father. She had chocolate-brown eyes, a tiny mouth, and (unlike Elizabet, who had the Solís nose) her aristocratic nose jutted out from her heart-shaped face. Her widow's peak was shown to advantage when she brushed back her thick dark hair. She had a tiny waist, full hips, and short, skinny legs. She kept her toes painted a bright pink.

Ronnie was an obedient daughter who never talked back to our parents. She was said to be my father's favorite, which she also believed. She was easy to get along with, easy to know. Unlike the rest of us, Ronnie was not a reader and rarely discussed anything other than clothes. She was not as knowledgeable as Elizabet or Nora, but she was friendly, pretty, and popular.

All of my sisters were extremely generous, Ronnie more than the others. At the church bazaars, jamaicas, she would give Josey and me

money to spend on popcorn and peanuts. At Christmas she would
pitch in to buy dolls for me and toys for Josey.

Ronnie never did much housework, a thing that irked Trina. Unlike Elizabet, who was always cleaning and cooking, Ronnie, backed
by our doting mother, delegated the dirty chores to Trina and me.
When Ronnie did cook, the menu was predictable: meat loaf, mashed
potatoes, and green peas. She rarely deviated from this, nor did she
experiment with recipes, but now and then she fixed a carrot-and-
raisin salad. Mostly she kept busy moving furniture around.

Ronnie was the artist in the family. In high school she was encouraged by her art teacher to major in art. She worked well with every
medium: charcoal, pen and ink, and watercolors, but she was especially good with oils. Her paintings were exhibited in school, much
to the delight of our mother, who unfortunately never saw them.

Ronnie was also an expert at arranging flowers. She instinctively
knew which flowers went well together. She preferred tall, stately
varieties: gladiolus, iris, and calla lilies. She trimmed the leaves, then
stuck the blossoms inside a "frog," an iron dish with spikes. Around
them she arranged ferns or other greens. We always had fresh flowers
in our house.

In our family it was said that artistic abilities came from the Solís
side, intellect from the Ponces. Although Ronnie looked like the
Ponces, she was very creative. She was constantly moving our furniture around, never quite satisfied with her surroundings. She would
group pictures together and sew pretty cushions for our faded sofa.
Unlike Elizabet, who wore tailored clothes, or Nora, who liked print
dresses, Ronnie doted on peasant skirts, which she whipped up on
our mother's trusty sewing machine. She wore them with frilly white
blouses of batiste or cotton. One of her favorites was a white eyelet
blouse worn off the shoulders.

In high school Ronnie was exempt from much of the housework.
From the time she was sixteen, she worked part-time as an usher-
ette at the San Fernando Theater and was in fact the first Mexican-
American girl hired there. She worked after school and on weekends
and would allow no one to loiter in the theater aisles. Most evenings
my father picked her up.

Ronnie was flirtatious but sensible. She had a lot of boyfriends, many of them Berney's friends, who hung around our house. She took care with whom she dated and rarely stayed out late. Ronnie did not want to disappoint the parents whose expectations of her knew no bounds. Of all the girls in our family, only Ronnie had a big wedding; apart from working at a factory job, that was all a Mexican girl could aspire to at the time.

After high-school graduation in the 1940s, Ronnie attended Los Angeles City College on an art scholarship. She would take the bus from San Fernando Road to the city. She rarely talked about her classes, but appeared to like being una artista. Within a year she decided she should earn money, however, and quit college. I think she felt guilty about not helping out at home.

All of my older siblings contributed at home. Early on Nora set the example for taste and generosity. She bought Easter bonnets and frilly dresses for Trina and me and rompers for Josey, as well as much of the family furniture. Elizabet helped buy a stove and washing machine for our mother. Berney and Ronnie also gave mi mamá a portion of their earnings, not so much as room and board but out of respect. This was common in the barrio, where those who worked usually helped their parents with money.

Years later, when our mother was seriously ill, Ronnie (then married and working outside the home) gave my father her weekly salary to pay for the private hospital where my mother was confined. She was following the example set by my father; when Rosalía and Rito were en el sanatorio, he mortgaged our home to pay for the medical treatment.

I never went anywhere with Ronnie. She had her own set of friends and could not be bothered with a pesky kid sister. We shared few things, other than the moving of furniture (I was hefty and liked to push). Ronnie was of the World War II generation and experienced fully the new freedoms given young women at that time. She, Elizabet, and Nora went to dances given at el Salón Parra as part of the war effort. Encouraged by our new progressive priest, they invited soldados to the church bazaars that soon teemed with men in uniform. Dark-eyed sailors and soldiers flirted with my sisters; I envied them their newfound freedom.

Ronnie never worked in an aircraft company. By the time she left college, most airplane factories were laying off workers. She got a job at Gladding, McBean & Company, a ceramic factory in Glendale where few if any Mexican-Americans worked. She was hired because she had an artistic background and could hand paint the dishes the company was famous for. She helped many of her friends find work there, too. In 1949 she married a handsome sailor and moved to a small town southeast of Pacoima.

Trina and I aspired to have a house like Ronnie's. Although her first house was small, she and her husband built and paid for it piece by piece. They then built two more, each one larger than the last, and finally settled into the prettiest one, a custom-made house with pegged floors, wide shutters, and pretty wallpaper. We admired the beautiful maple furniture in the bedrooms, lamps, coffee tables, the refrigerator, the freezer, and the outdoor barbeque. Each time I visited Ronnie, I took inventory to see what was new. None of her friends equalled Ronnie's material gains; she had everything.

Norbert was born after Ronnie. Like Elizabet, he had a flat nose, chato. He was not as handsome as Berney nor as rambunctious as Josey, but he was kind and sensitive. During the war he was still in high school, so he did not get to play soldier. He read a lot but did not frequent the library or snitch books from Nora. Norbert was short and husky; his terrific build was due to weight lifting.

He and his friends, guys he called "my buddies," wore tight Levis and white tee shirts and spent hours fixing jalopies passed down to them by an older brother. Norbert worked well with his hands; he loved to fiddle with car engines, carburetors, and fuel pumps. At supper Josey and I sat across from Norbert, who as I recall never had to sit on the bench with the kids; because he was un hombre, he got a chair.

Norbert preferred animals to people. He also had a fascination with names and even wrote his name on my father's truck. He wrote it as Norbt., a peculiar abbreviation, and also as Norb or Bert, but never as Norbert.

As a teenager he worked for O'Meara of the Valley, a landscape gardener who would pick him up each Saturday morning. He knew all about plants and how they grew best: in sandy or rich soil, sun or shade. Once instead of wages, Norbert brought home a Chinese willow tree.

The day Norbert brought home the weeping willow tree was terribly exciting. He ran in, eyes shining, hair tousled, to tell my father he had a Chinese tree for the front yard. As Josey and I watched, Norbert and my father unloaded the tree, taking care not to disturb the roots encased in burlap. They sat the tree down, then Norbert grabbed the garden hose and drenched it, saying that providing it got plenty of water, anything could grow. Even polliwogs.

Norbert walked around the yard, his Levis caked with dirt, trying to decide where to plant the tree. He inspected the back, side, and front yards, rubbing his curly head, unable to make up his mind. Now and then he sunk the hoe into the ground as if testing the soil. Finally he decided the willow would look best in the front yard, a little to the right of center. Supervised by my father, Norbert dug a hole.

"¿Así?"

"No, más grande."

I watched as he dug the hole with the square shovel. Once he had a grip on the handle, his hands never shifted, or else they might get calluses. As Norbert worked, our dog, Duke, ran between his legs, excited at having another tree to pee on.

"Gosh, Josey, no one else has a Chinese willow."

"In the whole world?"

"No, stupid. They gots them in . . ."

"China?"

Often Josey exasperated me with his questions. When I wasn't looking he would read my schoolbooks and scribble his answers to math problems in my writing tablet. He beat me at marbles and wanted a *World Book Encyclopedia* to show he could memorize things better than I could. As we watched Norbert, Josey paid close attention; should I ever plant anything, bury an ant even, Josey would be ready to instruct me.

By late afternoon Norbert was ready for the tree. He wet the roots again, then slowly lifted the tree and placed it in the gaping hole. My father was concerned that the precious tree not grow lopsided; he held it ramrod straight as Norbert filled the hole. His muscular arms gleaming with sweat, his face damp with excitement, Norbert then turned the hoe upside down and punched holes around the roots to let the air escape. Finally he made a watering trench around the tree that from afar resembled Elizabet's pie crusts.

My father watched as Norbert added a concoction, given him by O'Meara of the Valley, to keep the tree from going into shock, then walked off, satisfied with Norbert's handiwork.

The tree was beautiful; its moss-green leaves swept to the ground. That evening my friends on Hoyt Street came by to see it.

"Gosh! Did it really come from China?"

"No stupid, from a can."

"Shut up."

"You gonna make me?"

For a time the tree thrived, then little by little it began to shed its leaves. The slender branches turned brown. Poor Norbert didn't know what to do. He watered it even more, added fertilizer and vitamins, but still the tree drooped, its once green branches now dry and brittle. Mr. O'Meara came by to give advice. He snapped a tiny branch off the tree, looked at it, then shook his head. Soon the tree died.

A broken-hearted Norbert dug up the tree and carted it to the back; just before he dumped it in the trash, he inspected its roots. Later my father said the tree had rotted from too much water. Soon after, my father brought home a palm tree. Norbert pitched in to plant it, although compared to the Chinese willow, the palm was ugly and added nothing to the yard. I hated this tree and secretly hoped it would go the way of the willow, but it survived.

Another time Norbert brought home a pretty cocker spaniel. Eyes full of happiness, dog clutched tight against his chest, he placed it at our feet. I picked up the yapping, squirming bundle of caramel fur. Josey too latched onto the dog, although we both knew he was Norbert's special pet and not a replacement for el Duque, who had recently died. Norbert, who took his time about most things, did not immediately name the dog; he thought and thought about it. He wanted something that fit the dog's personality. Josey and I offered suggestions: Spot, Brownie, Perro. Norbert shook his head. He named the dog several times, then changed his mind. Worried that this dog might join the long line of Duques, he finally named the taffy-colored dog Fawn. A perfect name, pretty and poetic. He bought the dog a collar, then sat in the warm sun to brush its fur. He was always happy around Fawn.

Norbert joined the air force while I was still in grammar school.

He signed up, he said, because the air force guaranteed him an education. Although he was one semester from high-school graduation, he refused to wait. I often felt that Norbert, the most intelligent of my brothers, wanted something more than Pacoima had to offer; he wanted to do things, to see the world.

Norbert spent two years in Munich, Germany, where he learned to speak German and made master sergeant. In his letters (which I read aloud to our mother), he explained that if he were married, he would qualify for off-base housing. I understood only that he was enjoying himself and seeing something of the world.

As the family's official letter writer (now that Elizabet was gone), I wrote Norbert long, chatty letters. I liked to write, and since I was willing, my mother asked me to write on her behalf. In his brief letters Norbert sent photos of the pretty *frauleins* he met in Munich.

Once after not hearing from Norbert for almost a month, my mother was in a near panic. She consulted Elizabet (everyone consulted Elizabet), who suggested that we get in touch with the Red Cross. A few weeks later we received a bundle of letters from Munich. Much later, when Norbert came home, he told us about his embarrassment and anger when he was instructed by the company commander to "Write home, now!"

Mostly Norbert wrote to me. One Christmas he sent me a German radio and camera in a fancy case. When the postman delivered the cardboard box I ran outside, grabbed a pair of pliers, and tore at it, but was called inside. Just then a friend of my father's drove up and smashed the box, which was lying in the driveway. The radio was now a jumble of wires and tubes; the shiny camera though, was untouched.

The camera, a Zeiss-Ikon was perfect! It had numerous dials and settings for distance and height and a thick, wide lens. I learned to photograph moving objects by setting the camera for 0/seconds, bought rolls of black-and-white film at the corner store, then took pictures of everyone and everything. I carried my camera to school and to the beach. I could identify the detailed pictures taken by my Zeiss-Ikon; I had a fit when Trina snitched photos I knew came from my camera. I charged the film and development at the market, where Maggie, a friendly girl, wrote out receipts for the purchase of stewing beef. When my mother found out, I took the film elsewhere. I had the German camera for years; it was my most precious possession.

When he returned from Germany, Norbert drove me nuts with the foreign words and expressions he had picked up. He no longer said "hi!" but what sounded like *vee-gates*. He called Josey and me *dumkoffs*, swine even! My parents became *Frau* and *Herr* Ponce; my sisters *frauleins*. He sang American songs in German, too, his eyes twinkling with merriment as Josey and I listened in awe. When Josey and I fought, Norbert would come between us, saying: "At ease." I think he missed military life—and Germany.

After Norbert came Trina, a tall, girl who resembled Berney. Although we were only three years apart, the distance between us was great, because from the time I was three, I slept next door with Doña Luisa. We never got to know each other. We neither shared dolls, buggies, or secrets.

Trina was moody and difficult to like. She hated catechism and the nuns, gave not a whit for Girl Scouts, nor cared to sing in the church choir. Although she was a good student and brought home *A*'s, we never did homework together. I didn't know how to act around this sister.

There was little for Trina to aspire to. Caught between the popular Ronnie and a kid sister who was gaining on her, she did not aim to please. Nora was the family beauty, Elizabet had the brains, and Ronnie was una artista. Trina had a hard act to follow.

My sister Trina, I often thought, was caught up in the many changes that followed the end of war, a time when everything seemed to change: clothes, hairdos, cars, and attitudes. Trina and her friends criticized their parents for being "old fashioned" (later I did, too). They made fun of Mexican dichos and traditions, chewed wads of gum, and drooled over "cool cats" who were "hep to the jive." Few parents in our town understood the needs of these new teenagers who yearned to be like the girls in the movies, las Americanas in tight skirts and cardigan sweaters who spent hours listening to music. On screen teenagers drank and acted tough. The guys wore tight Levis and cussed a blue streak. They didn't give a hoot about what parents thought. Popular songs were terribly suggestive and urged kids to rebel. Parents who could not control their teenagers called them mal agradecidos with no respect for God or their parents. If a girl came home past midnight, she was said to be bad, bad enough to be sent to juvenile hall.

Our pastor preached against the new ideas and new freedoms. He abhorred the tight skirts worn by girls like Trina, calling them disgraceful. He felt they could only lead to occasions of sin. He frowned on modern dance styles, too, claiming there was nothing wrong with the waltz, which allowed room for a book to pass between the dancers (his way of measuring a proper distance). He hated teen jargon and cringed when he heard "cool cat," "hep to the jive," and "all reet-tweet."

It was as teenagers that Trina and I bonded. Once I left Doña Luisa to live full-time with the family (at the age of twelve or so), we shared a bedroom and giggled far into the night. We wore the same size clothes and shoes; we shared plaid skirts, pastel sweaters, and saddle oxfords. Often Trina talked me into letting her wear my new clothes. When later my friends commented on my sister's new sweater, I would have a fit, insisting the sweater was really mine. We scrutinized movie magazines for beauty secrets and spent our money on Max Factor pancake makeup (#2), Tangee lipstick, Maybelline, and rouge. Now and then we went to town together, but once there Trina would take off with her friends.

One summer night Trina and I went to a beach party at Zuma Beach, the "in" place among teenagers. We packed bathing suits, towels, and makeup, then met our friends near the corner. We got home past midnight. The back door was locked; Trina and I climbed in through the kitchen window. Just as I brought my knees up to the window sill, Berney drove in. With Trina pulling I jumped, scraping my legs on the floor. I limped to bed, while she secured the window. Minutes later Berney barged inside and peeked into the bedroom, where Trina and I, still in our wet suits, pretended to be sleeping. Later Berney hid Trina's favorite skirt, the one with the slit up the side. He stuck it behind a closet, but I found it and gave it back to her. When Berney saw her in the dreaded skirt, he frowned, once more acting like the older brother.

To my family I was Nena. Not María Elena or Mary Helen, but Nena, Nanny-goat, Nena-llorona, and what only my father called me, Malena. Although I liked my Spanish name, I was never attached to it. While my friends and I spoke Spanish all the time, we liked our names in English best, never questioning teachers who, rather than struggle with our "foreign" names, quickly deduced their American counterparts and entered them on our school records. In time we identified only with our names in English and even forgot how to spell our Spanish names.

Not even Doña Luisa, who spoke only en español, called me by my proper name, mi nombre propio. Father Mueller once said my French name was Marie Hélène, which sounded pretty, but so did María Elena. When the Mexican waltz "María Elena" (translated into English from the Spanish) became popular, I identified with the romantic lyrics, but this affectation did not last. I was never María Elena.

I was called "la llorona," crybaby, because I liked to cry. I would cry at least once a day. I cried when my brothers threatened to tease me, cried harder when they prepared to tease me, and screamed in earnest when they did tease me. Doña Luisa, exasperated at my continuous wailing, said that if I continued to cry my eyes would shrink. Se te van a cerrar los ojos, she argued, her voice hoarse and cross.

I began to examine my eyes in the bathroom mirror, peering closely at the pupils. With my index finger I measured the length of each eye, then compared measurements. Thinking they might shrink too, I began to measure my eyelids. Once in a photo my eyes resembled two slits. I stopped crying for a whole week. But I missed this form of expression and soon began crying again for any and all reasons.

Crying was something girls did. In the movies, including those shown at the church hall, women who cried got their way. Teary teenage girls were never spanked, but only sent to their room with a glass of warm milk. Husky cowboys fell apart at the sight of a girl in tears. In Mexican movies tough hombres were themselves moved to tears by those of their novias and mamacitas. Even big brothers like Berney gave in to sniveling siblings who wore Shirley Temple curls.

But I was a real professional and soon had an entire repertoire of wails. At church, especially on Good Friday, I sobbed along with Doña Luisa and the Trinidads, three viejitas whom my friends and I considered religious fanatics. When I began to whimper in my pew,

Doña Luisa quickly put her thin arms around me; by the time mass was over, I knew she would buy me my favorite sweets.

As la llorona of the family, crying got me out of numerous scrapes and household chores. If we were playing ball and I felt cheated, I cried in short, loud gasps, then took the ball and went home. I cried buckets when forced to accompany Ronnie to church against my will and screeched at Trina when she locked me out of the bathroom. Each time I didn't get my way, I first checked to see who was around, then took a deep breath and hit high C.

Josey, two years younger than I, was my favorite playmate. He had dark brown eyes, a tiny mouth, and hair that shone blue-black in the California sun. He was said to resemble our father, except that he was dark, muy moreno.

He was terribly spoiled. As the baby of the family, he was my older sisters' plaything. Like royalty, he was carried aloft while I followed at ten paces. Mis hermanas would parade him up and down the street as if he were a rare jewel. They tossed him in the air, smoothed his hair, tweaked his nose, and cooed in his ear, while I kicked at dirt clods.

As el más chiquito, Josey was kept spotless by our doting mother and Doña Luisa, who, when she looked at Josey, appeared to be seeing God. Once he was scrubbed clean and his hair brushed off his face, Josey was dressed in starched rompers and high-tops. He would follow me around the yard, rarely more than a few feet away. We would hold hands or chase each other, while Doña Luisa watched us from afar. We made up songs, dug holes, and climbed the walnut tree. I was his leader; Josey was my follower.

Together Josey and I explored the open field, el llano. We rolled in the moist carpet of grass extending the length of the lot and scraped our knees on protruding rocks. We poked at the numerous insects that lived here. Josey liked ladybugs but feared moscos; we would quickly return to the safety of our own yard. We ran circles around the pepper trees, los pirules. Now and then we would stray to the street to play with other kids, but we liked each other's company best. What I liked the most about Josey was that he obeyed orders: "Josey, get the ball," "Josey, gimme the bat." He always obeyed without complaining.

Josey was highly intelligent; in grammar school he was moved up not one, but two years! I feared he would pass me up; hoping to spot a mistake, I would watch carefully as he worked a math problem. He and I rarely fought. "I'm older and bigger," I pointed out. As he grew older, the dusky skin that in summer turned blue-black began to bleach out, but his hair, with nary a wave, remained thick and straight.

Josey was musical. Elizabet had once played the violin and Berney played a mean harmonica, but Josey had the better ear. He would memorize all the songs sung by the Andrew Sisters and he knew the name of every band, bandleader, and instrument played. He was forever tapping his fingers to an imaginary beat; he knew the difference between two-four, three-four, and four-four time. Once he learned to read music, he memorized scales, musical notes, and words like *fortissimo*, *allagretto*, and *pianissimo*. When he was about twelve, my father bought him a shiny saxaphone and drove him to San Fernando each week for music lessons.

Every day Josey practiced el saxofón. He began with scales, then attacked the lesson of the week. Up and down the scale he would go, his dark eyes bulging, his cheeks puffed out like a cobra's. He liked to rip, as he called the spurts of sound emitting from the sax. He discovered jazz. When he heard a familiar tune on the radio, Josey would grab his sax and rip along, never missing a beat. When he was done with a lesson, Josey polished the shiny instrument, then placed it in its coffin. He later got a music stand and a metronome. Once he found his calling, Josey quit playing ball in the street. If forced to he would help to field the ball, but he much preferred to fiddle with the saxaphone. He later formed a band that played at his high school prom. For years our house was filled with the sound of jazz.

Ours was a well-organized household. Because we were a large family and our parents liked to keep us busy and out of trouble, we were each allocated jobs according to our size and capabilities. Grumbling but respectful, we went about our work, intent on pleasing our parents, whose concern with cleanliness and order were evident in everything they did.

Saturdays were special. En nuestra familia each person had special chores on this day. While my mother boiled linens or ironed, all of us except for Nora would go about our work. (On Saturdays Nora slept late. As a "career girl" who worked long hours during the week, she was exempt from the usual, boring housework.)

Elizabet would retreat to the kitchen to concoct new recipes from scratch. She began with what was at hand, then improvised. Invariably she left dirty pots in the sink.

Ronnie's Saturday job was to sort and fold linens: sheets, pillowcases, and towels fresh from the clothesline. She would stack them in the hall closet as I watched, curious to see whether she folded towels as neatly as Nora or I. Ronnie could be as neat as a pin—providing she felt like it. Often she cared not a whit whether the sheets lay straight or not, but finished the job in record time. Saturday was also Ronnie's day to iron her school clothes.

En los sabados Trina cleaned the bathroom, grumbling as she scrubbed the tub, washbowl, and toilet seat. She would lock the door and turn up the radio she had hidden in the hamper while I pounded on the bathroom door. She would take her hidden makeup and slather it on her face. When she emerged at long last, the bathroom would be spotless, her eyes caked with Maybelline.

Josey, still coddled by everyone, would help my father outdoors. He swept leaves with the yardbroom, whose handle kept falling off. Josey mostly ran errands for the rest of us. "Josey, hand me the hammer, traeme el martillo." "Josey, you gotta go to the store." Josey was our little helper, providing we later rewarded him with his favorite candy.

My Saturday job was to dust, shampoo, and polish the six dining room chairs. I had this job for about three years and hated it for all of them, because it had bypassed my sisters. "Trina never did them," I complained to my mother. Each Saturday before I could attend catechism or play with my friends, I first had to clean all six chairs. All six! Perfectly, shiny, clean.

The chairs were of dark mahogany, upholstered in beige and maroon flowers. Four of the chairs had straight-backs; two had arms. Since our house lacked a dining room and a dining table, las sillas were used as occasional chairs in the living room; two were stuck in the hall. The somber-looking chairs were much too elegant for the kitchen, Nora insisted. Josey and I were not allowed to use them at supper; we continued to sit on the bench.

On Saturday mornings soon after breakfast, I prepared for the dreaded chore. I placed old newspapers on the porch floor, then took flannel squares (cut from old pajamas) from the rag bag under the kitchen sink; they absorbed the furniture oil and did not scratch the wood. The small brush used to scrub the chair seats was also kept under the kitchen sink, with a round pan. Once armed with the necessary tools, I was ready for the chairs.

I would lug the chairs to the porch, holding them aloft so as not to scratch the wood, set them down, then return for the rest. Using short, swift strokes, I brushed the dust off each chair; when I was finished I lined the chairs against the porch rail to inspect them for stains. Then in a small bowl I mixed furniture shampoo with water. I whipped the suds to a thick foam, then before they dissipated, I carried the foam-filled dish outside and placed it on the newspaper.

Next came the fun parts! I swished the brush back and forth in the shampoo, then cleaned the chairs with the foam. I swiped at the beige and maroon design, using the short strokes Nora had taught me, being careful not to soak the chairs. When I was satisfied that the chairs were clean of stains, I emptied the dregs in a nearby bush.

Once the chairs were dry, I took a soft cloth and saturated it with Old English Furniture Polish. I turned the chairs upside down, then went to work. My hands wound around each chair leg; I rubbed and rubbed, then attacked the back and sides. Then I went to find Nora. If she agreed that the chairs were finished, I carried them back to their designated rooms. If not, I pushed them against the porch and, after catechism, did them over again. And hated it.

On Saturday we also prepared for Sunday. After I returned from catechism,—and providing the chairs were done—I changed the bed linens. Elizabet, whose job this had once been, had taught me how. "Open the windows to let out los malos humores, dust the mattress, and change both sheets. Turn the ends under, or you'll have a lumpy bed."

As I grew older my Saturday jobs also included cleaning the cuartitos, a job I relished because it allowed me to pry into my brother's dresser drawers. I read the instruction booklets sent by Charles Atlas that Norbert kept hidden in a drawer. His dirty clothes were scattered all over the floor; Berney's white tee shirts sat in a neat pile. When I finished with the sheets, I would lie down on Berney's bed and fall asleep. Some Saturday mornings after listening to "Inner Sanctum," a scary radio program, I hated being alone in the men's rooms. I snatched the sheets off the beds, threw clean ones onto the mattresses, and bolted from the room, scared stiff that the monsters under the bed would grab my legs.

By midafternoon all was clean and orderly. It was now time for baths. As young children, Josey and I were bathed on Saturday mornings; we followed Trina in the bath order. I hated being dunked in leftover water and demanded agua limpia. This upset Doña Luisa, who was then forced to reheat water.

I especially remember one bath when I was about four and Josey two. We waited as Elizabet filled the tub next to the kitchen table, fetched towels, then undressed us. She tested the water, then put us into the tub. But she had neglected to clear the kitchen table. On it were mixing bowls, a measuring cup, and a large kitchen knife.

Josey and I splashed each other, while Elizabet unfurled towels and laid out clean underwear. Josey began to jump up and down, oblivious of the water that splattered on the floor. Suddenly he reached across the table and grabbed the knife. He waved it around, then dipped it in the water. I froze, not knowing what to do. Elizabet, busy cleaning water off the floor, did not look up. Fearing that he might hurt himself, I tugged at the knife, but Josey refused to let go. He kept jumping in the water, while I watched for a chance to take the knife from him. Just then he looked the other way and I yanked the knife, slicing Josey's finger in half.

"Ay, ay, ay," he cried, as the knife dropped to the floor. He screamed and screamed as blood poured from his severed finger into the water. Doña Luisa came running and Elizabet pulled Josey from the bright red bathwater. With Josey in her arms, she ran to find my mother, leaving a trail of blood on the kitchen linoleum. Doña Luisa wrung her bony hands, not knowing what to do. After inspecting Josey's finger, Elizabet pressed it together, splashed alcohol on it, then wrapped it in clean gauze and handed him to my mother.

While Elizabet and my mother looked after Josey, I was left in the bloodied water. When finally they remembered that I was still en la tina, Elizabet took me out, leaving my mother and Doña Luisa to comfort baby Josey. By now I too was crying, scared at what I had

done, afraid Josey would bleed to death. I could smell the bloody film
that covered my arms and legs; I begged to be washed off. Elizabet
carried me to the kitchen sink, turned on the faucet, and rinsed off
my arms, legs, and chest.

From across the kitchen table Josey looked at me, his dark eyes
full of pain. "I didn't mean to, Josey," I cried. Fue un accidente, I
wailed to Doña Luisa, now drying my hair. "It was an accident." I
felt terrible for having cut off my little brother's finger; I wanted this
nightmare to end. Josey quieted down, pushed his dark head into
Doña Luisa's flat chest, then asked to be put down.

Within the hour Josey's finger had stopped bleeding. "It hurts,"
he whimpered as we went outdoors, "it hurts." He started to pull at
the gauze, then thought better of it and held his finger up, as Elizabet
had instructed. I put my arms around him, being careful not to touch
his finger, and squeezed him tight. By late afternoon Josey and I were
once more together, chasing after el Duque. I never forgot the smell
of blood, though, nor the red water in the tub.

Years later my father installed a bathtub and shower (the first on
our block), where we could take leisurely baths. On Saturdays the
girls in our family took turns bathing and shampooing our hair. Trina
and I used Packer's Pine Tar soap; it smelled of pine and left our hair
squeaky-clean. After I towel-dried my hair, Elizabet would untangle
my curly mop in preparation for los rizos, the Shirley Temple curls
I liked to wear. On Saturdays while Elizabet worked on my hair, I
would close my eyes and submit to her willing hands, making believe
I was in a beauty shop.

Elizabet first brushed my hair to remove all snarls. Then she ran
the family comb through my hair, making it as straight as possible.
She parted it to the side, took a batch of hair, brushed it around her
finger, then released a curl that resembled a sausage. She repeated
this until my entire head was a mass of curls, then tied a pretty ribbon
in it. When she was finished, I would tear off to the bathroom mirror.
Satisfied with how I looked, I walked around like a zombie, afraid
to disrupt my pretty curls. But this affectation lasted only a short
time; there was usually a ballgame being played in the street. After
watching from the sidelines for a time I would join in, unmindful of
my curls, certain they would last until the following week.

When Saturday rolled around once more, our family again went about our assigned chores. I would clean the detested chairs, then scoot off to catechism to learn about sin. Later I would change the bed sheets in the men's rooms. After that it was time to take a warm bath and submit to Elizabet's ministrations. In our family, this pattern of el sábado as a special day remained for many, many years.

Doña Luisa

Doña Luisa was our adopted grandmother, an old, white-haired woman whom I dearly loved and with whom I slept for many years. She lived next door in a brown wooden house with a porch the length of the house. The house was large, with two bedrooms and a small kitchen; Doña Luisa shared it with Doña Nicolasa, an elderly widow whose married children lived in the next block. While different in temperament, the two women got on well.

Doña Luisa, whom I called Mita, was tall, thin, and flat-chested. She wore dark flannel dresses, belted in the middle, which hung from her skinny frame. Her lined skin was a rich brown; her hair, like white straw, was worn in a bun held in place by hairpins.

She wore a wrinkled scapular blessed by old Father Juanito (our deaf pastor who blessed everything people put in front of him) under her cotton undershirt; and long white petticoats she called naguas, full cotton slips like those worn by peasant women in the movies. Much to my mother's dismay, Doña Luisa refused to use our washing machine with the mangle and instead washed her slips by hand in a large zinc-plated tub. She scrubbed the puffy white petticoats on an aluminum washboard with Fels Naptha, the smelly soap used by my father and brothers to wash oil off their hands. The soap looked like damp clay and smelled horrid, almost like that made by our neighbor Doña Chonita, which I referred to as el veneno, poison. Once clean, the naguas were hung to dry on the clotheslines nearest the alley. Doña Luisa was adamant that the neighbors not see her undergarments flapping in the wind.

Doña Luisa, I heard tell, had been married twice! Her last husband, whom she had married in Mexico, had bequeathed her the brown house, which she later ceded to el condado, the county, in return for a monthly check. The kitchen had an icebox, a table and two chairs, and a tall pantry on one wall. The porch, whose cement floor was ideal for playing jacks, faced Hoyt Street and was big enough for several chairs and benches. She planted geraniums in two old buckets she had found in the alley; the red flowers and glossy leaves graced the porch where on summer evenings Doña Luisa and Doña Nicolasa sat talking.

Doña Luisa never spoke of her late husband, or of whoever came before him. Nor did she keep a picture of him atop a bureau and offer special masses for his soul. Still, her dark eyes grew misty when she remarked that she had been alone for most of her life. Until she found us, that is.

Doña Luisa had no children. She adopted us, as we adopted her, without conditions. Each of my older sisters had at one time slept over with this kind lady, not wanting her to be alone at night. Then it was my turn. When I turned three, soon after Josey was born, I was sent to keep this viejita company. I often felt I loved her more than my own mother, but kept this to myself. I went back and forth from her quiet house to my noisy one until I turned twelve.

I slept next to Doña Luisa in a double bed that sagged in the middle. She preferred to sleep on the edge near the trunk, the patequilla brought from Mexico, on which stood a kerosene lamp. We each had our own sheet and blankets. I never used a pillow, so I gave her mine. I liked being next to the wall, under the window that faced Hoyt Street. In spite of Doña Luisa's concern, I insisted on leaving the window open all night. While she huddled under the covers, I threw off my blankets; the cool night air lulled me to sleep.

Once she had secured the front door, she would admonish me to close my eyes . . . and would remain at the foot of the bed until I did. When she left the room, I stood on tiptoe atop the bed, then pushed aside the cotton curtains to peek beyond the wide porch to the dark street. I would also jump up and down on the mattress, trying to reach the ceiling, which is why the bed dipped in the middle.

Some nights Doña Luisa put me to bed and then stayed up to straighten her household. She folded and refolded the things kept in the trunk: old petticoats, lace handkerchiefs, torn stockings, and odd pieces of lavender soap. She also sorted the kitchen cupboard she shared with Doña Nicolasa, in which she kept tiny cans of Carnation milk, a small jar of grape jelly, and a can of sugar.

I loved Doña Luisa's house. Although our house was newer and better furnished, hers was dark and homey and was mine to enjoy. I ran in and out at will, took lazy naps atop the bed, and played paper dolls next to the trunk without interruption.

Unlike our house, Doña Luisa's casita did not have a bathroom, only an outhouse toward the back. She kept a chamber pot under the bed, which she faithfully emptied each morning. This bacinilla, bought in San Fernando, was of white enamel with pink roses on one side and blue trim along the edge. I hated to use the pot and even in the middle of the night insisted on being carried home to the bathroom. Doña Luisa, however, preferred the pot, and daily trekked with it to the outhouse that stood like a sentinel in her backyard.

She refused to use our bathroom, saying that someone was always in it. My mother said Doña Luisa was set in her ways. Rather than use our large bathtub, she always took a bath in the zinc tub she first filled with water heated on her wood stove.

I liked the wood stove. No one else on Hoyt Street had one like it. It was made of cast iron with four legs that curved inward, two round griddles, and, to one side, an opening for wood. *La estufa* was old-fashioned and different from our white stove with its four gas burners and wide griddle. On it Doña Luisa made delicious toast using white Weber's bread. She hated wheat bread and oleomargarine, and instead bought creamy butter wrapped in thin paper, which was kept in the icebox. She laid the bread in a straight row atop the stove, then dotted each slice with small pats of butter: one in the middle and two on each side, as if playing tic-tac-toe! When the stove got too hot the toast burned; the butter seeped through the crispy bread. Still I ate it, then wiped my mouth clean. Right before I bolted outdoors, I made sure to tell Doña Luisa that hers was the best toast ever.

Doña Luisa often sent me to fetch wood, a chore made easy by the abundance of wood in our lumberyard-backyard. She first checked it for nails, then let me place the wood in the stove. One by one I crunched the pieces of wood into the square opening, being careful not to burn my fingers or create sparks; otherwise Doña Luisa's house would go up in flames, and I'd be sent home to sleep with my sisters, whom I knew would put me in the middle. I thought it lucky that I found wood cut to stove size, until I realized my father, always kind to Doña Luisa, cut pieces of wood just for her.

Over her cotton dresses, our adopted grandmother wore aprons with pockets in which she hid lemon drops bought in San Fernando. She gave the candy to Josey and me during times of crisis—at least once a week. They were a treat! The drops were neither sweet nor sour but tart; they grabbed my tongue and made me want to spit them out. They were sold neither at the corner store nor at the movies held at the church hall, which is why they were so special. Once when Doña Luisa returned from town, she called me over and handed me a tiny white bag.

"Tóma."

"All for me?"

"Sí."

Although Doña Luisa catered to Josey, the baby of the family, and to el padre, I was her favorite. Because I stayed with her for more than ten years, people thought I belonged to her and not to my parents. It bothered me when my friends pestered me about Doña Luisa.

"How come you don't sleep at home?" Nancy once asked.

"I live at home, but I sleep with Doña Luisa."

"How come?"

" 'Cause she's old and . . ."

I hated having to defend Doña Luisa and explaining that I ate meals with my family too. In time my friends stopped asking questions and accepted that Doña Luisa was my adopted grandmother. They knew that if nothing else, Doña Luisa was on the side of kids, big and little. During street fights she came to my rescue, and when Josey and I fought she frowned at us both and appeared to scold *me;* but the minute Josey was out of sight, she hugged me tight, took me inside her dark, shadowy house and stoked the wood stove. She spoon-fed me warm milk and toast, then rocked me to sleep in her dry, skinny arms.

Doña Luisa helped my mother with housework and with the care of the younger kids. Although I never saw an exchange of money, my father gave her something each week. He paid her utility bills (we shared electrical wires) and fixed her roof when it leaked. He took care of her yard too, since it was part of ours, and kept her outhouse from tipping over. She was an important part of our family and was included in most things.

Her days revolved around our family. Although she attended mass each weekday morning, she also helped my mother in the kitchen. White hair flying, cotton apron wrapped around her thin waist, she crossed the yard that separated our homes in long, brisk strides, then came indoors, ready to be of service.

Each Monday morning Doña Luisa helped my mother with the family laundry. While my father uncovered the wringer-washer (a big, clumsy apparatus), which each washday was rolled out onto the back porch, black cord dangling, then connected it to the electrical outlet in the kitchen, Doña Luisa helped sort clothes. She and my mother then filled the zinc tubs with warm water for rinsing and placed them next to the machine. When all was ready, the washer was turned on and the machine, filled to capacity with hot water, soap, bleach, and a batch of white clothes, began to chug. Chug, chug, chug. Back and forth went the agitator, straining against the dirty laundry. Once the white clothes were done and in the rinse, the colored clothes went in—shirts, aprons, dresses. Last of all came the dark clothes. By then the water was a murky brown, the machine hot.

In the spring my mother and Doña Luisa stripped beds and washed not only sheets but blankets and bedspreads as well. If the weather was warm, they hung them on the line overnight to ensure that the germs accumulated during the winter were gone. Right before Lent and again before Christmas, our house was cleaned from top to bottom. Whenever one of us was sick, my mother, fearful perhaps of el TB, fumigated the room, then washed all the bedding in the trusty washing machine.

I was considered too young to help with the wash. Worse, I was afraid of getting my arm caught in the deadly ringer, so I would watch from the sidelines as each Monday my mother and Doña Luisa, and later my older sisters, went through the same routine.

From an early age I was allowed to hang clothes, provided I did not drag them on the ground. First I separated the towels and hung them side by side. Next came aprons, dresses, and Josey's short pants. I lined up clothes by color, too: a bright yellow skirt next to

a white one, a plaid shirt next to a dull gray, and all of Berney's tee
shirts in a perfect white row. There was little I could do with my
brothers' pants; the stiff Levis that were so cumbersome and heavy
to lift. Once the clothes were dry, I shook them free of dust and lint
and folded them: sheets in perfect squares, pillowcases and towels in
three sections. I threw the squares into the linen closet, watching to
see in what order they fell. This irritated my orderly mother. Doña
Luisa, exasperated at my pranks, tried not to laugh.

Doña Luisa used words my mother said were improper. She called
snot "mocos," a word used by rowdy kids. When she spotted a shiny
film on my nose, she would chase me around the yard.

"Venga para limpiarle los mocos. Come here so I can clean your
snot."

"Not snot! My nose."

"Pués, la nariz, okay?"

"Okay."

She held me against her dry knees, then with the red handkerchief (like the one my father used) that she kept in her apron pocket,
wiped my nose clean. She was careful not to rub too hard, or else I
would cry and accuse her of hurting me, a thing that brought tears
to her dark eyes. Often I asked why she used men's handkerchiefs
rather than the pretty ones we gave her at Christmas (now lying in
the trunk), but she ignored me.

Doña Luisa also helped cook, or tried to. My mother rarely encouraged her to help in the kitchen, mostly because Doña Luisa
never remembered to wash her hands, a thing my mother could not
tolerate. My older sisters, all of whom helped prepare meals, knew
enough to scrub their hands in hot water before touching any food,
but not Doña Luisa. She had her own way of doing things.

While paring potatoes she skipped the holes. Her tortillas were
shiny with lard, raw in the middle, and burnt on the edges. She forgot to drain the fat from meat and clogged the drain with coffee
grounds. When folding laundry she dragged the sheets in the dirt and
did not care whether the squares were even. She mopped the kitchen
without first sweeping and rarely scrubbed the bottoms of pots. But
not everything she did was wrong; Doña Luisa was an expert at
saving me from Berney.

Berney was always out to get me, mostly for nothing; or so I insisted to my parents. On lazy afternoons when he tinkered with his jalopy and assorted radios, I made sure to keep my distance. When he wasn't around, I would sit inside his current car to listen to the radio. I sat for hours, singing songs I recognized in a loud voice, trying not to lose the beat. Later, when his car refused to start because of a low battery, Berney would vow to get me. The chase began. I sprinted across our yard, Berney hot on my heels.

"Mita, Mita, Berney's gonna hit me." I ran as if being chased by the devil, screaming at the top of my lungs. "Abra la puerta! Open the door!"

With the speed of lightning, and from years of practice, Doña Luisa opened the door, then, once I was safely inside, shut it in Berney's face. This was repeated at least once a week, with Berney vowing to get me when I came out.

Once, feeling especially brave because Berney had not caught me, and knowing that he would not violate my sanctuary, I waited until Doña Luisa locked the door, then leaned out the window and yelled: "Ha, ha, you can't get me."

"Oh yeah?" Berney, hazel eyes narrowed, mouth set in a snarl, and hands clenched at his side, moved toward the door and began to pound on it. Alarmed, I screamed for Doña Luisa, who unlatched the door, stepped outside, and then berated Berney in her hoarse voice.

"No tiene vergüenza . . . un hombre queriendole pegar a esta pobre niña. You should be ashamed . . . a grown man wanting to hit this poor child." Berney, then all of seventeen, shuffled his big feet and lowered his eyes.

"Hit him, Mita." I screeched from my perch. I stuck my tongue out at Berney.

Knowing full well that my father would hear of this, my brother, eyes blazing with anger, shuffled off, looking contrite. He and I both knew the game (or fight) would continue; but for now Berney gave in to Doña Luisa. When, later in the day, I ran into him, he said nothing, nor laid a hand on me. Still his gaze was enough to send me running back to Doña Luisa.

Doña Luisa was a walker. She walked everywhere in her sturdy black shoes with mismatched laces: to the store, church, post office across the tracks, and to the city of San Fernando, six miles to the north. It amazed me that someone so slight, and so old, could walk so much and at such a fast pace. Most people on Hoyt Street, even teenagers like Berney, drove to town. Rather than take the bus, Doña Luisa walked and walked. She was strong, too, and liked nothing more than to carry me on her thin shoulders.

When on Thursday nights during the rosary I fell asleep, she would pick me up as though I were a sack of flour, throw me over her bony shoulder, and down the lane she would stagger toward her house. When at times I became too heavy, she would try to put me down, but I refused to walk. I screamed and clung to her spindly knees until she caught her breath, then once more lifted me up and continued the long haul. Once at home she would undress me, tuck me in, then sit to rub alcohol on her sore shoulders.

Doña Luisa was also an expert at picking tunas, the tasty prickly pears that grew in the back of most Mexican yards. She could tell when the fruit was ripe and ready for picking and delighted in feeding Josey and me tasty chunks of the sweet fruit. One time, when I was about six and Josey four, she let Josey stuff himself with tunas.

It was the time of year when the cactus in our backyard and those of our neighbors on Hoyt Street sprouted the delicious fruit. The tunas were red and yellow and free. To the children of the barrio they were a wonderful treat. Rather than check with a neighbor or the *Farmer's Almanac,* kept in a kitchen drawer, Doña Luisa merely walked around the nopalera and poked at the prickly pears. Satisfied that they would soon be ready to pick, she bided her time until the fruit almost burst. Often the ants beat us to the fruit that fell to the ground overnight; by midmorning they were covered with a moving red blanket.

Doña Luisa prepared for the tunas with care. She raked the dirt around the cactus, taking care to pick up any and all rocks, fearful perhaps of tripping on a rock while knocking down the fruit and flying headfirst into the sharp spines. Rather than knock down the fruit with a hoe or shovel, Doña Luisa liked to improvise and made her own tool. The tuna stick, as Josey and I called it, was a broomstick with a kitchen knife on the end of it, secured with a piece of cloth.

Some neighbors whacked at the prickly pears with a shovel or struck at them with a piece of hose, then spent the day picking fruit from the ground. Not so Doña Luisa. Although older than anyone else on our street, she had the eyes of an eagle and the hands of a woman who had once worked in the fields, which is why she was such an expert at tunas. She had great aim and rarely split the fruit in half.

On the morning of Josey's escapade, Doña Luisa rose early and went into the yard. While Josey and I ate a breakfast of oatmeal and toast, she raked the ground beneath the cactus plant, then walked around, testing the knife. Once done eating, Josey and I charged out the kitchen door and down the steps, colliding with Doña Luisa, who was busy adjusting the knife. She scolded us with a smile, then walked toward the cactus plant near the alley. Josey and I followed at a distance.

She pushed her white hair off her face, secured her cotton apron, then hooked up the stockings that sagged around her ankles. She circled the cactus, tuna knife in hand, careful not to snag her stockings on a spine. Like a gladiator she tested the knife with long, calculated thrusts. Josey and I followed close behind, as did el Duque, who knew from experience when something good was about to happen. While Doña Luisa stood against the fence to size up the position of the sweet fruit, Josey and I danced around her, tugging at the long dress that flapped around her thin, dry ankles.

"That one, Mita."

"No, that one."

"Ya déjenme. Just leave me be," she protested in Spanish, as she paused to push back the scraggly hair from her wrinkled face and adjust her apron. She rarely got angry, only impatient. Now and then when she paused to catch her breath, she walked back to Josey and me. Her dark Indian eyes enveloped us with love.

Once she made up her mind, she took a firm step forward and, with a giant thrust of the tuna knife, swung at the cactus. One by one Doña Luisa cut the tunas, as Josey and I jumped up and down with excitment. She cut the cactus at an angle, picked the fruit off the ground, then gently laid them atop a sack tucked inside a wheelbarrow. When the wheelbarrow fairly bulged with fruit, she pushed it to the water faucet next to the kitchen, then dumped them into a tub filled with water. Sometimes, anticipating her next move, Josey and I would run to the wash shed where my mother kept a washboard and old tubs, yank out a tina, turn it over to check for holes, then drag it to the faucet and fill it with cool water, anxious for the prickly pears. Once she dumped the fruit in the water, Doña Luisa took the kitchen broom and with swift, precise strokes, brushed off the bristles that clung to them.

Back and forth went the broom, lightly brushing across the scarlet tunas that bobbed up and down in the water. Within minutes the spines, some as big as my thumb, rose to the top and mixed with the fruit. They looked treacherous, deadly even. Doña Luisa emptied the dirty water, making sure the fruit did not fall to the ground, then refilled the tub, as el Duque licked both the faucet and Josey's legs. She cleaned the tunas until few spines were visible in the water. The fruit was now ready. Although we loved tunas, we feared gagging on a spine.

The tunas were of the common variety: red with a crown of spines at the top. They came in all sizes: from as small as Josey's hand and to as large as a big orange. They tasted different too: some were as sweet as honey, while others, cut perhaps before their time, were as sour as lemons. Josey and I found it hard to tell which of the tunas were ripe, so first we squeezed, then handed them to Doña Luisa— or threw them at el Duque, the only dog in the neighborhood who flourished on prickly pears.

Once Doña Luisa gave us permission, we walked around the zinc tub, turning the red fruit over with a stick, comparing it in size. At times Josey and I coveted the same one. Feet streaked with mud, hands lashing out at the water, we elbowed each other until one of us, usually me, scooped out the tuna, a triumphant snicker on my face. I handed it to Doña Luisa, making sure she did not confuse it with Josey's selection. With one stroke of the knife, Doña Luisa cut off the fruit's crested top and then the sides, to expose the heart, el corazón, which I quickly gobbled up.

If we were lucky, Josey and I got to eat yellow prickly pears too. These were especially sweet and did not grow in our yard but were given to us by a neighbor. The yellow fruit was smaller in size, but what it lacked in size it made up in taste. Josey and I fought over the yellow pears too, but not too often. We had already developed a taste for the common red tunas that each spring brightened our back yard. We were content to eat the juicy fruit cut for us by Doña Luisa.

In our family only Josey and I liked tunas. Trina preferred the red popsickles sold at the corner store. Rather than wait for Doña Luisa to knock down the juicy fruit, Trina would trek to the store, dark hair flying, to buy her favorite sweets. She would come home to stand in front of my brother and me, licking the cold popsickle while Josey and I waited to stuff ourselves with tunas.

Doña Luisa had always spoiled Josey. She let him ride atop her thin shoulders as I trailed behind. She gave him his way with toys, let him eat toast made on her wood stove (which I always felt was my special treat), and rarely chased after him to clean his nose. On the day of the tunas she sat him on her lap, his short legs sticking out from his rompers, and hand-fed him all the tunas he could hold. Josey, little pig that he was, gobbled up the ripe red pears as well as the yellow ones given us by the neighbors. He ate so much he could barely walk.

When he began to complain of a stomachache, my mother rubbed him with olive oil until he felt better. Three days later, when Josey had become bloated and still could not go to the bathroom, my mother and Doña Luisa decided that Josey was constipated, or as was said in the barrio, tapado, stopped up. My mother, her round face pale and worn, sought to find a remedy that would cure her baby, fearful that el más chiquito would burst, while Doña Luisa prayed nonstop.

First the two señoras gave Josey hot cinnamon tea with lemon, then rubbed him with olive oil heated in a spoon. As they rubbed his stomach, they prayed in Spanish; their soft voices filled the room. "Compadece de este niño, Señor, Have pity on this child, Lord." They prayed and prayed, as Doña Luisa wrung her skinny hands in despair, then wiped Josey's flushed face with a warm towel. The praying continued far into the night.

Josey lay on the bed, scared stiff at the strange incantations spoken by my mother and Doña Luisa, his fear intensified by the stench of oil that permeated the stuffy room. His small chest, shiny with perspiration and oil, rose and fell; his sunken eyes glowed like dark coals. His face was pinched and yellow.

"Am I gonna die?" Josey asked, his voice hoarse and tight.

"No, but you better go to the bathroom soon, or . . ."

When the oil and prayers did not cure Josey, my mother and Doña Luisa gave him great quantities of warm water to drink. When he had had his fill, and had spat the water out, they picked him up and ran with him to the outhouse. They sat him on the smaller hole; Doña Luisa stationed herself outside the door. While Josey sat on the wooden seat, scared stiff at falling in, I circled the outhouse, tracing my steps around and around.

"Puje, mijo," Doña Luisa told Josey. Grrrrr, Uhhhhh.

For three days they sat Josey in the outhouse, bringing him in when he cried. His nalgitas became swollen from sitting on the smaller hole; his eyes were rimmed with shadows. Neighbors came to give advice and peek at a bloated Josey atop our mother's bed. In desperation my mother undressed Josey, then put him in a tub of warm water. She told him to bend over. Doña Luisa gently shoved a long sliver of soap into his behind. She moved back just in time. After that Josey hated tunas and his new nickname: el tapado.

Each night I thanked my lucky stars and all the saints in heaven for bringing Doña Luisa to live next to us on Hoyt Street. She never learned to cook, nor did she remember to wash her hands. What Doña Luisa did best was to love.

La Doctora Barr

By the time Josey and I came along, it was fashionable for pregnant women, even those with countless children, such as my mother, to consult a doctor. Since few doctors came to the barrio, everyone consulted Dr. Barr.

Josey was delivered at home by la Doctora Barr, who had also delivered me. Two of my older siblings were born when our parents lived in Ventura; the rest came into this world without a doctor in attendance. Only Doña Luisa was there to greet them.

Doctor Barr practiced medicine in the nearby town of "Burbanque," as we called Burbank, but also came to the homes of gente mexicana to deliver babies. She worked independently and was not affiliated with the clinic in San Fernando that sent out nurses to instruct barrio women on health and hygiene. The public nurses, most of whom were dedicated to improving our lives, were often critical of how we lived, what we ate. They made Mexican women feel uncomfortable. Not Doctor Barr; she enjoyed working in our pueblito, and in her halting Spanish made herself understood to the women. I regularly saw her car chugging down Hoyt Street on the way to a neighbor.

Doctor Barr was of medium height, plump, with soft brown hair worn in a bun, from which wispy tendrils escaped to form a halo around her cheerful face. She wore little makeup and needed none. Her cheeks were a bright red; when she smiled they appeared to be two apples. The wire-frame glasses she wore over her kind eyes often slipped down her nose, leaving her to peer over them.

"Well, playing ball again, I see."

"Sí Señora Barr."

"Yes, Mrs. Doctor."

"And are you helping your mothers at home?" she asked, as she pulled a worn black bag from the seat of her '38 Dodge. "Are you helping your mother?"

"Yes ma'am! I wash dishes, sweep the kitchen, and make the beds."

"Liar! I make them."

"I make them," I insisted, as la doctora disappeared into a nearby house, black bag in hand. "I make them."

On Hoyt Street, and all over town for that matter, new babies were a common thing. Every time I turned around, someone was having a baby, or several. Every woman on our block, beginning with my mother, had from five to ten children—and thought nothing of it. Still it was exciting to know a doctor who considered babies special. Dr. Barr, I heard, approached each birth as a miracle of the highest order. She treated all pregnant women with respect and never once implied that they had too, too many children. She realized that most expectant mothers gained too much weight, but because she also was plump, did not dwell on it. Rather she left folks alone to do the best with what they had. When they were offered, she would eat tortillas hot off the griddle sprinkled with salt and would leave a house with a stack of hot tortillas wrapped in a white cloth, saying it was her dinner.

Unlike Anglo women who sought out a doctor during the early stages of a pregnancy, the expectant mothers of our town did not consult la Doctora Barr until the pregnancy was well into its final months. Few families had money for prenatal care, let alone the bus fare to Burbank. Folks on Hoyt Street went to the doctor only when seriously ill or when they needed an operation. Still pregnant women, even first-time mothers, knew what to do during un embarazo. Most went on with their daily work, caring for home and children until the first labor pains, then alerted a neighbor. The neighbor in turn notified un señor, who rushed to the one phone booth (on Van Nuys Boulevard and San Fernando Road) to call Dr. Barr. In the meantime neighbor women would bring out sábanas limpias, crisp, clean sheets; put water on to boil; and farm out kids to relatives or neighbors to spare them the confusion that accompanied a birth. In large families the younger children slept in the same room as parents, but it was not considered proper to have them around during a birthing; so off they went.

When the doctor arrived, all was in readiness: the expectant mother lay on clean white sheets, face washed, hair combed back in a bun or braid. In her hand was a clean rag to bite on when the pain became unbearable. To scream aloud was said to be muy ranchero; rather than appear low class, a woman in pain muffled her cries. A bottle of alcohol, clean towels, and a pan for the afterbirth were kept nearby, as were the clean rags used as sanitary napkins.

For poor Mexican women, sanitary napkins were a luxury. Not everyone could afford this product, which was not sold at la tienda de Don Jesús, but was readily available at the Pacoima General Store. When money was scarce, and the doctor still to be paid, women used what was available without complaint: old sheets and clean rags cut into strips.

Not everyone in our neighborhood believed in a scientific approach to childbirth. Few women knew how to read or write in Spanish, let alone English, so they couldn't read the pamphlets given them by Dr. Barr. They knew only what they had learned from their mothers and abuelitas, the common sense that had generally served them well.

While most señoras believed in eating nutritious foods and remaining active, they actually had little choice in what foods they ate. If a family was limited to beans and tortillas, that was what the mother-to-be ate. And because of the numerous children they cared for, pregnant women had no choice but to get up each morning to care for la familia. Few took naps, but merely collapsed at night next to husbands equally tired. Doctor Barr understood the problems faced by poor women; she rarely chided them for their starchy and limited diet. Now and then, however, she did suggest that women lay aside old Mexican customs and do things the "American way."

Among the women who disdained la doctora's advice was Juana, said to be una india because of her dark skin, high cheekbones, slanted eyes, and the facility for delivering babies without a fuss every nine months. Unlike other pregnant women, who waddled when they walked, Juana carried her babies high against her chest. Not even in her last months did her stomach protrude. Back straight, arms akimbo, she strode through our dusty streets, belly tucked underneath her ribs, followed by a bevy of dark-haired kids. Her recuperative powers were amazing, and the talk of the town.

One time I was playing ball with Concha, my best friend, when Emma, a neighbor woman, came for Doña Placencia, Concha's mother. Juana was about to give birth.

"Doña Placencia, Doña Placencia. Juana says it's time . . ."

"Avísale que ya voy, tell her I'm coming." Doña Placencia removed her apron, washed her face and hands, combed her greying hair, grabbed a bottle of alcohol, and off she went to aid her friend and neighbor.

Concha and I, busy palying a game of jacks in the dirt, ran after her mother. We were curious to be around someone about to give birth, a subject discussed by our mothers with sighs of "Jesús, María y José" but not when we were within earshot. I caught up with Doña Placencia and, in my best Spanish, volunteered to help carry the towels and alcohol now in her hands. She ignored me and kept on walking, a smile on her face. Still I persisted, as did Concha, who from experience knew that her mother would eventually give in. We followed her to the small dark house with flowered curtains where Juana waited.

Once at Juana's, Concha's mother opened the door without knocking, took the towels and alcohol inside, checked on Juana, then shooed us out. She closed the wooden door in our faces, then drew the latch. Rather than leave, Concha and I stayed close to the house, kicking at dirt clods, in hopes of being asked to run an errand. Soon we resumed our game of jacks, all the while looking toward the latched door. Finally, unable to stand the suspense, we dashed back to Juana's and knocked on the door with clenched fists.

"Mamá, mamá!"

"Señora Placencia!"

When Doña Placencia finally came to the door, we pushed our way past her, but she yanked us back. Still we refused to leave. By this time Concha and I had agreed to use any pretext to get inside the door.

"Tell her your stomach hurts," I suggested, "and you think you're gonna die."

"Neh, she won't believe me," answered Concha, wiping her nose with the hem of her dress.

"Can you make your nose bleed?" I persisted. "You know, real bloody . . ."

"Only if you hit me!"

We decided to say we needed money for candy and gum. This sounded like a normal, everyday thing, and would not arouse suspicion. Back we went.

"Mamá, we wanna go to the store."

"Oh?"

"Sí, we need some money . . ."

Concha's mother pretended to be pleased at our request; we rarely asked permission for anything! Only her smiling eyes betrayed her. She unlatched the door and let us into la sala, the front room of the small house, then went to fetch the handkerchief in which she kept loose coins. While Concha waited for her mother to return, I tiptoed into the next room and peeked inside.

The room was dark; I could barely make out the figures of two women: Juana, bending over, her long braid hanging across her face, and a woman I did not recognize but thought might be Emma, standing behind her, towels at her feet, hands outstretched. Their voices were barely audible.

"Púje, púje. Push, push. Just a little bit more."

"Ay! It hurts!"

"Pués . . . this isn't the first one . . ."

"Ummmm. I hope it's the last."

"Yes, but first you must push."

I stood mesmerized, peering into the room, trying to focus on what the two figures were doing. Just then I heard Concha's mother approaching from the other direction, and I quickly moved back to where Concha stood, my heart thumping loudly against my chest. Doña Placencia gave me a look that spoke volumes; her eyes narrowed, then crinkled at the edges. She said nothing, but merely handed Concha two dimes and quickly shooed us out the door.

Later that evening we heard that a son had been born to Juana, a bouncing boy named Juan Manuel. Early the next day she was seen outside, new baby strapped to her back, hanging diapers on the line! Later that week she came by our house, dressed in a pink cotton dress. She looked as slim as ever, her stomach flat, her waist just a bit swollen. In her arms she carried the new baby, while her numerous children trailed behind.

Women on Hoyt Street shook their heads in wonder (and disgust) at los modos rancheros de Juana, the way she went about birthing. They compared her to backward women stuck in a ranch. They could not understand how throughout her many pregnancies Juana neither asked for the doctor nor followed la dieta afterwards.

One of the few areas of conflict between Dr. Barr and our women was the traditional diet new mothers were supposed to follow. La dieta, as it was called in Spanish, pertained not only to food but also to the aftercare following a birth. For all her goodness, and often in direct contrast to her earlier advice, Dr. Barr became exasperated when her patients insisted on following Mexican traditions and customs rather than her instructions, which she felt to be more "wholesome." In her halting Spanish, Dr. Barr would encourage women to get up, walk around, and bathe soon after a birth. Mexican custom dictated otherwise. In order not to catch cold, frío, a new mother should neither bathe nor wash her hair for at least six weeks! Foods such as lemons, avocados, and carne de puerco, which might sour her milk were to be avoided at all costs. A new mother should drink neither extremely hot nor cold foods, except for homemade chicken soup, which was good for any and all illnesses.

Once she expelled the afterbirth, a woman who had just given birth was made to wear a wide band (made of old sheets cut in strips) around her stomach. This was to ensure that the womb, la matriz would soon return to its normal size. Heavy lifting was prohibited, as was mopping floors and scrubbing clothes on a washboard. This, then, was a time for women like my mother, who worked hard all her life, to be waited on by family and neighbors. In time la dieta was forgotten. Not everyone could afford the luxury of lying in bed for six weeks, nor did women want to do without a bath. While old ladies shook their heads in amazement and issued dire warnings, young women who wanted to be *como las americanas* did as the doctor suggested. They got up on the third day, took a bath and washed their hair, and generally went about their daily chores. It seems that Juana, illiterate and "backward," knew what she was doing all along.

The Three Trinidads

On Hoyt Street lived three elderly women we kids considered religious fanatics: Doña Caridad, Doña Magdalena and Doña Clarissa. We poked fun at this trio of señoras and called them names, many of them thought up on the spot: "las religiosas," "las santuchas," and my favorite, "the three Trinidads." The three were members of the Altar Society and each morning walked to Guardian Angel Church in a group. Once there they split to clean the various altars, dust pews, or polish the communion rail. When not busy with these tasks, they knelt to pray to a favorite saint, then left the church together.

They were very competitive. Often when on the way home from la iglesia, they argued in Spanish about who among them had prayed more and had done the most good deeds.

"I finished my novena to Saint Francis."

"Poś, I lit three candles to . . ."

"I fasted all day yesterday and now feel sick."

"Jesús, María y José!"

Doña Cari

Doña Caridad, called Doña Cari by kids, was the leader of the pack. She was a widow who lived across the street from us. She was of medium height, heavyset, with a round face and several chins that wobbled when she spoke. When it was directed at me, her high-pitched voice gave me the shivers. Her thin gray hair was held in place by hairpins sold at the five and dime. Every three months her hair changed color; it went from gray to blue-gray. Often the hair dye did not rinse off but remained on her neck. When teased by the others for tinting her hair, Doña Cari became angry: her teeth chattered, her chins wobbled. She adamantly denied using dye, a thing considered frivolous for women her age, insisting that the inferior bathsoap sold at the store caused the change in color. No one dared disagree with Doña Cari; frivolous she was not.

She wore shawls of light wool: a soft lilac interspersed with white, a silky rose with a short fringe, and my favorite one, a gossamer-like yellow shawl that smelled of lemons. All were gifts from her grandchildren. In autumn, when the weather turned cool and a light breeze rustled the pepper trees on Hoyt Street, Doña Cari piled shawls atop her ample shoulders, saying "soy muy friolenta."

Doña Cari turned up her nose at the black rebozos worn by other women, shawls of coarse cotton and heavy flannel. She considered them too common, cheap-looking even. I once heard her say she preferred to be swaddled in shawls rather than appear low class.

Doña Caridad lived in a roomy house left to her by Don Esteban, her late husband. He had been much older than Doña Cari it was said, but had worshipped the ground she walked on and satisfied her every whim. She owned two other houses on the block. One was rented out to Don Policarpio, an elderly man who wore a patch over one eye. In the other lived her widowed daughter Petrina with her three children: Santos, Anthony, and Jemina, called Jemmy.

Jemina was Doña Cari's favorite. She was husky with thick ankles, a pert nose, and a smattering of freckles on her full cheeks. Her auburn curls complimented the myopic, hazel eyes that peered from behind inch-thick glasses. Jemmy was extremely obedient and once, in a moment of weakness, promised her doting grandmother she would never cut her hair. At fourteen Jemmy's hair grew past her knees.

Jemmy was a bookworm, a phenomenon among her teenage friends, most of whom spent their waking hours playing Frank Sinatra records. Jemmy read *real* books, hardcover books of hundreds of pages with nary an illustration. She hated the comics read by most kids and turned up her nose at books of less than three hundred pages. She read books in alphabetical order. Each summer she checked out at least twenty books from the San Fernando library, to be read before school began. She was up to the *g*s and was already bored. Her constant reading worried la abuela, who feared her favorita would go blind. She insisted that Jemmy's eyes be examined each school year and that Jemmy be fitted with new reading glasses. Everyone deferred to Doña Cari; no one dared contradict her. Whenever she played in the street, Jemmy kept one eye on the ball and the other on her grandma's door.

The two older boys neither drank nor smoked in front of la abuela. At their confirmation, dressed in white shirts and dark pants and coached by their grandma, they renounced Satanás and all his works, vowing not to smoke or drink until they were twenty-one. Doña Cari feared they would take to el vicio and forever be lost to a life of debauchery. From that day forward they grew in stature on Hoyt Street, where being disrespectful to parents was the norm.

When war broke out, Santos, then all of eighteen, joined the Navy and went to the Pacific. Each week he wrote V-letters to his grandma and included a postscript for his mother.

Antonio Francisco, called Tonio by his grandma and Tony by Jemmy, was named for Saint Anthony of Padua and Saint Francis of Assisi, the protector of animals. This, I often snickered, was really funny, because Tony was neither saintly nor did he care for animals. He was mean! Mean to the neighborhood dogs and cats he pelted with rocks, and mean to kids smaller than he. Josey and I hated him. More than once Tony had stoned el Duque, just for fun.

Like all good Mexican mothers (and abuelas) Doña Cari was constantly on the alert for what she perceived as the works of the devil. She was constantly harping on las malas compañías and urged her grandson to avoid those who might lead him astray. Each morning she joined the other Trinidads in prayer and lit candles to Saint Anthony, asking him to protect Tony from evil.

Although Doña Cari had her own house, each evening at six sharp she walked to her daughter's to eat dinner entre familia. There at the formal oak table, out of deference and respect, Doña Cari was served first, followed by Tony. Jemmy and her mother came last.

Before anyone could eat, Doña Cari insisted they say grace. First she lit candles to Saint Francis, then the praying began. She prayed for the pope, the bishop, and Santos. Jemmy never dared complain of the prayers that each year took longer, while dinner got cold.

Like most of us, Jemmy used street talk and pachuco slang. Words like "cool," "simón," and "hep to the jive" made her feel grown-up.

Often however, she slipped up, then paid dearly, for her mistake. One time at dinner Jemmy answered her grandma with her favorite slang.

"Quieres más pastél, Jemina? Do you want more pie?"

"Simón, Granma."

She was sent to her room to escape being slapped by Tony, who allowed no disrespect for his grandma.

Unlike Marta, a middle-aged widow who lived on Carl Street and who remarried three months after her husband died, Jemmy's mother seemed destined to remain unattached. I once asked Jemmy about this.

"How come your amá don't get married?"

"She can't."

Jemmy shuffled her feet, then explained that once Doña Caridad had caught influenza. Claiming she was at death's door, she insisted that a priest hear her confession, then made Petrina promise never to marry while she was still alive.

"And then what happened?"

"She got well, that's what."

According to Jemina, her grandma had made a last confession more than once. Each time I heard Doña Cari giving Jemmy orders in her high-pitched voice, I marveled at how alive she sounded. As if she could live forever.

Jemmy's mother, Petrina, was a pretty woman with light brown eyes like those of a friendly cow. She worked as a hair stylist in a beauty shop; with the tips she earned, she bought pleated skirts and pastel sweaters for Jemina. She had a nice smile and a disposition to match. I often marveled at how someone this nice could have mothered a son like Tony.

At seventeen Tony was tall for his age and quite handsome. His thick black hair, saturated with pomade, was worn in a ducktail; his brown eyes missed nothing. From his small, spiteful mouth emanated the worst cusswords heard on Hoyt Street or in the entire neighborhood.

He attended high school in San Fernando, hated books, teachers, and the principal, and thought he was tough. When Doña Caridad wasn't looking, he wore pleated pants called "drapes" to class. Once, sent home to change pants by an irate teacher, he refused to return and spent the day smoking in bed and reading comic books. Feeling that Tony had been singled out for punishment, Doña Caridad forced Petrina to plead with the principal, whom all the Mexican kids hated. Tony was suspended for two days, which he spent in bed with the girlie magazines he hid under the mattress.

Whenever he ditched school, he made it a point to head for home when school let out. Textbooks cradled in his husky arms, he would leave the poolhall to merge with other students, afraid of having his grandma see him with las malas compañías.

Toño was clever and liked to pit his grandma and mother against each other, knowing he would benefit from any arguments between the two. On school days they fought over who should fry eggs for Tony and who best ironed his white shirts. On payday, Jemmy told me, her mother gave Tonio a school allowance matched by Doña Cari, who then slipped Tony more dollars with which to buy Fats Domino records.

"And how much do you get?"

"Uuuuhh."

Tony spent his money on friends, cigarettes, and booze, making sure to hide the whiskey from Jemmy. Petrina tolerated Tony's bad habits, most of which she said were inherited from her late husband.

One time Tonio was in the back alley smoking and drinking beer with his teenage friends. Jemmy, busy hanging wash on the clothesline, saw him light a Lucky Strike. Tony walked over to Jemmy, blew smoke in her face, and pulled her hair, while his friends snickered. Eyes smarting behind her thick glasses, Jemmy ran off, screaming for her grandma. By the time she returned with Doña Caridad (whose chins were already wobbling), Tony, alerted by his friends, had stomped on the incriminating cigarette, but did not exhale the last puff. While his grandmother ranted, he held his breath.

"Lookit him, granma!"

"No tienes vergüenza!"

Doña Cari finished the scolding, then, wool shawls dragging, she walked across the yard and into the house.

Although the scolding took but minutes, Tony began to gag on the smoke. He coughed and coughed, unable to take a deep breath. His eyes and nose began to water; his face turned a splotchy red. His friends were scared stiff at this turn of events. They smacked him on the back as an alarmed Jemmy, hair flying, ran off to get her grandma once more.

Doña Cari, used to family emergencies, rose to the occasion. She grabbed the garden hose, yanked it across the alley, squirted Tony in the face, then lashed out at las malas compañías, who ran down the alley at a fast trot.

They half-carried Tony inside the house; Doña Cari cradled his head while Jemmy supported his shoulders. Doña Cari sat him on a velvet chair with a lace doily and ordered Jemmy to remove his shoes, fetch a pillowcase (embroidered with birds), and a glass of water. When he had fully recovered from el susto, Tony took to his bed to listen to Fats Domino, while in the next room his grandma lit candles to Saint Anthony.

Later that week, swaddled in a lilac shawl with pink rosebuds and flanked by the other Trinidads, Doña Caridad walked to church to offer a mass of deliverance for Tony, who had suddenly lost his taste for cigarettes.

Doña Magda

Doña Magdalena, the oldest of the three Trinidads, lived five houses down from us in a green clapboard house she shared with her niece Amparo. She too was a widow, but unlike Doña Caridad, had no natural children, only Esteban, an adopted son who was in the Marines. Her plain house was not as elegant as that of Doña Cari nor as full of plants as that of Doña Clarissa, except for the pink geraniums that grew along the porch. The front of her house was painted the same sick green as ours, but the back was a faded yellow. The green paint, it seems, had run out once the front and side walls were finished. Still and all, the pretty flowers gave the house a festive look. In the back was the outhouse, painted the same obnoxious green; around it grew more pink geraniums.

Unlike Doña Caridad, Doña Magda was friendly and had lived on Hoyt Street longer than my parents. She always smiled when she went by. As a young woman she had been tall, but age and arthritis had shrunk her body. Her olive complexion was dotted with birthmarks, lunares, that to me resembled the Milky Way. Her thin grey hair, like fine silk, was worn in a long braid that in summer was pinned atop her head or wound around her ears.

She dressed completely in black. During the week she wore cotton dresses; on Sunday she wore a shiny gabardine dress that had seen better days. Her arthritic shoulders stuck out through the dress, so that from afar she appeared to be wearing shoulder pads. The dress sleeves hung down to her gnarled hands, on which dangled three copper bracelets bought in Mexico, said to alleviate the pain and swelling of arthritis.

While Doña Cari wore flowered dresses and Doña Clarissa dark skirts, Doña Magda was the most severe in her dress. Only the beige of her coarse stockings broke the expanse of black that extended from the neck of her somber dress to her sturdy black shoes. On cold days she wore a roomy black coat given her by Amparo. In a gusty wind, the coat swirled around her thin frame.

Underneath her dark dresses Doña Magdalena wore scapulars and holy medals collected for years, which she claimed protected her from the devil and the evil eye. The scapular she tucked into her dress was of thick cotton, almost like cardboard, with a cross in the middle. This was worn to ward off el demonio. The medals were pinned to her slip with large safety pins; when she walked the medals swung back and forth, *chink, chink, chink*. They sounded like the loose change in my father's pants pocket.

Doña Magda believed in miracles and in paying mandas in person. It was said that her dearest wish was to visit Rome to meet el papa. Each day she listened to a Catholic radio station that kept her abreast of the miracles taking place throughout the world, all of which she believed on the spot.

She felt that in addition to prayer, one should make penance at every opportunity. Her novena to Saint Filomena was going on its third year; her nightly petitions to St. Augustine kept her up till late. She ate nothing but bread and butter on Fridays. Given the opportunity she would have dragged herself to church on her knees.

Doña Magda was the most traveled of the Trinidads, a fact that irked Doña Caridad but didn't faze Doña Clarissa. Each month she visited St. Vibiana's Cathedral in Los Angeles with a church group. At one time she and Amparo had traveled to Mexico City to lay flowers at the feet of the Virgin of Guadalupe. Inside the basilica, Doña Magda swore she felt tremors in her arthritic hands, so she threw herself down on the floor. Once revived by a frightened Amparo, she fasted and prayed without ceasing, certain a miracle had taken place. Upon her return to Pacoima she went straight to our new priest to share the good news and to show him her hands, now less swollen. But he became angry, livid almost, and showed her to the door.

The Trinidads believed her, however, saying that God had chosen to heal Doña Magda because of her piety. They rubbed her hands as though testing the miracle and all but wept with emotion. They resolved to pray to the Virgin of Guadalupe each Tuesday and to light candles to Our Lady of Perpetual Help. Doña Clarissa promised to pray an entire novena in Latin, certain that this language was of more value than Spanish, let alone el inglés. Doña Caridad dug up a bottle of alcohol, mixed it with holy water and dried rosemary, and offered it to Doña Magda. When her hands began to swell once more, Doña Magda was not too unhappy, but even welcomed the pain, feeling that this too was a penance.

Early on Doña Magda had converted her small bedroom into what resembled a tiny church, with three altars in one room! A small altar dedicated to El Santo Niño de Atocha (a short, fat saint who wore bloomers) was to the left. Toward the back wall, adjacent to a tall window with sheer curtains, was a large picture of la Santísima Virgen del Perpetuo Socorro. She wore a light blue gown over a white tunic and to my eyes resembled the Virgin Mary, except that she did not have stars at her feet. A small statue of the dark Virgin of Guadalupe graced the largest altar in the room. The ceramic statue, brought in Tijuana for $2.99, was beginning to crack. From afar Guadalupe's dark Indian eyes looked down at the crack between her toes.

Inside the crowded room, votive candles of all sizes, bought at a religious supply store in Los Angeles, flickered throughout the day. Next to them was an assortment of flowers: dahlias, cosmos, and Shasta daisies grown by Amparo. Doña Magda religiously changed the water every third day.

A profusion of religious artifacts filled all four walls of Doña Magda's bedroom: framed santos, shiny medals, braided palms collected on Palm Sunday, and strings of rosaries. Atop her bed sat a plump cushion embroidered with the word *PAZ*.

As a young woman, Doña Magda began to collect rosaries; she now had the most extensive assortment of rosarios in the barrio. Atop her dresser (and on nails stuck along the walls) hung rosaries ordered through a catalog published by a missionary society. A rosary made of Philipine mahogany and sent by Esteban was said to bring good luck in ten days. The one made of glass beads was said to come from the grotto at Lourdes, where many miracles took place. I liked best the jet-black rosary bought for her Tía Magda by Amparo, which, according to the catalog, was blessed by none other than the Pope himself! Each time I touched the dark beads I felt terribly holy!

Doña Magda was forever fingering the rosary that hung from her waist as she murmured "Jesús, María y José." When my friends and I saw her coming down the street, we hissed "Jesus, Mary, and Joseph; here comes the Holy Trinidad!" We said this in a hushed tone, because Doña Magda, daily involved in making novenas or repaying sacred promises, was considered on Hoyt Street to be something of a martyr. Martyrs were respected in the barrio, even by little kids.

In our parish certain religious groups (and some individuals) competed to see who could appear to be the holiest, the most dedicated to God. They made a big show of lighting votive candles, and praying novenas, and when requesting a mass for a dead relative, insisted that our priest announce the sponsor's first, middle, and last name. Folks knew who gave to the collection basket and who did not.

One year during the Easter Vigil, the Trinidads and members of Las Hijas de María and the Altar Society almost came to blows at Mary's altar, when it was discovered that both groups were scheduled for the six o'clock vigil. After much haggling they made room for each other in the third pew. Still Doña Caridad, chins wobbling up and down, was furious. Doña Clarissa began to pray aloud in Latin, hoping to impress the interlopers, while Doña Magda fingered her black rosary.

Up until the coming of our new pastor, the women in the barrio worshipped the old-fashioned way, in the language and traditions of Mexico. El Padre Juanito, who was then in his sixties, rarely criticized the viejitas, but assured them that a place in heaven was reserved for those who paid a penance on this earth. Father Mueller changed things. Out went the old hymn books, dusty saints with funny names, and processions. But some customs still persisted.

On our street Doña Magda held the record for paying off personal petitions made to God and all His saints. Doña Magda, kind soul that she was, liked to repay petitions in public. She was not alone in thinking that a public demonstration of piety had more merit, nor was she the most vocal; she was only the most persistent. Folks on our street said she was merely following a common, Mexican tradition, but others said she was vain and wanted attention. Her stiffest competition came from Doña Remedios, a sour-faced busybody with four sons in the army, a situation that kept her praying nonstop. More than once the two women came close to colliding near the church entrance after they had crawled through the streets to pay a penance or a promise made to Nuestro Señor.

During the war many men from our town were drafted and sent overseas. Their relatives at home, many of whom were viejitas, like Doña Magda, felt it their sacred duty to offer mandas in return for their loved ones' protection. While some vowed to attend mass on the first Friday of each month, pray novenas, light candles, or wear a religious medal, many more preferred to pray at a shrine to the Virgen of San Juan de Los Lagos in the town of Sunland.

There were unwritten rules about how to repay a manda. To arrive at the shrine (located about seven miles from Pacoima) in a comfortable car was not considered a sacrifice, nor was walking the last mile. What counted was to drag oneself on one's knees, de rodillas, to hurt, suffer, and hurt some more. Thus when Doña Magda insisted on repaying a petition in the old way, folks saw this as a noble gesture, un sacrificio. The Pacoima streets, littered with rocks, indeed made this a sacrifice.

One time Trina and I were on our way to eight o'clock mass (the later mass was said to be for the lazies). As we neared the corner, I saw Doña Magda inching her way down the street on her knees. Her grey head, hidden beneath a black shawl, was bowed low; her dress wrapped around her dusty ankles. I was terribly impressed, certain that she was on her way to Guardian Angel Church. Her knees, I knew, would be bloodied and her dress full of dirt by the time she reached the church door. This was almost like the Vía Crucis on

Good Friday, I thought. All Doña Magda lacked was a cross.

Trina began to snicker, her dark eyes full of merriment; I lagged behind, staring at the dark form coming up the street. Just then Trina yanked at me, her hand heavy on my arm.

"Come on."

"No," I screamed, kicking out with my oxfords.

"We'll be late," she hissed, tugging at her new belt.

"No we won't," I countered, moving toward the street.

I wanted to watch the show! I was determined to be on hand when Doña Magda made her triumphant entry into the church. I stood my ground.

A crowd gathered, including the rowdies who never went to church but who knew when something was about to happen. We stood on the sidelines, not unlike runners in a relay race who greet the anchor. We pushed and shoved, each wanting the best view. I staked out a spot near the door, as Trina and her friends snickered at the martyr of Hoyt Street now coming up the road.

Trina and her friends, my mother often said, were at an age where they lacked respeto, respect for their elders and for Mexican traditions. They made fun of parents, teachers, and Mexican dichos, folk sayings, which they claimed were old-fashioned and un-American. The girls acted like voladas too, chasing after boys, their olive faces thick with the makeup bought at Thrifty's in San Fernando.

That day Trina and her friends stood in a small cluster, laughing at the dark bulk that was Doña Magda. I remained on the church steps, determined not to give up my place. My mouth felt dry, my eyes stung, as I focused on the snaillike figure. Suddenly a loud commotion was heard inside the empty church. The doors flew open and out stormed Father Mueller, his steel-blue eyes narrowing, his chasuble bunched around his knees.

The startled crowd, surprised at the sudden interruption, parted like the Red Sea. Father Mueller's face was beet red, his ears a deep pink. He walked over to Doña Magda, leaned down, and hissed.

"Por favor, señora." He appealed to her in his best Spanish, about to choke on the words. "Please, Doña Magda, this is not necessary! Please stand."

"Pero padre . . !"

"Come, come. This is no longer in vogue," he emphasized, his voice hoarse and angry, as he tried to ignore the crowd now gathered. "Our Lord is content with your prayers," he concluded. He then bent down and lifted up the martyr of Hoyt Street, ushered her into the church, and then walked briskly toward the sacristy to prepare for mass. The crowd, like a flock of sheep, followed el padrecito inside.

Later that week parishioners grumbled aloud, upset at the reaction of our new priest to what was a common practice. Doña Magda, folks said, should be allowed to repay the manda for Esteban, fighting in Corregidor, any way she chose. Members of the Altar Society, Doña Caridad among them, called on our pastor to voice their objections. But Father Mueller, adamant to the end, reminded the women that we now lived in a modern world. Our modern priest loved us for our piety, yet frowned on the ancient rites of sacrifice. After that no one dared pay a manda in Pacoima but sneaked off to the Los Angeles placita and to the Sunland shrine to repay a sacred promise.

Each Sunday morning a profusion of dusty cars headed up Foothill Boulevard toward the Sunland shrine of the Virgin of San Juan, which was closer than la placita. The road to the foothills was scenic, dotted with orange trees. The shrine was inside a house next to a taco stand. From the outside it looked like any other house, with a front door, two windows, and a small front yard. Inside the living room (now the shrine), the floor was covered in dark linoleum streaked with heel marks from the many visitors. At the back was a homemade altar painted white, with a statue of the Virgin. She wore a gold-cloth outfit and a crown with golden spikes like that worn by ancient Phoenicians. In her hands was a tiny scepter, and at her feet (and along the altar) were pink and red roses, carnations, geraniums, and, here and there, a stately gladiolus. A profusion of candles was mixed in with the flowers: tall ivory tapers, votive candles in red glasses, and small blobs of yellow wax.

Some people got off near Foothill Boulevard, then arrived at the stucco shrine on their knees. Others, bolder, drove into the driveway adjacent to the shrine, car doors slamming and car radio blaring, then stomped their way to the holy shrine. Many left within minutes, sauntering off to Sunland Park to ride the carousel or to picnic on the green grass under the tall oak trees.

When Father Mueller heard of the renewed popularity of the Sunland shrine, he had a fit. The following Sunday he reminded parishioners of their obligation to the parish and the parish priest. He droned on and on, his perfect Spanish lost on the mute figures before him, all of whom, the minute mass was over, would hop into their cars for the short trip to Sunland.

It was some time before Father Mueller realized that people preferred to honor a personal manda in ways not acceptable to him, the archdiocese, or His Eminence, the bishop. In time, however, they became modernized and adopted new ideas. They did as my sister Trina did: made fun of simple folks who followed simple customs. In time the shrine of the Virgin of San Juan became a tourist attraction. The taco stand converted to a fast-food restaurant where people zipped in and out in record time.

Then one day Doña Magda stopped paying mandas. No longer could we ogle her public feats of sacrifice. Dressed in her flapping dark dresses, she continued to attend daily mass and take communion, but she no longer knelt in the street, only in a pew. She told the Trinidads she feared to offend our pastor, but they didn't believe her. They claimed Doña Magda had lost faith in the Almighty.

The story was that Doña Magda received a telegram from the Navy saying that Esteban had abandoned ship, was AWOL, but was believed to be in the Hawaiian Islands. A second telegram informed her that Esteban had returned and, after a light reprimand, was back in the Navy. Upon hearing this a mortified Doña Magda fell on her knees to pray, then fasted on bread and water.

Soon after he sent Doña Magda a picture of his new wife, a dark, full-bodied woman in a red and white sarong. Up close the woman was quite pretty and resembled a hefty Dorothy Lamour. Doña Magda took one look at the picture, then stuck it behind the small altar. "La Hawaiana," she hissed to the Trinidads, "esta muy prieta." Not only was Esteban's wife too dark, but she was also a Jehovah's Witness, which to Doña Magda was the worst anyone could be. She took to her bed for days.

Shortly afterward, Doña Magda experienced a change of heart. When on Mother's Day Esteban sent her a pretty card, her heart melted. She burst into tears, went to confession, then placed Esteban's picture next to San Martín de Porras; she placed a red votive candle in front of la Hawaiana.

Doña Magda was a typical Mexican mother who loved her son

with a passion. It was said of her, "es una santa; sufre por su hijo," she suffers for her son. On our street, this was the ultimate compliment to a mother.

Doña Clarissa

The least likely Trinidad was Doña Clarissa, a sweet-faced woman with a thin, ascetic look and thick hair worn in a chongo. Behind the bifocal glasses, her alert eyes missed nothing. Her mouth was thin, with lips like twin peaks that moved up and down when she spoke. When she was agitated, her thin nose quivered like that of Flicka, a horse in the movies. I considered her the most intelligent and least religious of the three Trinidads.

It was easy to spot this lady from afar. Her left leg was shorter than her right, so that she swayed to and fro. She used a bordón, a cane bought in a San Fernando hardware store, to help her navigate to the corner store and to church. Her handicap did not deter her from other activities. She helped the Trinidads with the church upkeep but liked best to sort the dusty music books stored in the choir loft. She was very independent and would refuse Don Sebastian's arm when climbing the church steps.

Doña Clarissa's clothes resembled those worn by Italian peasant women in the movies. She wore heavy wool skirts of brown, black, or navy blue, all of which looked old. Up close the mended holes were faintly visible. Atop her head she wore a kerchief, similar to a babushka. Doña Cari found this muy ranchero, so she offered Doña Clarissa a pretty wool shawl from her vast collection; it was declined.

The kerchiefs were of the same material as the skirts, except for the fringe along the edge, and quite different from the rebozos worn by other women on Hoyt Street. Her shoes resembled those worn by Doña Chonita (black with stubby toes and low heels), and were bought from the Mason Shoes catalog. Because of her limp, the right shoe wore out first. One Easter Sunday I spotted white shoes on Doña Clarissa's feet and complimented her on them; except for the fancy stitching, they resembled nurse's shoes. Claiming they made her feet look too wide, she had them dyed black within the week.

She lived on the corner of Hoyt and Carl streets, in a neat white house surrounded by shrubs and trees. Many Tuesdays she walked either to Doña Caridad's or Doña Magda's to listen to the Rosary Hour, which, even though it was in English, was easy to follow. But often she skipped this ritual to stay home and listen to opera and to review the stacks of music she kept on a bureau.

Doña Clarissa was half Italian; her Italian mother had married a baker from Monterrey, Mexico. Her name, she often reminded people, was spelled *al modo italiano,* with two *s*'s, rather than one. Although Spanish was her primary language, as a child she spoke fluent Italian; she had learned Latin in school. Of the three Trinidads, she alone knew the correct responses to prayers said at rosary and mass; during Lent, she sang the "Pange Lingua" by heart. Unlike most of us, Doña Clarissa knew what she was praying.

She liked nothing better than to pray the Latin mass along with our pastor, a thing that bothered Doña Cari, who said only un sacerdote should pray the mass, and who delighted in chiding Doña Clarissa about impersonating a priest.

"¡Áy! ni que fueras sacerdote!"

"Hummph."

During the misiones held each November at Guardian Angel Church, Doña Clarissa sat in the front row, to make sure the visiting missionary would hear her Latin response. On the last night she would send him baked goods wrapped in waxed paper and tied with string.

At one time Doña Clarissa sang in the choir, along with other viejitas who neither read music nor kept the beat, but sang from memory. Since her voice was low and deep, she was placed in the back rows to sing alto. Now and then she sang the part assigned to the men, her chin pressing against her chest to flush out the low, low notes. When told she could either sing with the women or con los hombres, she snorted, picked up her cane, and never again climbed to the choir loft.

Whenever someone in the neighborhood died, Doña Clarissa was asked to recite the rosary, a thing that made her feel terribly important. She was received at the grieving family's door almost with honors and was given a prominent chair, smack in the middle of la sala. She recited el rosario from memory, and she knew each Mystery

by heart: Joyful and Sorrowful, the Litany of the Saints, the Anima
Cristi, and the correct responses to our pastor's mumblings. Once
our priest arrived at the home, she was asked to give up her seat.

Unlike the other Trinidads, Doña Clarissa often skipped Sunday
mass. "Good deeds count more than prayers said in a stuffy church,"
she often said. She donated clothes to charitable societies and twice
a year dragged herself (and her leg) through town to collect clothes
for the poor.

"Hi, Doña Clarissa!"

"Buenas tardes to you!"

"I been saving my clothes for . . ."

Certain that good deeds would secure her a place in heaven, Doña
Clarissa stuffed clothes given her by friends and neighbors into cardboard boxes, then sent them off to los pobres. She mailed money
to missionary societies and once asked me to address the envelopes
for her. Afraid that someone would see the money and steal it, she
wrapped waxed paper around the dollar bills. Her dented mailbox
was usually clogged with pamphlets and petitions, the envelopes
printed with pictures of thin, starving children.

I once saw Doña Clarissa on the porch with a packet of envelopes
clutched in her hands, as tears streamed down her lined, parched
cheeks.

"How come you're crying?"

"Por los pobres niños"

Each spring Doña Clarissa made cajeta de membrillo, quince jam,
which was a rare delicacy on Hoyt Street. Most women on our block
only made apricot and peach jam. Cajeta was a challenge, or so Doña
Clarissa implied. She recited the problems in making this jam to the
other Trinidads, all of whom knew the litany by heart. She prepared
for this chore as she did for most things, by laying in a large supply
of the ingredients.

The quince was bought from a neighbor, a troquero who trucked
fruit from Fresno to the Los Angeles produce market; when he was
finished he would take home the overripe fruit. El membrillo, Doña
Clarissa claimed, should be ripe yet firm. Once the fruit was stacked
indoors, she trekked to the corner store to buy a five-pound sack of
sugar. She assembled all the necessary cooking utensils: a huge, cast-
iron pot; assorted cooking spoons; a paring knife; and a shallow

pan in which to lay the fruit. She washed strips of muslin stored in a cardboard box, then waited for the weather to stabilize.

Covered from head to toe in a canvas apron, Doña Clarissa cleaned and pared the fruit, cut it in pieces, then threw it in a pot of boiling water. She ripped open the bag of sugar and scooped sugar into the pot. She flavored the quince with nutmeg only, saying that cinnamon did nothing to the taste. With a wooden spoon the length of my arm, she stirred the fruit, making sure it did not stick to the bottom. She stirred and stirred, waiting for the jam to sputter.

"Tiene que hacer shhhht," pursing her lips to sound like fruit sputtering. "Shhhhht." Doña Clarissa stirred the jam all day long, waiting for it to "shhhht." She dared not stop for dinner, but munched on sesame bread and goat cheese. Her face wet with perspiration, and with one eye on the weather, the expert on cajeta de membrillo would work far into the night.

One time Doña Clarissa let me help with the cajeta. She spread the cooked quince to dry on muslin squares, which were then secured on a wide board kept in the garage. The quince-filled board was then set to dry on top of the garage, while Doña Clarissa went inside, satisfied that, providing the weather remained clear, the jam would harden within two days. When it rained the next day, Doña Clarissa was forced to bring the cajeta indoors and reboil it in the blue pot. Once more she waited for the "shhhhht." Finally the weather cleared, and out went the jam once more. The next day when Doña Clarissa checked la cajeta, she was outraged to find bird pecks on the fruit.

She ranted and raved and even threw rocks at the birds still in the tree. Undaunted, she brought the jam inside, pounded out the pecks, cut it into squares, wrapped each piece in waxed paper, then stored the squares in her trusty icebox.

At Christmas she presented the other Trinidads, Doña Luisa, and my mother with quince jam. She tied a bright ribbon on each square, gave it a twist, then went off to deliver cajeta. My mother offered her jars for the jam, but she refused, saying glass made the jam taste funny. She never mentioned the bird pecks.

Uncle Nasario

Up until the time Josey was born, I was la más chiquita, the baby of the family. This term of endearment for the youngest was common in Mexican families. Often when referred to this way, I pouted and pretended to cry, until Doña Luisa took me in her arms. Still I liked being referred to as the baby of the family, especially by Uncle Nasario; even after Josey came along, he called me by this special name.

Uncle Nasario was my mother's first cousin, and apart from Uncle Louie (who lived in Pacoima), he was our closest living relative in this country. He lived in la colonia, a Mexican barrio in Oxnard, where he settled when he first arrived from Mexico.

He was of medium height and weight, with broad shoulders and a flat stomach. In summer his complexion resembled smooth copper; his eyes, like those of my sister Ronnie, were chocolate brown flecked with black. His nose was straight, and behind his sensual lips were the whitest teeth I had ever seen. Folks said he was bien parecido, very handsome, a fact that did not escape his sad-looking wife.

He wore linen shirts, bright-colored ties, and, in winter, a blue fedora. In summer he wore a snappy Panama hat with a flowered band. He drove a late-model car, which he kept shiny clean.

Uncle Nasario was terribly vain. He watched his weight, wore elevator shoes (ordered through a catalog), dyed his hair, and was the only man I knew who wore perfume. My brothers used after-shave lotion, sold at the corner store, and doused their hair with Three Flowers brilliantine and hair pomade, but Uncle Nasario exuded a special scent. He smelled of lemons and mint.

Unlike my father (whom I could see was far better looking than my vain tío), Uncle Nasario dyed his hair. Determined to stay young, he experimented with different colors, bought when his wife wasn't looking. When he picked me up and swung me around, I could see the roots the dye had missed. At other times the dye dribbled down to his ears, where it remained for weeks. On one visit his thick hair shocked even my mother! Indoors it looked a healthy brown, but in the sun it glowed like a neon sign. Each time he visited, I stared and stared at his hair, curious about the current color.

My mother once caught me observing her favorite cousin's hair and gave me a pinch. But she couldn't get to Josey in time.

"Uncle Nasario, how come your hairs are orange?"

"Qué? What you saying?"

"He means you look elegant, primo!"

"Ah, sí!"

Uncle Nasario visited at least once a year. He never wrote to let us know of an impending visit, assured that, as family, my parents would receive him with open arms. He arrived unannounced, the horn on his latest coupe blaring. After he had greeted my parents, he would pick me up in his husky arms and throw me in the air. Dress flying, hair ribbons askew, I squealed with delight at this handsome man who brought such happiness to our mother. He twirled me until I cried out for mercy, then put me down, and wiped his face with the linen (initialed) handkerchief he kept in his shirt pocket.

"And who is the prettiest?"

"Ummmm. I don't know!"

"Ha, ha. Don't tell me you don't know! Come on, tell me . . . who is the prettiest?"

"Me?"

"Sí!"

He complimented my sisters and commented on their eyes and hair, which he said were inherited from our mother.

Whenever he visited Uncle Nasario brought presents: a plant for my mother, red wine for my father, and for us kids, pinole in tiny sacks and the raw peanuts which he himself grew. He would beam with pride as he told us how he cultivated los cacahuates in his backyard. "It's important," he would say in his clipped Spanish, making sure he had our attention, "to plant the peanuts in a mound, in full sun, or between rows of sweet corn."

He dug out a peanut that he described as an example of a healthy nut. He rubbed it back and forth in his wide hands, while he explained how he nurtured the peanuts with estiercol, cow and chicken manure, and compost he kept in a big hole. Peanuts, he claimed, should be watered slowly, so as not to dislodge the shallow roots; a small trickle was right. Once he had our attention, and after he and my father had opened the wine, he would drone on and on about the peanuts.

Once Josey and I sat down, our handsome tío prepared to dole out the dreaded cacahuates. Josey and I hated the small, hard, home-grown peanuts, which resembled the garbanzo beans my mother fixed during Lent. They tasted like rancid walnuts, and worse. We had already developed a taste for the roasted nuts sold at the corner store. When Uncle Nasario offered us a handful of peanuts, we accepted them, rather than offend him and our parents.

From past experience I knew enough to tell Uncle Nasario how good the peanuts tasted. "Ummm! Yummy! Qué buenos! I would munch on a solitary peanut and then, when Uncle Nasario wasn't looking (and while avoiding my mother's eyes), I would spit it out and run to the water faucet.

Uncle Nasario was as vain about his avocados as about his looks. On our rare visits to his house, immediately after we removed our coats, he took us on a tour of his backyard. Taking care not to step on the budding plants, orange hair dangling across his eyes, he described every bush, tree, and plant.

"Miren mis tomates!"

"Ummmm."

"And these are chiles."

"Where are the peanuts?"

"In the store. Aha, ha, ha."

The backyard was pretty, very pretty, with flowers, trees, and shrubs covering every inch of ground. Uncle Nasario grew trees of every kind: apricot, peach, plum, cherry, and nectarine. Toward the back fence stood a lemon tree with yellow-green leaves; next to it were orange trees with their dark green leaves, and fragrant flowers that kept bees busy in the summer. I liked the orange tree best; it reminded me of our tree at home, whose branches in spring drooped with waxy orange blossoms. When Uncle Nasario wasn't looking, I stretched up to a branch, cut off a twig, and stuck it in my hair. The heady perfume of azahares made me dizzy.

Most of the trees and plants were given to Uncle Nasario by friends who worked on nearby ranches. Although he worked in agriculture, Uncle Nasario never described what he did en el fil, other than to say he picked his jobs with care. He nursed the tree shoots in his garage all winter long, first wrapping the fragile roots in hopsacking. In the spring, when the seedlings could withstand the cold Pacific air, he planted them alongside the grown trees in his yard. He folded chicken wire around the bottom, then hung cloth strips from the top branches to keep off the birds.

Tío Nasario also grew vegetables. Unlike my father, who grew mostly chiles and tomatoes, my uncle's garden boasted plants that neither Josey or I had ever seen or tasted: eggplant, jícama, tomatillos, crookneck squash, okra, and rhubarb. Planted in neat rows were tall onions, chiles, tomatoes, and bunches of cilantro. Along the wooden fence grew pumpkins and green and yellow squash. It was difficult to tell the difference between pumpkin and squash, because the wide leaves were similar. The tomato vines resembled sweet peas, except that they reeked of tomatoes.

Uncle Nasario preceded each yard tour with a short lecture. "Some plants are from the same family," he would explain, his face serious. "Just as your mother and I are both Solíses!"

"Pero yo soy Ponce!"

"No, no! Eres Solís!" he insisted, then stooped to examine Josey's nose, which he claimed was similar to his. That ended the discussion. I yearned to ask about the peanut family and wondered if cashews were their cousins, but the tour continued with a detailed account of avocados.

"In order to grow the best avocados," Uncle Nasario began, as he guided us to a clump of tall trees, "one must have a certain touch, water sparingly, and feed them plenty of iron." His incessant and detailed descriptions of aguacates sown in the past bored Josey and me. He spoke of trees as people and never tired of extolling the virtues of the climate he said contributed to his prized crop.

"Avocado trees are either male or female," he explained, a grin on his face, "and must be planted close together."

"Why?"

"Uhhh, to help each other, para que los dos . . ." He squinted up at the sun, then continued with the educational tour. "Pues, avocado trees will not give fruit if planted alone," he concluded, as he wiped his hands on a red kerchief, "because they need a mate." I thought this most interesting. So did Josey.

Once the adults went inside, Josey and I walked around and around the avocado trees, trying to tell which were male and which were female.

"That one's a man!"

"How come?"

" 'Cause it's bowlegged."

"And that fat one is you."

Folks in la colonia lived in homes similar to those in Pacoima; in each yard grew fruit and vegetables, including avocados. Still, Uncle Nasario argued that his were unrivaled and if allowed, he would have held an avocado contest. Once a year he picked the fruit (making sure it was firm), wrapped it in newspaper, then arranged it in wooden boxes stacked in his crowded garage. He then held court. First he invited friends and neighbors to join him in a glass of wine and then, as though conferring a great honor, he would hand out fruit to the tipsy men.

"For you and you."

"Ay! What pretty avocados!"

"Pos, it takes mucho fierro.

"Hmmm."

He would point with pride to the nails dumped at the foot of each avocado tree, which provided the iron. While Josey and I watched, he would kick at the rusty nails with his shoe, making sure we saw the rusty spikes, then continue with his story. He regaled Josey and me with accounts of his experiments with fruit trees, then would let us peek inside what Josey and I called Uncle Nasario's hideout.

In a shed behind the house, Uncle Nasario kept an assortment of gardening tools: spades, hoes, shears, and clippers. The large pruning shears were oiled and sharpened each winter, then used to cut back trees in early February. A pole with a short saw at the tip cut dead branches from los arboles in the front yard. The small shears with the red handles were for trimming hedges and for snipping off suckers, the small shoots that sapped a tree's strength. On a special shelf, Tío Nasario kept tools used for grafting fruit trees.

While he had no formal training in any kind of agriculture, he had taught himself how to graft peach, apricot, and plum trees. He claimed that the nectarine resulted from the grafting of a peach and a plum tree, and implied that if he'd had the time (and money), he might have been the first to produce this fruit. At one time he had joined an apricot tree to a peach tree; its blossoms were a variegated combination of pink and white. The fruit, however, turned out hard and bitter; even the birds refused it. Uncle Nasario never spoke of failed experiments, but steered Josey and me clear of the compost heap that overflowed with dead plants and twigs.

Whenever he visited us, Uncle Nasario would treat us to pinole, roasted blue corn, ground with cinnamon into a fine powder, then mixed with sugar and sold in tiny bags. It was terribly sweet and tasted like Mexican bread in powder form. Often Josey and I shared a bag, but because I was older (and bigger) I got to tear a hole in the bag and taste it first. I then poured pinole into Josey's outstretched hand. It was impossible to chew the powder as we would candy, nor could we "drink" it at one gulp. Because we feared choking on the powdery stuff, Josey and I ate it slowly, one pinch at a time.

My mother delighted in the company of her handsome cousin. Once flushed with wine and surrounded by us kids, Uncle Nasario would go on about how he and my mother, both surnamed Solís, shared certain family characteristics. Los Solíses, he insisted, were ethical, hard-working, church-going folks. Each time he alluded to a Solís family trait, he and my mother laughed, as though sharing a secret. He never mentioned vanity.

In Mexico my father and Uncle Nasario had been close friends. They grew up on adjoining ranches and attended primary school together. As youngsters they worked side by side in the cornfields and gathering mesquite for firewood. Don Pedro Solís, my mother's father, was general manager of a large ranch, a man greatly respected in the community. When my father expressed an interest in my mother, Uncle Nasario spoke on my father's behalf. Thereafter, each time he visited, he teased my father about having married la hija del patrón. Although this was done in jest, my father blushed and stammered, while Uncle Nasario roared with laughter.

Although he and my father agreed on most things, Uncle Nasario disdained Mexicans who wanted to become American citizens. He was still attached to Mexico and returned often to visit his relatives in Guanajuato. He often teased my father about becoming un Americano, a thing *he* vowed never to become. During the sixteenth of September fiestas, he pinned a tiny Mexican flag to his lapel.

Tío Nasario rarely spoke of his romantic escapades, but as a young man he had a reputation for being muy enamorado, a lover of pretty women, cousins included. Astride a frisky horse, he chased after the young girls in the ranch, all of whom admired his pearly white teeth. He once told of how, minutes before the irate father of a young girl came after him, armed with a rifle full of buckshot, he fled the ranch, only to fall in a ditch.

"What happened, Tío?"

"Pos, he almost shot my foot, but when he saw me limping, he said nothing."

He liked pretty women of all ages. He often took my face in his hands and asked: "And are you going to be the prettiest?" "Yes," I answered, delighted with my uncle's flattery. He then said the same thing to my sisters, all of whom blushed and stammered.

When Uncle Nasario left after a Sunday visit, the sun seemed less bright, less warm. He would back up past the pepper trees, then turn right on Hoyt Street. Cheeks flushed, gray fedora atop his orange hair, he sped past in a whirl of dust. Next to him sat his wife, frowning.

Falcón

Sometime in the 1930s, my father began to work for himself. Tired of working en las limoneras and of the cold, damp weather in the Ventura area, he wanted to be other than a laborer. Although he rarely spoke of it, he and my mother blamed el frío that permeated the work camp for the tuberculosis that later developed and killed *Them* (my two older siblings). One rainy day his employer, a kind lemon grower, heard my sister Rosalia coughing.

"Eh Ponce, you want your children to live a long life?"

"Sí!"

"Then I suggest you move outta this damp place."

Soon after that my father packed his family up and moved to the small town of Pacoima.

My father liked to grow things. At one time he wanted to farm; he and his brothers Felix and Gabriel, both older, leased five acres of land in what later became Panorama City. They cleared and fertilized the ground, planted lettuce, then waited to become rich. They never counted on the weather changing; everything grew in sunny California. But that spring the weather was especially cold. Just before harvest time, a rain storm swept through southern California and ruined la lechuga. The brothers were devastated, their dreams of independence now a sea of mud. They returned to working in the citrus groves to pay off their debts. But my father believed in himself and in a country where, providing he worked hard, he could make a good living. More than anything, he wanted to be his own boss.

His options were limited; he spoke little English and could barely read and write el inglés. But he was ambitious and determined not to return to el fil. His most important asset was the flat-bed truck with which he had moved his family to Hoyt Street. He was certain

85

he could earn a living with it. And since our house sat on a double lot with room to spare, he had plenty of storage space. He decided to buy and sell wood from our home. How he arrived at that choice was never clear to me. Either he suspected that lumber was a thriving business, or this was all he could aspire to. Our backyard became a lumberyard. Soon he hired a helper named Falcón.

Falcón was of medium height and weight, with long arms that appeared to hang to his knees. He was fair, with eyes that changed from hazel to murky green. He wore a wool cap over his light brown hair and baggy pants held up by suspenders. He hired out by the day, which was agreeable to my father, who could afford little else.

Falcón lived on the other side of Pacoima, in a plain white house with pretty rose bushes. When there was work to be done, my father walked to Falcón's house to inform him of the time work would begin. Early the next day, the men drove to the railroad yard on San Fernando Road in Glendale. There my father bought the shipping crates used to ship heavy equipment from the East. He picked only the best crates and paid a minimal price. He and Falcón dismantled the cajas on the spot, piled the wood atop our truck, and brought it home.

The wood was dumped next to the fig and walnut trees, near the clothesline that separated Doña Luisa's yard from ours. My father and Falcón checked each board for cracks and nails, then stacked the wood in a pile according to length: long boards on the bottom, short ones to the side.

Eager to help my father, Josey and I would trail after him and Falcón as they worked. Josey enjoyed jumping up and down on the wood until he either got a leg caught entre la leña or he became bored. I disliked working on the woodpile; while lugging boards from one side to the other, I tended to scratch both my hands and knees. But I was determined to show that although a mere girl, I could work like any boy—or better.

As soon as the truck was empty of wood, Falcón swept the flat bed in preparation for whatever else came along. He then went off to work with my father while Josey and I waited to see what was next.

When sorting wood, my father set aside los palos replete with nails, pieces he or Falcón had missed. When he became tired of Josey and me pestering him, he put us to work removing nails from the planks, hoping this would hold us for a time. He gave us each a claw hammer, then walked off.

Although Josey's hands were smaller than mine, he was better with the hammer. He set a board against the stack or the walnut tree, then held it down with his knee while he pulled and pulled at the nail. His tiny mouth set in a firm line, Josey would pull out the nail, then stop to wipe his brow. He tossed it into a coffee can, then began on the next one. While Josey yanked nails to his heart's content, I too put the hammer to use. Unlike Josey I threw out all the nails that were not perfectly straight, and those that were rusty and left behind an orange stain. But Josey was out to save each nail. His specialty was to straighten nails on the iron rod my father kept in the garage.

I liked to watch Josey at work. He banged away at a crooked nail, determined to make it straight and usable once more. When he and I got tired of this chore, we would jump up and down on the wood stack, until either he or I fell down; then we'd go off to play at something else. Sometimes Falcón volunteered to help Josey and me with the nails, but for the most part we worked alone. I think this was my father's way of keeping us busy and teaching us to be thrifty at the same time.

I liked the smell of the wood, especially after a rain; as it dried, the wood appeared to smoke. I watched in fascination as tiny puffs of warm air rose to the sky. Once the sun was out and the wood was dry, the mist disappeared.

Now and then a piece of madera, different from the common planks, got mixed in with the pile. These small, isolated pieces, a little darker than the others, were easy to spot. Once I found such a piece. It was a rich brown, soft and fragrant; I wanted it for myself. My father then told me it was cedar. This soft wood was used to make the hope chests that girls on Hoyt Street pined for. I hid the wood underneath the other planks, in the hopes that someone would make my doll a sweet-smelling crib; when next I looked, the cedar was gone.

My father dumped the rusty, crooked nails Josey was unable to fix at the foot of a tree. He explained that in this way the trees would get iron, the fierro necessary for a tree's growth. Often he reminded me of Uncle Nasario.

People in the neighborhood knew they could count on my father for a good piece of wood at a fair price. He and Falcón were prompt in delivering an order of lumber, and if a board cracked in the process, it was quickly replaced. My father often extended credit to folks in need of madera. The men were honest, and once they were able to, they came by our house to pay off the debt.

Sometimes we were allowed to ride with our father to drop off wood. Once the boards were loaded, Josey or I ran to the truck cab for the red flag kept there.

"I got it!"

"I had it first."

"Apá, she's hitting me!"

"No I'm not."

We handed the red rag to our father. While Falcón watched and tried not to snicker, my father let Josey attempt to tie the rag. When this failed he took el trapo, tied it in a knot, then let Josey and me pull each end. We pulled and pulled, wanting to ensure that the rag would not fall off the board, or my father would get un tíquete.

Falcón was friendly and smiled as he worked. Much to my father's consternation, he preferred to pull out nails alongside Josey and me. Each time this happened, my father would walk over, give him a tug on the arm, and lead Falcón to where the real work lay.

According to my mother, Falcón had one bad habit. He spent his pay on pies and cakes that he alone ate, then went home empty-handed to his hungry and growing family. When my mother saw him sitting near the walnut tree, gorging on pies and cakes, she teased him in a friendly way.

"Hmmm, qué pastelito tan bueno, Falcón. Creó le gustaría a su familia." She commented on the delicious pie, and that his family, too, might enjoy eating the pastries. Falcón ignored her, intent on chewing the berry pies that left his mouth a dark blue. Josey and I watched how Falcón then hid the pie wrappings underneath a piece of wood. He would wipe the pie crumbs off his mouth and walk off to join my father.

On payday Falcón stuffed the odd dollars paid him by my father into his shirt pocket. He would cut across the open field to the Pacoima General Store, then exit out the back door and into the alley. One time I was in the store and saw him come in. He headed straight for the bakery section. He walked up and down the aisle, his work shoes scraping the linoleum, his calloused hands brushing against the packages that lined the shelf: chocolate cupcakes, apple fritters, creamy lemon pies, round spice cakes. He filled his scrawny arms with an assortment of cookies and donuts. Rather than head for home, he then found a soft spot underneath a pepper tree, leaned back, and gobbled up los pasteles.

More than once my mother suggested to my father that Falcón's pay be sent directly to his wife. She felt this would allow his wife to buy food for the entire family before Falcón spent it all on himself. One day she approached my father in the lumberyard.

"Fuera bueno mandarle el dinero a la esposa de Falcón."

"Así no fue el arreglo."

"Que lástima. Los pobres niños tienen hambre."

"Lo siento, pero . . ."

My father continued to work as my mother persisted. She argued that Falcón's children needed food more than Falcón needed pastry. Still my father refused to heed her advice. "I can't withhold his pay," he told my mother, his voice firm, "that was not part of the arrangement." I felt that perhaps my father knew that eating cakes made Falcón happy and a good worker, so he allowed for this. More than that, he felt that women should not meddle in the affairs of men. Nonetheless my mother was determined to do what in her eyes she felt was right.

One sunny day, fully aware that Falcón was still sorting wood in the backyard, my mother sent Elizabet to deliver Falcón's wages to Doña Eufemia, his wife. When la señora Falcón received the money sent to her by my mother, she burst into tears. Falcón, it seems, had not been home for days. The children were hungry and she had nothing other than tortillas to feed them. She thanked my sister profusely and in a faltering voice called down blessings on my mother: "Ay Santísima Virgen, gracias te doy por este milagro." She walked my sister to the street. "Tell your saintly mother that I am most grateful for her kindness." Upon hearing this, my mother was quite moved. Later that day, when questioned by my father, she pretended not to have known that Falcón was in the backyard.

In the following weeks my mother continued to send Falcón's wife a portion of his wages. She would wait until my father was out on an errand, then send Elizabet, or whomever was around, to Falcón's home. I was never sent, because I was too young and adept at dropping things; but I trailed Elizabet on this mission of mercy. In time this became such a habit that Doña Eufemia would meet my sister at the door.

Doña Eufemia remained my mother's loyal friend for life. And Falcón continued to work for my father. Now and then, on the way to the store, I would see him near the pepper trees, in one hand un pastelito, in the other a quart of milk.

The Day Rito Died

 I remember well the day my brother Rito died. He died of tuberculosis in Olive View Sanatarium, where he had been confined for as long as I could remember. I often forgot I had such a brother, except when on Sundays I was left at home while my parents and older siblings visited him.

Rito had caught cold, frió, as we said in the barrio, which settled in his lungs. He lost weight, and when tuberculosis set in, he became weak. I only saw him a few times. I remember most that he wore blue cotton pajamas.

My parents visited Rito each Sunday. When he became worse after lung surgery, they visited during the week too. Soon afterward his condition became critical, and he was moved to a private room in the infirmary, to make sure he would not contaminate others. When he took a turn for the worse in the winter, my father arranged to be notified, day or night, of his condition.

We had no telephone. Few folks in the neighborhood, other than local merchants and the Anglos who lived across the tracks, had telephones. All emergency calls from the sanatarium were relayed to our parents by Mr. Jameson, owner of the Pacoima General Store, and Mr. Tamez, of the Tamez Grocery Store. They were good, kind men who did more than sell food. They extended food credit to la gente mexicana, those unemployed or sick. Sometime previously both men agreed to relay to my father any message they received from the sanatarium.

One night or early morning, Mr. Tamez came with the message that Rito was near death. I woke up when el Duque began to bark at the car that drove up and woke our household. Doña Luisa immediately got up, lit the kerosene lamp kept on the metal trunk, and got

dressed. I saw the lights came on in our house; the kitchen bulb illu-
minated my father's form. I heard voices coming from my mother's
room, soft, murmuring; there was never panic in our house. The engine of the Dodge sputtered, then came to life. I heard the car pull
out of the driveway, my father at the wheel, the tires crunching on
the hard dirt. I then went back to sleep, lulled by Doña Luisa, held
tight in her thin arms. When I awoke the car was back. A deadly
silence permeated our home, broken only by the sound of muffled
crying.

I don't remember who told me Rito had died. I don't remember if
I cried. I was a child and barely remembered the handsome stranger
with eyes so like my father's, who had been in Olive View half of his
life. In the morning I saw shadowy figures enter and leave our house:
friends, neighbors, and relatives, dressed in dark clothes, came to
give my parents el pésame. The women brought food, which was
put on the kitchen table next to the enamel coffeepot that was kept
filled by Elizabet. Inside the large kitchen, neighbor women warmed
tortillas and beans for those who were hungry, but first they fed us
hot cereal and toast. Quietly they shooed us out the kitchen door.

Curious as I was, I refused to stay in the backyard, so I found my
way to the side of the house near my mother's bedroom window. I
heard whispers, muffled crying, comforting words in both Spanish
and English. Within minutes Uncle Louie, my mother's cousin (who
wore bib overalls all his life), came to the door dressed in a dark
shirt and pants. I barely recognized him. He came and left through
the kitchen door, a red handkerchief held to his face. That afternoon Uncle Nasario, that jovial, outgoing man who always made
me smile, drove up in his shiny car, his handsome face strained and
lined. He went to my mother, held her tight, then turned away to
hide the tears that filled his light brown eyes.

I didn't see my mother for the rest of the day. She remained in her
room, where sad-eyed women, most of whom I knew, arms laden
with rubbing alcohol and hand towels, entered and left, as if on cue.
Outside, near the garage, the men stood, among them my father and
uncles, who huddled together. They spoke in Spanish; their short,
muted sentences were hard to hear, but appeared to comfort my
father.

Among the men was Berney, now in his early teens, a tall, strapping boy who, because of the seriousness of this ocassion, was allowed to be con los hombres. Some of Berney's friends stood in the circle, among them Danny, a handsome boy who it was said had a crush on Ronnie. Norbert stayed in the men's rooms, talking with friends who cut school to be with him. Ronnie and Trina, in clean dresses, remained indoors, helping with the guests that filled our house. Josey, I believe, slept most of the day. Now and then, tired of the inactivity (and knowing well I had to be quiet), I scrambled up on a chair to peek outside. Except for Uncle Nasario and a bibless Uncle Louie, I failed to recognize the men with my father.

Toward evening a small fire was built in the backyard where the men congregated. From the kitchen door I saw one of them sip from a small bottle, which was passed around to the others. When the bottle was offered to Berney, he declined the whiskey with a jerk of his curly head. My father, I knew, did not encourage his sons to drink, not even on this somber occasion. Around suppertime the women who earlier had ministered to my mother went home to feed their own families, saying they would return for the wake. Uncle Nasario and my father came indoors to eat the food prepared by Elizabet and two cousins from Oxnard whom I had never seen before.

The men remained around the fire, warming their hands and softly talking, as el Duque circled them. The yellow flames cast deep shadows on the men; their sad faces took on an eerie, deathly pallor. The Mexican tradition was that they remain until late at night, out of respect for my father.

Mexican families like ours had little money to spend on wakes or funerals. The funeral mass was offered free of charge; the cemetery plot was paid for in installments. The mortuary bill, which included la caroza and the coffin, was also to be paid in installments. Funerals were kept simple, not because of tradition but due to lack of money. The viewing of the body was done in the home; this was not only convenient, but less expensive. Early on it was decided that Rito's wake would be held in our front room. My siblings and cousins put things in order. They cleaned and dusted, wanting the sala to look worthy of my brother. Once more I was shooed out the back door.

That evening I went to sleep with Doña Luisa as usual. She tossed and turned all night long and in the morning continued to sniffle, her dark eyes full of sadness. She put on her best black dress, one that came to her ankles, fed me avena y pan tostado, then went to our house to help prepare for Rito's wake.

I was playing hopscotch toward the back of the house, where I wouldn't be seen or heard, when the hearse came to deliver my brother's body. I was about to jump a square when I looked up to see a long black sedan, the length of two regular cars, approaching. The driver leaned out and asked, "Is this 13011 Hoyt Street?" "Yes," I answered. Before I could ask what it was they wanted, I heard movement inside the house. Suddenly the front door opened; out came Elizabet and cousin Mary, dressed in dark clothing. Cousin Mary, who was most proper, wore a navy blue dress with a white collar and cuffs; a short string of pearls was at her throat. Their loud and clear voices, so unlike the crying of before, drifted across the yard to where I stood. The driver, a pale man wearing thick glasses, backed up the hearse until it was parallel to the front door, then slammed on the brakes. The hearse appeared to let out a sigh, then came to a stop. The driver got out, door slamming loudly, then opened the back door and pushed back his hair, as if about to make a delivery. By now my father and my uncles Louie and Nasario were on hand to pull out the long silvery box that I knew was the coffin in which Rito lay. They yanked it halfway out, squeezed it through the door, then carried it inside.

Anxious to see everything, I kept getting in everyone's way. Rather than stand aside, I walked alongside the men, my hand resting on Rito's box. When we neared the porch steps, I stumbled, nearly tripping Uncle Louie. Elizabet pulled me aside and began to scold.

"Stay in the back."

"But I want to see!"

"This is only for grown-ups."

"But . . ."

Doña Luisa came to the rescue; with promises of lemon drops, she convinced me to stay in the backyard. Accompanied by the faithful Duke, who for all the sadness of the day still wagged his tail, I went toward my favorite fig tree, then waited for Josey to join me.

When next I looked the black car was gone. Relieved of its cargo, it slipped away down Hoyt Street, raising no visible dust, and onto Van Nuys Boulevard. I played with my dolls, one eye on the kitchen door, hoping to be called inside where the grown-ups were. In the cold, wintry yard everything seemed so still. Duke lay on the dirt, his tail looped around his scruffy legs, his long ears drooping across his face. Not a branch moved in the eucalyptus trees that cast huge shadows over our house. High above a lone cloud drifted across the blue sky, then disappeared.

I heard crying from inside the house. Soft, folorn. From near the fig tree, I heard my mother's anguished cries. "Hijo mio. Ay hijo mio." Her cries came and went like waves. Even el Duque was subdued. He kept to the back of the house, his tail between his legs.

Toward afternoon neighbors and relatives came to pay their respects: the Garcias, Jaramillos, Montaños, Solíses, Reyes, and others. Among them was Mrs. Goodsome, principal of Pacoima Elementary School, which my siblings attended. She was a good, kind lady who liked our family, especially Rito, whom she claimed was an excellent student. When I saw her inside, I too wanted to be part of the crowd. I pushed my way in between the mourners to the front of the room. It was then I saw Rito.

He lay inside a silver coffin lined in white material. The quilt-like material looked soft, comfortable. Rito's coffin was on top of the wooden bench that normally sat near the garage. The upper half was open, so that we could peek at him. Rito was dressed in a dark jacket and a snowy white shirt. I think he wore a tie. His curly hair shone with pomade, and was combed to the side, with one limp curl over his clear forehead. His lovely green eyes, now closed forever, were fringed by dark lashes that brushed his fair cheeks. His pale hands were clasped together as if in prayer; the tapered fingers entertwined with a black rosary were as still as death.

Behind the coffin and on both sides of the wall hung crisp white sheets. Pinned to them were velvety gardenias, their dark green leaves shiny and fragrant. Large candles were set at the head and foot of the casket; inside the dim room they glowed warm and bright. Next to the casket and on the floor stood zinc buckets and cans with fresh flowers: roses, carnations, gladiolus. The flowers, brought by friends and neighbors, were surrounded by crespón, a mossy green fern that grew in our backyards. From a distance the home-grown flowers looked quite pretty, and not at all like the stiff, formal arrangements found at most wakes. I think Rito would have liked them.

On top of the closed half of the coffin lay a small silver crucifix.

Next to it was a funeral wreath of gardenias and white stock. A white ribbon enscribed in gold letters lay across the wreath: *Nuestro Hijo Querido*. Bowls of buttercups, called tasa en plato, sat close by; they were pretty but gave off a strong smell. Their aroma, combined with that of the creamy gardenias, was what we kids referred to as olor a muerto, smell of the dead. The stifling odor and the sad eyes of the mourners forced me to leave the room, but not before I sidled up to Mrs. Goodsome, who hugged me, called me a sweet child, and admonished me to obey my mother.

That night Father Juanito came to pray the rosary. He first gave my parents el pésame, then knelt to recite the rosary. He prayed the Ten Soulful Mysteries. The women who throughout the day had been praying inside my mother's room gave the response. "Ruega por el, Pray for him." When he finished with the rosary, Father Juanito recited the Litany of the Saints, then concluded el velorio with the prayers for the dead. "Requiescat en pace," he intoned. "Amen," we responded. He then took his hat with the pom-poms (brought from his native France), set it on his greying head, and left.

That night I was allowed to sleep in my mother's bed. There was no room elsewhere, or so I was told. The relatives from Oxnard who remained overnight were given my spot on Doña Luisa's lumpy bed. Excited about the attention I was now getting, I began to jump up and down on the bed, until Doña Raquel came into the room, tucked me in, and in a gentle voice told me to go to sleep. She stayed with me until I did.

In the morning everyone looked haggard and somber in their mourning clothes. Even Uncle Nasario's ruddy cheeks and friendly eyes appeared sad and drawn. Inside the kitchen my sisters and cousins served hot chocolate from an enamel pot atop the stove. They filled platters with the sweet Mexican bread brought earlier by Uncle Louie. Just then the church bell began to peal. Everyone began to gather coats and hats for the walk to church. Without being told, Uncle Nasario and our male relatives went into the living room. They pushed aside the limp sheets with the wilted gardenias and smelly buttercups that had made me sick. They picked up the silver coffin and Rito, hoisted it onto their shoulders, and went out the door, followed by my mother, now dressed in a dark winter dress and her best hat. Neighbor women, black dresses to their knees, huddled around my mother, then escorted her down the porch steps and to the street. My older siblings checked our clothes and hair, then herded us children out the door toward Hoyt Street. I stumbled along with Doña Luisa, who appeared to lack her usual vigor. We caught up with the procession at the church door. Suddenly the bells began to peal again. *Dong. Dong. Dong.* Even the bells sounded sad.

At the entrance to the church, Father Juanito awaited Rito's body, which he blessed, while we crowded around. The high requiem mass followed, beginning with the "Liberame Domine." During communion friends and relatives received the host, which was offered for the soul of the our dearly departed one, and which I knew would ensure that Rito's soul would ascend straight to heaven.

When mass was ended, we followed Father Juanito and the silver coffin down the aisle. Once more our pastor blessed my dead brother, then sang "In Paradisum." This last hymn signaled the end of the service and was something like la despedida, the farewell sung at Mexican parties. The coffin was then placed in the waiting hearse, the same one that had brought Rito home for the last time.

I did not attend the funeral; they said I was too young. I walked home trailing after my mother, who did not go to the cemetery. "I cannot bear to see my son interred," she whispered to my father, her voice lost and forlorn; my sisters, however, went in her place. My mother now walked with my cousin Mary, who appeared to hold her up; their dark listless forms inched their way down the empty street.

When the big black hearse went by, my mother wavered in her step, then stopped. She stood deathly still until the hearse had passed, then slowly pulled back her hat veil. "Adiós hijo mío," she murmured, then resumed the long, slow walk.

I stayed behind, slowly picking my way between the rocks and grass on the path next to the street, my eyes glued on the big black car that finally turned left and disappeared.

Sacrifice

Most Thursday evenings I accompanied Doña Luisa to Guardian Angel Church to pray el rosario. Church was only a block away from my home; I knew every bump and ridge along the path, most of which I had helped make. Once the first bell rang, Doña Luisa removed her apron, threw it atop the trunk in her bedroom, and called to me "Es tiempo para el rosario."

"I know, I know! Just let me kick the ball to Concha."

"And wash your face, eh?" she would caution in Spanish, her voice hoarse and low, "Lávate la cara."

I ran indoors, Concha's voice bouncing off the ball as she and my friends continued to play in the street. In the bathroom I shoved Josey aside, closed the door, and splashed water on my grimy face. I ran a damp towel over my knees, then grabbed a dress that did not appear too wrinkled. I knew well that one should wear clean clothes to church as a sign of respect. If time allowed I ran the family comb through my curly hair, plunked my favorite beanie on my head, and off I went to meet Doña Luisa.

Doña Luisa's dress rarely varied; she got ready in minutes. Other than to run a comb through her grey hair and pull a dress over the white naguas that clung to her skinny frame, there was little else she could do. She kept a black shawl handy on a peg near the door. In one swift motion she yanked it off and wound it around her head and skinny shoulders. She sometimes changed her shoes, which amused me. For although she was always after me to look clean for church, Doña Luisa was not too fussy about herself. She inevitably went to church in her scruffy everyday shoes, shoes that had seen better days.

We would leave soon after the second bell rang, not wanting to be late. I trudged along behind Doña Luisa, trying not to envy my friends still in the street. My beanie secured with bobby pins snitched from Trina, I sometimes ran ahead of Doña Luisa, skipping over the huge rocks in the street, then ran back. But mostly I walked alongside this dear woman, trying to keep up with her long strides. As she walked, she appeared to slide forward; her slender torso was constantly striving to catch up with her legs. Near the front door she would pause, waiting for me to catch my breath, then she would take my hand and lead me down the main aisle to our favorite pew, three rows back.

Few people, other than the Trinidads, Doña Luisa, and I, attended Thursday's rosary. On Hoyt Street most folks went only to Sunday mass, except when someone was dying; then whole families filled the pews, only to disappear again. My friend Nancy said that the rosary was boring, the prayers repetitious. She preferred the misiones held in the fall, when we got to light candles and listen to the visiting missionary screech about Satan, hell, and damnation.

Another reason the church was half-empty on Thursdays was because "Inner Sanctum," a radio series of spooky stories, came on at the very time our pastor was reciting the rosary. The program began with a squeaky door that sent chills up and down my arms.

Once ensconced in my seat, I would begin to fidget, but I was quickly silenced by Doña Luisa. At home she allowed me to be loud and sassy, even to talk back, but church was another matter. In The House of God, we were told in catechism, one should act accordingly. Tired of waiting for the priest to appear, I would sit back to contemplate poor Jesus of the Bleeding Heart, whom I had known for all of my five years, surprised that in all this time he had not bled to death.

Doña Luisa rarely had to coax me to attend the rosary; I was more than willing. Going to la iglesia got me out of washing the supper dishes. As I slid out the kitchen door, leaving her to clear the table and wash the dishes, Trina would give me a dirty look.

"You think you're so holy!"

"No I don't!"

"I saw you take a nickle from . . ."

"Liar! I didn't steal . . ."

"You better tell that to the priest."

The thing is, I liked church! I liked to be inside the quiet building filled with the smell of incensce. I enjoyed looking at the flowers arranged by Mrs. Barrera, a kind lady whom I liked. She had no children of her own, only a nephew who now and then visited. When I arrived extra early for rosary, she let me watch her fix the flowers. I helped to fill vases with fresh water and clean the flower stems.

"Take off the extra leaves. Like this, see?"

"But they look bare!"

"Sí, but they last longer."

Doña Luisa appeared to resent the attention I gave Mrs. Barrera. When I returned to the pew, a wilted flower in my hand, she would snort and purse her lips, and be slow about letting me get past her naguas and dark dress. Once, upon taking my seat, I saw tears in her eyes and quickly put my hand in hers to reassure her that she was the person I loved most. She took my hand, raised it to her lined lips, and kissed it. I sat looking at my hand, which felt warm. When next I glanced at Mita, her eyes were dry.

Nancy is right, I often thought, el rosario is boring! It was not like the Vía Crucis that took place during Lent, when we knelt and stood, knelt and stood. The rosary prayers never changed, other than the different Mysteries. Often I closed my eyes and fingered my rosary, a small version of Doña Luisa's black one except for the blue beads. It was blessed by Father Juanito and kept atop the trunk in Doña Luisa's bedroom.

I hummed church hymns under my breath, hoping the choir would sing something other than "Bendito, Bendito." At that time Father Mueller had not yet been assigned to our parish; old hymns were still sung by the choir of old ladies with weak voices. Doña Luisa appeared not to mind, or even hear, the music. She kept her dark eyes on the altar, her fingers twitching the black beads back and forth.

While waiting for our pastor to emerge from the sacristy, I would try to memorize each Station of the Cross. These were made of wood and, like everything else in our church, were old. When I squinted my eyes and concentrated, I could see the figures of Jesus and Mary, as well as the Roman soldiers, wearing silver helmets on their heads. I disliked those stations of the crucifixion. Poor Mary looked so sad, her pretty blue eyes full of tears. Jesus looked worse! His face was streaked with dirt, his feet, I knew, were scratched and cut from the long walk. Pobrecito. The wooden cross on his back looked like the boards in our lumberyard, except that it lacked nails.

I tried to memorize the names of the flowers on the altar, but knew only those found in our garden at home: Shasta daisies, roses, carnations, gladiolus, and my favorite, the beautiful tiny pink rambling roses with their prickly thorns.

As I sat waiting for el rosario to begin, I came to realize how much I enjoyed the silence, the mystery, the beauty within our church. Unlike our noisy household, our church was quiet, peaceful, empty. I studied the shadows cast by the statues atop the altar, whom I knew by heart and greeted like best friends: Guardian Angel, Saint Joseph, the Virgin Mary, and the fat Niño de Atocha. Church for me was a wonderous, silent place.

Doña Luisa and I had sat in the third pew for as long as I could remember; I could find my way in the dark. We sat with the women, on the right side; the left was for the men and boys. I knew every scratch and indentation on this pew and yearned to scratch my name on the wood so that others would know it was ours. Nancy often bragged about having scratched her name on three pews, but I never believed her.

"Gosh Nancy, did you use a nail?"

"No stupid, I used my finger. Ha, ha."

"But when did . . ."

"When nobody was looking . . . with a big nail, see?"

It angered me when others sat in our place. After all, I reasoned, Doña Luisa and I practically owned that spot! Doña Luisa appeared not to mind, and when on some Thursday evening others sat in our pew, she merely moved to the next empty one. This however, rarely happened, since during the rosary most of the pews were empty.

The three Trinidads too, staked out a spot inside Guardian Angel Church. Directly in front of us sat Doña Magda, clutching a rosary from her extensive collection. Doña Cari, swaddled in shawls, head held ramrod straight, sat next to her. Doña Clarissa, who now and then broke from the pack, sat alone in the second pew. Sometimes she was joined by Doña Nicolasa and her grandaughter, who, once she had spotted me, would defect to the third pew. Directly behind us sat Doña Cruzita.

Doña Cruzita was a short, stubby woman who resembled Santa Claus. Her hair was like spun sugar, white and fluffy. Her cheeks, like those of a chipmunk, had a small bulge on each side. Her small beady eyes were constantly peering around, as if trying to focus on something. Kids on Hoyt Street said Doña Cruzita was almost blind, which was why she blinked and stumbled. She was not active in the church nor on friendly terms with Doña Luisa, let alone the Trinidads.

She lived far from the church and attended services only when a nieto walked her there. Still everyone in our town looked out for her. Polite boys guided her up the church steps; snotty-nosed kids took her arm. When services were over, folks waited with her at the door until her grandson returned. When necessary more than one person would offer to walk her home. Even Don Malacara, a grumpy man who drove a dusty Ford, sometimes offered to drive her home.

Doña Cruzita liked to sing. Once the organ began to sound, she prepared herself. She peered around, took a deep breath, then puffed out her fat chipmunk cheeks. Unlike the rest of us, she rarely waited for Father Juanito to sing the first stanza, but would start right in, once she recongnized the hymn.

Her squeaky voice sent chills up my arms. Mundo the street bully and altar boy said that Doña Cruzita sang like a stuck pig. Concha said she sounded like her new puppy, a little dog that yelped all night. I insisted that Doña Cruzita sounded like a tethered goat, una chiva amarrada. When the music began, and providing Doña Luisa did not restrain me, I would move as far away from her as possible. It was upsetting to think that people might mistake her voice for mine.

Doña Caridad considered herself a soprano; she looked down on those who sang the lower range. During rosary devotions (and much to Father Juanito's amusement), she and Doña Clarissa strove to outdo each other. They sang hymns by heart, as if to test their faded memories. Doña Cari's chins wobbled as she reached for a high note, while Doña Clarissa's chest heaved with emotion—and the strain of trying to keep up with the competition. No one cared to compete with Doña Cruzita, who not only had a unique voice, but also a stomach that made funny noises. During prayers she either burped, gurgled, or farted—or all three.

One night during a special rosary, when the church was quite full,

I clearly heard Doña Cruzita pass gas. I knew it was her! She was unwell and often cut wind without noticing. El pedo, as we called it, was not only loud, but smelly. I turned to glare at her, and was about to hold my hand to my nose, when Doña Luisa jerked me around. By this time everyone could smell the fart. I sensed people looking at me and began to protest to Doña Luisa.

"Yo no fui!"

"Púes, calle. Well, hush then."

"But it wasn't me," I wailed, as around me friends started to giggle. "It wasn't me."

I pleaded with Doña Luisa to listen. I hadn't farted; I shouldn't be blamed! I pointed to Doña Cruzita and was about to scream my innocence to the entire congregation, when Father Juanito raised his hands for the benediction.

Everyone stood; everyone but me. I remained in my seat, pouting and kicking at the front pew, but Doña Luisa ignored me. She would never admit that Doña Cruzita had farted, but was blaming me to save face! Doña Cruzita's! The stuck pig! The tethered goat!

Finally I stood, trying to hold back the tears of resentment that streamed down my angry face. My friends would hear about this I knew, as would everyone on Hoyt Street. I would never live it down. I begged Doña Luisa to get me home, but it was too late. As we neared the front door, Doña Remedios, a busybody who never missed anything, came up to me.

"Aha, is she the one who farted?" she asked in Spanish, her beady eyes staring me in the face.

"Sí, pues es niña," answered Doña Luisa, her dry hand on my arm. "She's only a child."

"Ha, ha, you farted," hissed Josey as he went past.

"Úhule, what a smelly fart," laughed Mundo, as he secured the church door. "I can still smell it!"

Mortified at this exchange, I pressed my face against Doña Luisa's knees, as tears ran down my face to land on my pinafore. When Doña Cruzita went past, my sobs grew louder.

We walked down the dusty, dark street, then cut across the rocky path next to the street. I clung to Doña Luisa, softly crying. She stopped to wipe my eyes, then we continued walking. Once at home I undressed and went to bed. Just before I dozed off, she hugged me tight, her wrinkled face close to mine, eyes full of love and compassion.

"Ya duérmase," she whispered. "Go to sleep."

She said nothing more. We both knew I had been sacrificed to save the dignity of una señora de edad, a sick old woman who died the following year. Doña Luisa knew I would forget and in time forgive her. Which I did. Out of respect, and love.

Kid Ponce

My brother Berney was a boxing fan. He faithfully followed all boxing events as reported in the paper and considered himself an expert on championship matches.

Berney and the neighborhood boys faithfully listened to what were called "elimination bouts," which were almost as important as championship fights. They would sit outdoors next to Berney's car, to listen to his scarred radio, placing bets on their favorites. They cheered on Mexican-American boxers, some of whom they knew, and also those imported from Mexico with the nicknames *el águila* or *el pajarito*, none of whom resembled an eagle or little bird. The boxers were flyweights and welterweights, skinny guys with dark hair and brown eyes who looked like our neighbors. Most were knocked out in the first few rounds, much to the despair of the fickle Mexican crowd, who first cheered them on, then slung water balloons at them.

"Pendejo!"

"Gallina!"

"He can't fight! Get someone dat can!"

They would cheer an opponent and heatedly argued over whether a TKO was as good as a knockout, often demonstrating on the spot. Once a fight was on, Berney and his friends refused to budge from beside the radio.

The Saturday-night fights were transmitted from the Olympic stadium in Los Angeles, a huge white building where the most exciting boxing events took place. Sometimes Berney and his buddies drove to the fights, but not often, since Los Angeles was a long way off, and it was expensive. When they did go, they pitched in for gas and then each boy paid an entrance fee. One and all got to see the bout.

Joe Louis, called the Brown Bomber, was a favorite on Hoyt Street.

Berney and the others spoke of Joe Louis as though he was a personal friend.

"Ya gonna watch the Brown Bomber tonight?"

"Yeah. He better win, or else . . ."

"Or else what?"

"I'll quit talkin' ta him."

It was exciting to know that an ordinary guy like Joe Louis could get to be world champion. Everyone on Hoyt Street, it seems, was caught up in cheering for el Joe Louis.

Berney liked to box and although somewhat slender, he considered himself tough. He spent hours locked inside the garage, blasting away at the patched punching bag that hung from the ceiling. Hazel eyes glued on the leather bag, legs spread apart, brow bathed in sweat, Berney attacked the bag, moving in and out with slow grace.

Boxing was fun and very popular in the barrio, where young men dreamed of becoming rich and famous through the use of their fists. While championship fights were held at the Olympic, Berney and his friends also patronized those held nearby, mostly because they featured local boxers.

The Valley Gardens Arena was located on Vineland Boulevard in North Hollywood, about six miles from Pacoima. It was a big, barn-like stadium, with a marquee like a movie theater that announced who was fighting. Round neon lights, like those used in Christmas decorations, decorated the entrance. At the back was a huge parking lot that accommodated the jalopies of guys like Berney who lived for boxing and wouldn't think of missing a fight.

On most weekends one or another of Berney's friends was scheduled to box. As amateurs they boxed in what were called preliminary bouts; these were the least important of the night's events and took place before the main fight. The preliminaries were open to those who had a trainer and the necessary connections to get their names on the program. The process was quite democratic; everyone had an equal chance. Young guys who had the guts to face an unknown opponent used this golden opportunity to become known, hoping to be contracted for future training and future fights. Few went the full four rounds. Many were unprepared for the hard blows and soon began to bleed from the mouth or nose. If nothing else, Mexicans-American vatos had pride; they hung on until the last round. Although every boxer wanted to win, what most mattered was showing what they could do in front of the whole town. Now was the time to put to use the grueling hours spent with the punching bag and sparring with friends, and to leave the ring like a real man, on your two feet. The excitement of being in the boxing ring was a reward in itself for most of the young boxers.

Early in the week the young men of Hoyt Street got together to plan strategy and place bets. On Thursday evenings Berney's friends would come by, honking loudly enough to startle Duke, who ran around as excited as they. The guys were dressed "to the nines" in two-tone sport jackets, spotless white shirts, and dark pants. When Berney was ready, and all bets had been collected, they piled into the cars. Their bright eyes flashing, their hearts full of hope, they tore down the street, tires spinning, laughing at the world.

The fights were advertized each week. Much to the disappointment of local boxers seeking fame and fortune, only the names of well-known boxers appeared in the newspaper. Not to be outdone, young men promoted their own fights with flyers printed on cheap white paper. Each week a flyer with a boxer's picture and boxing name would be passed around. My brother was billed as "Kid Ponce."

The first time I saw Berney's picture on a flyer, I was terribly impressed! My brother, the future world champion! In the photo Bernie looked ferocious! He held a boxing glove to his chin; his eyes squinted toward the camera. He looked mean and tough. I ran off, the flyer clutched in my hand. This is too exciting, I thought, to keep to myself. Visions of my brother as the next Joe Louis filled my head. Come next Thursday, Berney would box in the Valley Gardens Arena, to the acclaim of his peers. He would be famous, of that I was certain. I showed the flyer to Concha, Beto, Virgie, and Mundo, making sure they did not crumple it. All appeared impressed except for Mundo, who claimed the guys from San Fernando were tougher, better boxers. He took off before I could hit him.

On the night before the fight, our backyard was a flurry of excitement. Berney's buddies came and went; the radio blared louder than usual. Berney remained inside the garage, while his friends gave him last-minute coaching. He wore black shorts and black, high-top "tenis." His thin frame, outlined by the hanging lightbulb, darted in and out. He sparred with his friends, all of whom were more experienced than he.

"Keep yer chin down!"

"Ya gotta protect yer face!"

"Ya gotta dance on yer feet!"

"Dance?"

"Yeah, move around, like dis."

When he was ready, Berney went indoors, a white towel wound around his neck, looking just like Joe Louis!

My parents did not approve of Berney's boxing career, nor of his boxing buddies, although most were nice guys from the neighborhood. It was common knowledge that they smoked and drank beer after the fights! Often they dragged home at all hours, twin pipes blasting as they rounded Hoyt Street. Berney however, was considerate of my parents: he came home from the fights at a reasonable hour and sober.

Among Berney's friends was a certain Ponciano, a short, husky guy with a broken nose and a thin moustache. He wore layers of brilliantine on his ducktail, draped pants that ballooned like skirts, jackets with huge shoulder pads, and shirts with French cuffs. The snazzy red convertible that he always drove with the top down was usually packed with pretty girls wearing high pompadours and thick Maybelline.

Ponciano was not a pachuco, but almost; or so my parents claimed. My mother disliked him. Ponciano, she said, was too slick, had shifty eyes, and laughed too loud. She tried to discourage Berney from las malas compañías, friends she felt were a bad influence, but she did not always succeed.

One night the police came to arrest Berney. A car had been stolen and witnesses had mentioned a certain "Ponce." Since Berney's surname was Ponce, and he fit the description of "young, Mexican male," he was a prime suspect. A sleepy Berney was taken to Van Nuys jail and booked "on suspicion." My father, visibly upset, followed in our two-tone Dodge. He returned later that night and, as my sisters listened outside the door, explained to our upset mother that there had been a mixup; the person sought by the police was Ponciano, not Berney. Knowing that Ponciano and Berney were friends, and unable to find Ponciano, the police had arrested Berney. Unless my parents posted bail, they informed him, Berney would remain in jail for seventy-two hours.

I never knew whose decision it was to let Berney remain overnight in jail. My mother, my sisters said, pleaded with my father to bring Berney home. But because it was already late, or perhaps to teach him a lesson, my father decided to let Berney remain in jail until morning. A taste of jail, he reasoned, might forever cure Berney of las malas compañías.

When Berney was released, the next day, he kept to his room, too embarrassed to face the family. Tenía vergüenza. The shame was felt by us all. No one in our family had ever been arrested, let alone sent to jail. "He didn't do it," I screamed at my friends, who pelted me with questions, once they knew of the arrest. "It was a mistake." Few people thought anything of the incident. Guys from our town, even nice boys like Berney, were constantly being hauled off to jail on suspicion of this or that.

Within days Berney was cleared of all charges. Although young men his age were into pachuquismo, Berney was never part of a gang. Mostly he stuck to fixing cars and radios in the garage and listening to boxing matches on his old radio. In time, much to my mother's relief, Berney forgot his friendship with Ponciano-of-the-red-convertible. He quit boxing, too. One balmy night at the Valley Gardens Arena, with the whole town watching, el tigre Fuentes, a hefty boxer from San Fernando, knocked Berney out in the first round. Still I remember the flyer with his picture on it—"Kid Ponce."

Kindergarten

By the time I was four and Josey two, I was tired of playing with my little brother. Chasing after el Duque offered little challenge. Playing in the open field was too safe; I knew every rock and hole by heart. Even our treehouse, recently fortified with new boards, was no longer fun. I wanted to be in kindergarten!

Each morning I watched my older sisters in their starched dresses, polished oxfords, and cardigan sweaters leave for Pacoima Elementary School. Their dark wavy hair, secured with barrettes and bright ribbons, shone in the warm sunlight. Each carried a pencil case and paper tablet. Clutched in their hands were the math or English books they had used for homework.

Each morning I begged to be taken along. I too wanted to be in school, a place said to be more fun than anything! Kids at school, I had heard, were allowed to read books, sing new songs, and tell stories. Each morning and afternoon, as part of something called "recess," they were sent outside to play with kickballs, baseballs, and even a tetherball. Yes, I thought, school sounds like fun!

I began to count the months until I would turn five and begin school. I was anxious to play new games, tired of the frayed kickball and assorted cans used in "kick the can." My inventive brothers nailed empty cans onto long boards to make stilts, sancos, which I couldn't balance. Playing jacks in the street was no longer fun. Each morning my sisters patted me on the head and smiled.

"I wanna go to school!"

"You have to wait till you're five."

"But I'm four now."

I accompanied them to the back gate, bade them goodbye, then went looking for Josey, who was always willing to play. I took to counting the days on the kitchen calendar until my fifth birthday. Unlike others, who began kindergarten in the fall, school for me would begin in midsemester, since my birthday was in January. Away from Josey I wrote *A, B, C* in the dirt and drew pictures of a girl walking to school. And then finally I turned five, and off I went to kindergarten.

That mild winter morning Doña Luisa woke me. I splashed my face clean, then went home to eat hot oatmeal and toast. I was happy to be of kindergarten age and anxious to get going. While my sisters shoved each other in the bathroom, I struggled into my school clothes, one eye on the clock. I wore a blue dress, blue ribbons atop my Shirley Temple curls, and shiny oxfords bought in San Fernando. My sisters Ronnie and Trina, one on each side, walked me across the alley, past an empty lot, and on to the school. Behind us followed Concha and her two sisters. As we walked I looked around at the mossy green grass beneath my feet, and up at the cobalt-blue sky. The mild January sun was warm on my face.

I carried the gifts I had received for my birthday; the pencil set given me at Christmas by Elizabet was left behind. In my left hand I carried pencils, a box of crayons, and a ruler, all tied together with string. I wanted to take the pencil set, but I could only carry so much. In my right hand, clutched by Ronnie, I carried a clean hankie.

My sisters walked me to Room K, then each went her separate way. I stood among my friends, giggling with excitement and fear. Fat Lupe, a girl on our street who wore pretty frilly dresses, kept shoving a smaller girl. Concha stood twisting her dress belt. Elvira, a tall serious girl who lived on the other side of town, shuffled her feet. The boys, dressed in long pants, kept elbowing each other; their black hair stuck up like a brush. Even Beto, a kid who hated to take baths, looked clean—and scared. We were nervous, anxious to be accepted as "school kids."

"I got new shoes."

"I wanna go home."

"Crybaby."

"Shut up."

From the first I loved kindergarten. Everything was like magic. Room K was the largest in the school; a wide ramp led to the wide door. A square cotton rug covered the shiny clean linoleum. The child-size tables and chairs that filled the large room were unlike any

I had ever seen. From a corner hung the red, white, and blue American flag, which we saluted each morning. Along the wall facing the ramp were wide, wide windows that let in the sun. Atop a bookshelf sat a bowl in which swam a fat goldfish; next to it was a vase with yellow daisies. But what most held my interest was the bookshelf. It was full of books! Books of all sizes with pretty covers.

I loved school, the teacher, my new friends, and our large, airy room. From the windows that faced the ramp, I could see across to where the bluejays sat. On windy days huge puffs of wind blew stray leaves across the open corridor, and right up to our window. When they were opened, the windows leaned back at an angle, secured to the frame by a small chain. During story time, sprawled on the rug, I was afraid to sit under the window; I mistrusted the chains and only felt secure next to windows like those at home.

It was exciting to have so many books to choose from. I was in love with words, and even before starting school I would browse through my older siblings' books. I knew my ABCs and could count to one hundred. I knew the names of our first presidents and liked Abraham Lincoln best; except for his coat, he looked like the statue of Saint Joseph in our church.

During the reading hour, I would flip through the books, noting page numbers, looking for words I already knew, such as *it, the* (which appeared more times), *he, she,* and *I.* Already I could print the names of everyone in my family except my father. *Tranquilino* was too long, too foreign, and too difficult.

Our kindergarten teacher was Mrs. Paddington. She was of medium height, pretty but frail. Her mousy hair hung without direction. Her limpid brown eyes were steady and kind. Because we were from poor Mexican families, she was considerate of our lack of knowledge, hygiene, and manners. Still it was her duty to teach us to speak el inglés. She was firm, yet kind, while instructing us to "speak English, English!"

Mrs. Paddington wore flowery dresses that swished back and forth when she walked, so that we could always tell when she was near. Her shiny black shoes had a buckle and short heel; her stocking seams were never straight. She was as eager to teach us as we were to learn. Each day before we napped on the square rug, Mrs. Paddington read to us in a soft, melodious voice.

My favorites were the Mother Goose stories. Before beginning, Mrs. Paddington would tell us something about the story; for some kids the characters and themes were new. In time we came to understand that Mother Goose was not really a mother, but was "make-believe." I lay on the rug, my arms entwined around my head, to listen to the teacher's soft, soft voice. I was soon lost in a world of fantasy and happiness.

I laughed with delight at the antics of the three little pigs and was overjoyed when Little Red Riding Hood outsmarted the sly wolf. I loved that particular story; among Mexican people, grandmothers were also revered. It was perfectly natural that a young girl would visit her grandmother and take her a basketfull of "goodies." I was allowed to take this book home to read (and explain) to Josey. He too liked the story, but was afraid of the "big bad wolf."

Within a week I was made office monitor, a job that allowed me to become familiar with Pacoima Elementary School.

The school office, entered from the right, faced Norris Street. The office faced the front lawn, where all important functions took place. The flagpole stood directly across from the office. Each morning promptly at eight thirty, Mr. Putty (the custodian) raised high the Stars and Stripes. We recited the Pledge of Allegiance in loud, clear voices; and when we said "the flag," we extended our hands forward, as in a salute. We sang *The Star-Spangled Banner*, a song we kids knew better as "O Say Can You See."

Inside the main building was the office of the principal, Mrs. Goodsome. Her room was really a small cubicle within the larger office, but Mrs. Goodsome alone sat at a large oak desk. In the front, facing the lawn, sat Emma, the school secretary, a pleasant lady with reddish hair and freckles across her nose. At the other desk sat a woman who took care of school forms, but I never knew her name.

On Mrs. Goodsome's desk was an oak plaque with her name etched in long, flowing letters: Prudence L. Goodsome. My friends and I thought the name Prudence sounded terribly odd. I wondered about its origin and Spanish counterpart. The teachers and secretaries called Mrs. Goodsome something that sounded like "Pru." That's a mistake, I thought; no adult would ever be called "Pru." However, we accepted her, funny name and all, just as she accepted our foreign-sounding names, strange customs, and lack of English.

Each morning when I brought in the attendance sheets for Room K, Mrs. Goodsome looked up from her desk and smiled.

That first week Pacoima Elementary seemed enormous. The main building loomed high above me. I felt dwarfed by the eucalyptus trees that appeared to grow to the sky, and I got lost more than once. Within the school were around ten classrooms, an auditorium, and two bathrooms, one for boys, one for girls. Two large corridors ran the length of the building. Unlike other schools, ours did not have a cafeteria, certainly none that I remember. Food was brought in for students who bought lunch tickets.

The playground, a large dirt area, faced Norris and Herrick streets. It was surrounded by a chain link fence that had a gate close to the drinking fountains and bathrooms. To the right was a sandlot where the younger kids played on the monkeybars and swings—or threw sand at each other. To me the playground seemed enormous; now and then I chased a ball to the back fence, then ran back to the safety of the sandbox. I feared being stranded so far from my friends and our teacher.

The auditorium was big, with rows and rows of chairs. The faded velvet curtains, pulled open and closed by ropes hung from pulleys at each end, skittered across the stage to meet in the middle. This cavernous room, empty most of the school year, was off limits to kindergartners except during Christmas, when all the grade levels participated in a holiday program. Sometimes on my way to the office, I took a shortcut to the auditorium. I would open the heavy door, then stand looking into the dark, stuffy room, trying to imagine the exciting events I had heard took place in there.

The year spent in kindergarten was the most exciting and carefree of my life. I played new games, learned new words, sang new songs, and made new friends. Better yet, I read piles of books: picture books, story books. Not a day went by that I did not check the bookshelves for new works. I memorized titles, covers, and sizes and was soon able to find my favorites with little effort. I also learned to write.

Cursive writing, we were told, began in the third grade; for now we were taught to print. Each day Mrs. Paddington handed out the lined paper on which we were taught to write. She passed out shiny yellow pencils with sharp, sharp points, saying we should keep these pointed down to avoid an accident. Seated at the small tables, we began with the first three letters of the alphabet, then moved on to simple words like cat, dog, hat. In my writing pamphlet, I faithfully traced over the letters of the alphabet until they appeared perfect. The one letter I could not master at first was the small *b;* I wrote it backwards, like a *d.* I persisted however, and soon got it right.

Mrs. Paddington made us feel good about learning. She gave out gold stars for "excellent" work; the silver stars for "good" work were not as cherished. I quickly scanned all papers returned to me for this mark of excellence! I walked home, papers in hand, anxious to show these to my mother and Doña Luisa, neither of whom read English; but they smiled and murmured, "Ummmm, bien. Good."

That first year at Pacoima Elementary passed all too quickly. Soon it was time to pass from kindergarten to B1: the first half of grade one. During the last week of the semester, Mrs. Paddington reviewed the ABCs, checked writing pamphlets, and wrote new words on the blackboard. She dispatched notes to the parents of children who were slow learners, pinned to their clothes lest they lose them. She ordered us to sit on the multicolored rug, reviewed school rules for the last time, then walked us to Room 1 to meet Mrs. Nelson, the first-grade teacher. When the introductions were over, she marched us back to our room and the faithful goldfish.

The last day of kindergarten was terribly exciting! Mrs. Paddington wore an especially pretty dress. Her eyes shone with excitement as she lined us up against the far wall. "Hush, hush," she admonished, a frown on her face. "I have many things to do and cannot be distracted."

I however, continued to talk with my partner. "Hush," our teacher hissed as she locked the back door and straightened tables and chairs. This made me giggle even more. Suddenly, Mrs. Paddington took my arm, and half-dragged me to the end of the line. Still I continued to talk.

I whispered to Fat Lupe, acting smart because she was on her way to being a first grader. "Kindergarten kids act like babies," Lupe hissed, pulling at her knee socks.

"I know," I answered, adjusting my hair ribbons. We were comparing shoes when Mrs. Paddington strode up to me and in an angry voice (one never heard before) cried: "The next time I talk to you, or anyone else in this line, none of you will pass on to first grade. You will remain in kindergarten for another year."

"Owwwww."

"I wasn't doin' nuthin'!"

"It's all your fault."

I began to cry; Lupe stared at her feet. "I wasn't talking," I cried, my hand to my eyes. "It wasn't me." My friends, angry at being stuck all morning in a stuffy room, gave me dirty looks. The boys, who blamed girls for everything, began to yank at my ribbon. Just then Mrs. Paddington, dress swishing to and fro, opened the door, and out we went.

Two by two we marched to Room 1 where Mrs. Nelson, a short, chubby teacher, awaited us. She introduced herself once more, then told us to choose a desk in which we felt comfortable, one in which we would sit the following year. She explained bathroom and recess rules (no pushing; wash your hands afterwards), then gave us a cheery smile. We smiled back, delighted at being in a room with real desks, a huge blackboard and colored maps on the back wall.

Fat Lupe, certain the worst was over, began to giggle; I smiled at the world. Finally I was in grade one. No longer would I be forced to go home before lunch, but would be allowed to remain until school let out at three. No longer would I be relegated to the sandbox and swings reserved for "babies." Best of all I would now have different schoolbooks to read, books said to be "lots harder." Feeling almost grown-up, with an easy step and a light heart, we scattered down the school steps, arms filled with left-over crayons, worn erasers, scratched rulers, and frayed books.

On the last day of each semester, old, tattered books marked "obsolete" were given to room monitors. I was lucky to get three and thrilled to see that they had been used by third graders. If I try hard, I thought, I can learn to read these, too. Unlike some of my friends, who disdained these leftovers as "junk," I thought of them as rich treasures. Few parents, mine included, could afford luxuries such as books, crayons, paper, or erasers. These were special; and at home would be put away in a safe place, then periodically be brought out to be looked at, touched, and in time, read. On that sunny day when I graduated from kindergarten to first grade, I clung to the tattered books, faded papers, and pencil stubs. I treasured them all summer long. I looked forward to the books I would read when school began in September.

REASON

Los Piojos

School was wonderful! Each day I learned something new and discovered new friends. The teachers were eager to teach us and often stayed after school to drill us in English and math, the two most difficult subjects.

My best friends were Nancy, who had changed her name from Natcha and thought she was "so big"; Virgie, who got in a fight with Mundo and lost, then was spanked by her father for fighting in the street; and Concha, who lived across the street.

Concha was considered timid by everyone in the neighborhood, especially the adults, because she never talked back to anyone, let alone teachers. She, like the rest of our generation of Mexican-Americans, was intimidated by the Anglo world, especially at school, where at times we felt like second-class citizens with our funny customs, hard-to-pronounce names, and bad English. At school we were constantly told: "Speak English, English only. You're not in Mexico now." While others such as Nancy, who talked back to everyone, gave teachers a smart retort, Concha just hung her head and said nothing.

We lived in two worlds: the secure barrio that comforted and accepted us, and the Other, the institutions such as school that were out to sanitize, Americanize, and delice us at least once a year, usually in the spring, when everything hatched, including lice.

During the spring months, just after the new semester started, we were checked for immunizations, tonsilitis, and any disease thought to be prevalent in the barrio that year, such as measles, el sarampión, or whooping cough. The public-health nurse visited our homes; the school nurse caught up with us at school.

At times I thought that the blessing of throats that took place en el día de San Blas in February was not a coincidence, that perhaps God was aware that we needed special protection from the school nurse and had appointed San Blas to intercede on our behalf.

I cringed when called to the nurse's office, a small cubicle next to the main office. Nurse Smithers had eyes that missed nothing. She knew each of us by name and reputation, since she visited twice a week. She was forever inspecting our ears, mouths and hair, and checking our records with a red pencil. She swabbed scratches with alcohol from a bottle kept on a tray, then dabbed smelly purple stuff on any area that looked infected. I hated the smell of iodine and the purple medicine that refused to wash off, which I felt marked me as "diseased."

Not all the teachers were sensitive to our lack of hygiene and manners. Some found it hard to accept our funny names, customs, and differences. More than once I heard them discuss our many illnesses and their causes.

"My stars! Did you say your girls are scratching their hair?"

"Dear me, yes, it's that time of year, you know. What else do you expect, them living like they do, sleeping ten to a bed. Nits do jump, you know."

"Must be the culture, just like bad teeth and that TB."

It seems that lice were part of our culture, along with poverty, shabby homes, low-paying jobs, and too, too many children. It seems that we Mexican-Americans, as we were then called, had so many things wrong with us that I wondered why it was we were happy. I, for one, lived in a loving home, did well in school, played "kick the can" in the street, enjoyed the church bazaars, and loved catechism; I lived what I felt was a good life. We felt content and could not understand why we had to be singled out as a group when it was suspected that one of us had lice.

Once when I was in the third grade, several girls thought to have lice were rounded up and marched to the school nurse. When word got around that nits had been found on our schoolmates, we cringed, for we knew we would all be suspect and forced to be inspected, whether we liked it or not. I dreaded having even a speck of dirt on my head. To the eagle-eyed nurse, everything visible on our dark hair looked like nits. Just to be suspected of having piojos was in itself a disgrace.

On this day the third graders were inspected room by room. Early that morning, right after attendance was taken, our room was marched off to the main building. Fat Lupe walked ahead of me, pulling at her socks, saying her father would be sure to hear about this. Nancy, angry because her comic books were taken from her, kept bumping into Lupe and calling her names. I walked alongside Elvira, whose dark hair, secured by twin barrettes, swished back and forth. We were told to wait in the hallway adjacent to the office. From there I saw white-clad Nurse Smithers, cap tilted to the side, inspecting my classmates' hair.

She parted, then peered into each strand of hair. She checked the backs of heads with her fingertips, as if touching a rattlesnake and afraid of being bit. Now and then she mumbled something to the office clerk, a pale, nervous woman holding several charts. When she finished the nurse gave each girl a shove toward a teacher, who smiled and gave the student a yellow paper to take home. Our Spanish-speaking parents did not understand the message written in English, but knew it meant they should take steps to delice their child.

On this day Concha's room was ahead of us. We began to talk.

"I hate it."

"Me too."

"Que vergüenza."

"Shut up."

"Jiggers!"

When it was Concha's turn to be inspected, she began to sniffle. More than once she had been found to have nits. She hesitated, looked around for an ally, then reluctantly stepped forward. The clerk handed Nurse Smithers Concha's chart. They whispered to each other as Concha, head bent, waited. The nurse then turned to Concha and carefully picked up a trenza. She held the braid aloft with the tip of her fingers and began to peer into it. Unfortunately for Concha the nurse spotted something white; she pushed Concha toward Mrs. Paddington, the kindergarten teacher, who now was assisting. Mrs. Paddington, limpid eyes full of concern, gave Concha the yellow slip, as though offering her a reward for having survived this ordeal. Concha was dismissed and sent to her room, along with other sniffling girls.

When it was my turn, I stepped forward like a defiant lamb not quite ready for the sacrifice.

"Mary Helen Ponce."

"Here."

"Hummm. Are you Trina's sister? and Veronica's?"

"Yes, ma'am. Elizabet and Nora's, too. They're all my sisters," I answered, fluffing my pinafore ruffle.

"Well, I doubt very much if you have lice. So far we haven't found any on your sisters. You may be excused. Next."

"But I want to be inspected!"

"Nonsense child, there's no need. You look clean enough," intoned the nurse, as she shoved me toward the line.

"But I itch!"

"Itch? Where? Just where do you itch?"

"Right here," I answered, then proceeded to scratch my Shirley Temple curls. "Right here."

"Tell me, do you play with anyone with lice?"

"Yes, ma'am," I answered proudly. "Concha Gomez is my best friend."

"Well fancy that! I suppose you got them from her."

"Yes. I mean no. I just itch," was my lame reply, as I waited to be handed a yellow slip. Mrs. Paddington, trying not to laugh, pushed me toward the door. Nurse Smithers pursed her lips, adjusted her cap, then snorted, "Next."

"Could I have one of those?" I asked, pointing to the yellow slips Mrs. Paddington held.

"Next," said the nurse in an irritable voice. "Next," echoed Mrs. Paddington.

In the hallway I encountered my classmates, Concha among them, all smiling and comparing yellow slips. We were once more together and could seek consolation from each other. We smiled as we walked to the room; the vergüenza, the shame, was over. We had survived another inspection, one we would later talk of as an event. It was time to return to our schoolwork, to pretend we were like the children in the books who lived in pretty houses and had never heard of lice.

This experience was part of our culture, of being Mexican-American—like having black hair and brown eyes. The inspections went with our identity, as did the yellow slips we wore home as badges of honor.

Later when Concha and I walked home, she refused to take part in the pushing game we usually played. I put my arm around her, just like best friends, and tried to make her smile, but she was not in the mood for fun. Concha knew she would have to endure the smelly petrolio, the only remedy known to kill lice, with the smell that lingered and made her dizzy.

After she was deliced and shampooed with Packers Pine Tar Soap, which we referred to as shampoo (and was all our parents could afford), she and I once more played together both at school and home. Black heads pressed together, sharing secrets, sharing life.

Los Calzones de la Piña

As children our daily diet consisted of simple foods: avena (oatmeal), potatoes, sopa de arroz, and flour tortillas. Besides our favorite pinto beans, these foods were the staples of our Mexican-American diet. Most families in Pacoima were large, with numerous children, and ours was no exception. We filled the kitchen at mealtimes, spreading out along the bench.

Parents in Pacoima bought food in large quantities. The huge sacks of beans and flour were lugged home from the market to ensure that if nothing else, la familia would have beans and tortillas. Like most women on Hoyt Street, my mother bought beans, flour, and sugar in hundred-pound sacks and lard in five-pound cans. The beans, sewn tight in dark hopsacking, were kept in the sack. An opening at the top allowed mi mamá to scoop out beans each day for the cooking pot. Sugar was stored in a wide ceramic bowl with a lid. The flour sack was emptied into a huge can (earlier washed out and dried), then stored in the pantry next to a sack of potatoes. When the pantry was full, all was well in our house.

My mother, never too fussy about what kind of flour she bought, did not appear to pine for the maize used in corn tortillas, but had become accustomed to the bleached wheat flour sold at the corner store. White flour, it was said, was healthier and cheaper.

The flour was sold under two trade names: Harina de la Piña (with a huge pineapple on the sack) and my favorite, La Espiga de Oro (decorated with a stalk of wheat). They were trucked in from Los Angeles and sold at all three of Pacoima's grocery stores. Often a dishtowel or piece of china lay hidden at the bottom. In this way women on our street put together a set of matching dishes. Once the sacks were emptied, my mother and Doña Luisa shook out the remaining flour, ripped out the seams, then washed and stored the sacks for later use.

Mexican women put the sacos to good use. They sewed aprons, curtains, dishtowels, and calzones (underwear) for girls. Although it was common practice to use sacking for clothing, no one in the barrio cared to admit that a dress or shirt was made of sacos. At times neighbors traded sacking. Doña Remedios liked best the short pieces with which she made tiny, embroidered cushions to give to her grandchildren at Christmas. One time she made heart-shaped cushions that resembled big, fat Valentines. She trimmed them with lace and sold them at the church bazaar, much to the delight of those women who, not knowing they were buying sacos, displayed the cushions in their front rooms. Doña Pepita made shirts from the sacos for her grandson, a husky boy named Rafa. He wore them when cleaning the yard.

My mother worked hard to clothe her large family. Each fall she checked our schoolclothes, then sat to mend torn slips, lower dress hems, and to reinforce zippers. When time allowed she went to work on the sackcloth, Doña Luisa at her side.

Preparing the sacos was in itself hard work. The first and most important step was to bleach out the pineapple and wheat stalk, then decide if the sack was to adorn the kitchen or our backs. A huge tub was filled with hot water, Purex bleach was added to the water, then they stirred and stirred the sacking until it appeared to be free of color. But often my mother would tire of stirring the cloth and would remove the sacos before the designs were completely gone.

Doña Luisa then emptied the tub in the back yard and hung the sacking to dry. Then the sacos were ironed and laid out on the kitchen table. When the supper dishes had been put away, the kitchen floor swept clean, and her children shooed out of the way, my mother cut aprons and calzones from the material.

My mother had learned to sew in Mexico, where my grandmother Martina taught all of her daughters the domestic skills that served women of the ranch so well. My mother knew how to cut, baste, and sew, and how to embroider.

At one time a teacher at Pacoima Elementary organized a sewing class for Mexican women of our town. This was part of a program organized by the principal, Mrs. Goodsome, who felt that all barrio women should learn to cook and sew "the American way." The sewing class was offered first. Women who completed the sewing class, Mrs. Goodsome said, could then learn how to bake.

Several women from our street signed up for the class, among them Juana, who lived across the way. From the start she told the teachers she was not interested in learning to sew. "Quiero hacer cak-es," she told the instructor. When she was told that yes, she could learn to bake cakes, cookies even, Juana enrolled, but only in the cooking session.

My mother would have liked to attend the sewing classes, but like other señoras in our town, she was embarrassed to admit that she could not read or write in English, and so could not understand the teacher's instructions. She preferred to sew at home and to make her own patterns. When a blouse or dress was old, she ripped out seams, ironed out creases, then created something new. I liked to watch the two women work: Doña Luisa busy at the ironing board, my mother's grey head bent over the Singer sewing machine with the foot pedal (which she faithfully oiled and kept covered with a doily).

One complication in using the sacking for clothing was that the pineapple was very difficult to bleach out. The wheat stalk disappeared after several boilings, but not la piña; the telltale yellow color remained. The only solution was to work around the pineapple: place it to the front, tuck it in a back seam, or hide it near the crotch.

The calzones de la piña had sat in the bottom drawer of the chest I shared with Trina for some time. I hardly noticed them until that fateful day when I ran out of clean underwear and was forced to wear "homemades." I tried to be a good sport as I hitched them up, appalled at how they ballooned around my buttocks. I hated them, but I hated hurting my mother's feelings even more. After all they were well-made, bien hechos.

The day I wore los de la piña to school, I was in second grade, Room 2. For some reason I was allowed to play kickball, a hard running game. This was a great treat, because when teachers knew that tuberculosis was prevalent in a family, the children were discouraged from playing "rough games," so as not to exert themselves. We were told to sit on the bench next to the chain link fence and watch the games. The other kids would point to us and call us los tísicos.

But on this day, a teacher who saw that I was a chunky, healthy-

looking girl with red cheeks, evidently decided I could benefit from
the exercise and picked me for a team. I jumped off the bench and
tore across the playground, hair ribbon flying, shoes kicking up dust.

I took my place among the circle of players and began to practice
kicking the ball.

Once the game began I kicked with all my might. I ran all around
the field, getting in everyone's way, excited at being young, healthy,
and full of energy, happy to be playing, happy to be part of the gang. I
never gave a thought to the stiff pineapple bloomers that were visible
each time I kicked the ball.

I played gloriously. I played hard. I played to win. I was so intent
on kicking the ball as far as the boys, that it was some time before I
heard the giggles and saw fingers pointed in my direction. I realized
the pineapple was showing, but I didn't know what to do. Just then
I felt a loosening at the waistline; the elastic on my bloomers had
burst! I could feel them beginning to slide. I was in a near panic and
yearned for the recess bell.

I then began to hook them up right before I kicked the ball. Around
me the kids began to call: "Mary Helen, Mary Helen." When I turned
they hooked up their dresses or pants and doubled over, convulsed
with laughter. This went on for what seemed like hours, with me
hooking up los calzones, my face hot and flushed. I was close to tears
when recess finally ended.

I walked to the classroom, my sweaty hands gripping my dress
at the waistline. I wanted to run home. Without a word our teacher
handed me a safety pin. I took it, slid into the girl's bathroom, and
pinned up my underpants. I returned to class full of dread at having
to face my classmates, ashamed to have them see how embarrassed I
felt. But they said nothing, merely avoided my glance.

Once at home I took off the calzones and stuffed them in the bottom of the drawer. I vowed never, ever to wear them again. I didn't
tell my mother about the incident, but after that I began to wash my
underwear by hand, to ensure that I would never again be forced to
wear underpants with a picture of a pineapple on the bottom.

El Jabón de Doña Chonita

 Doña Chonita Olivas lived in a roomy house that accommodated numerous relatives: sons, a cousin, and her daughters-in-law. She was my mother's friend. Unlike the Trinidads, Doña Choni, as she liked to be called, did not "live" in church, nor did she daily visit with the women of our neighborhood, but kept to herself. Until soap time, that is.

Doña Choni was very, very short, shorter than most of my friends! Even Josey towered over this lady. Her face was round, with a pointed chin and bushy eyebrows that met in the middle. Her brown eyes shone like round marbles when she was angry, which was quite often. Kids on our street called her a dwarf who looked like a wolf, con ojos de canica, eyes like brown marbles. Her wispy grey hair was worn in a loose braid and held tight with an orange rubberband. On Sundays, in anticipation of mass, her scraggly trensa was transformed into an elegant bun, held in place with a black haircomb.

I called her Grumpy, like the dwarf in Snow White, because she was always frowning. She frowned morning, noon, and night. When on an errand to Don Jesus's store I cut across her back yard, she would frown at me from the back stoop. During "kick the can," when I sent a can toward her fence, she grumbled and hissed, sounding like a water heater about to burst. If we talked back she threatened to tell our parents we were disrespectful.

Although grumpy, Doña Chonita was clean and neat, fastidious almost. She swept and watered her huge yard each morning, then rolled the hose and stored it in the shade. With a rag she washed the hoe used for weeding, dried it, then stored it in the shed, a small room at the back, shaded by trees and shrubs, that looked scary from afar. Whenever we hit the ball into the back of the yard, we left it there rather than go near the menacing shed.

Most weekdays Doña Choni wore cotton dresses that almost swept the floor. "She buys her dresses at J.C. Penny," Concha told me, "then cuts them in half. She makes aprons with the leftovers, con mucho rickrack." Not all her dresses were cut in the middle, though. She often tucked them under the belt that encircled her generous waist. The dresses, of pretty cotton prints with a collar and cuffs, made her look like a tugboat about to sink.

She wore aprons made to her exact size (short) by Lidia, her dutiful daughter-in-law, who it was said was afraid of her. Made of sackcloth, they were trimmed in colored rickrack, with large pockets on each side. When she walked Doña Chonita looked like a battleship with flags flying. On her round feet she wore stubby black shoes similar to those worn by young children, rounded at the toes. These were bought from a mail-order house in Chicago that catered to wide feet. Once a year she bought a money order at the post office made out to the shoe company, then waited for the brown shoe box to arrive.

Doña Chonita was a widow and ruled her family with an iron fist and stern looks from her ferocious wolf eyes, simply because she was the lady of the house, la mujer de la casa. Her married son Cristóbal still lived at home. He obeyed her every wish, as did her two unmarried daughters, sour-looking old maids who trembled when spoken to and who ventured out only for Sunday mass. In our neighborhood folks said that Doña Chonita lived for her children. They never mentioned how she dominated their lives.

Doña Choni's apricots were the juiciest, the sweetest fruit on all of Hoyt Street, or so we said when each summer they literally fell into our laps. They were guarded with a ferocity unmatched on our street, where most neighbors ignored kids who snitched fruit off their trees.

Doña Chonita's house sat back from the street; the front yard was dominated by a huge apricot tree. In the summer the top branches, where the roundest fruit grew, became top-heavy, broke, and scattered the fruit to the ground. Kids on Hoyt Street, including Concha, Virgie, and I, were always on the alert to snatch up the apricots that steadily dropped throughout June and July.

"Psssst, Concha, get the apricots on the ground!"

"Shhhh, she might hear you and . . ."

"I got one! Want a bite?"

"Mmmmmm."

The apricots were huge and tasty, their orange skins toasted by the California sun. I preferred them to those found in other backyards, ours included. On summer evenings when we played ball, I would deliberately aim at the luscious apricots. As I rushed to retrieve the ball, I would scoop up the delicious fruit, stuff it in my mouth or dress pockets, then run to polish it off in the shade of a pepper tree.

Sometimes Doña Chonita would hear us playing. Out she would march to the front gate, apron flying, marble eyes flashing. Concha, who was faster than I, would hide in a nearby bush, leaving me to take the blame. Unable to hide, I hung my head, watching Concha out of the corner of my eye. Doña Chonita scolded me in a hoarse voice that sounded like that of Duke, our dog.

"Y que haces aquí?" she asked, knowing perfectly well what I was doing.

"Nothing."

"Hmmm."

She stood at her full height of four feet, two inches (or so), and glared at me until I turned tail and ran. The minute she went inside, we returned to our game of playing baseball and snitching apricots.

Doña Chonita was also known for her jabón, homemade soap that she made once a year and sold for a nickel or gave to friends and neighbors. She used a secret recipe, guarded with the same ferocity as the apricots. I referred to the soap as el veneno, certain that it was a type of poison. Cut into bricklike squares, it looked and smelled hideous. I hated to use it. Rather than complain to my mother about her friend, however, I hid the soap that smelled like gasoline behind the woodpile.

When Doña Chonita sent out word that the soapmaking was about to begin, the women on our block began to save their fat drippings, an important ingredient.

"No se les olviden mi jabón." She reminded everyone about the soap.

"Do you take bacon drippings too?"

"No, no! Sólo manteca." She wanted only lard.

Early in the week, my mother took the tin of fat drippings kept atop the stove and inspected its contents. If the fat was rancid, it went into the garbage. If it was fresh and did not smell, she put it into a clean container and wrapped it with waxed paper. I was then sent over with our contribution of manteca.

"Doña Choni, my mama says here's the manteca."

"No speekee Spañol?"

"Sí! She said do you want more?"

I liked to watch Doña Chonita make the soap. She cooked it in a big zinc tub set atop a pile of wood arranged the night before by her older son Cristóbal, who called her "mi señora madre." He was married to Lidia, a frail woman whom Doña Chonita ordered around.

"Hand me a cup."

"Sí, Doña Chonita."

"And do the dishes again. They look dirty."

It was said that Lidia broke out in a rash each time she used her mother-in-law's soap, but she continued to use it out of respect, or fear.

The soapmaking took all day. Once the water boiled, Doña Chonita added more wood to the fire. She walked around the tub in a bright blue apron trimmed in red rickrack, tested the water, and poured in various ingredients, including eucalyptus leaves, which contained both oil and perfume. Last of all came the drippings. She stirred the soap with a short stick (cut to size), bending her small frame toward the fire, her long braid swishing back and forth. Now and then she stopped to wipe her brow and to scan Hoyt Street, her eyes returning to the prized apricot tree.

The jabón resembled Fels Naptha, a harsh, smelly soap used for heavy laundering and cleaning. Doña Chonita dared not leave the soap unattended, for fear of lumps, but stirred it until it was thick. At lunchtime the dutiful Lidia fixed un bocadito, a tasty dish for her formidable mother-in-law. Once the soap was cooked to Doña Chonita's specifications, it was allowed to cool and then cut into bricks and stacked alongside the washroom.

El lavadero was really a small shed, similar to others found on Hoyt Street. Most Mexican families had a washroom toward the back of the house, where they kept tubs, washboards, assorted soaps and bleaches, and wooden clothespins rolled up in a cotton hanger. The shelves held containers of the bleach used to whiten the shirts worn by men like the faithful Cristóbal.

Doña Chonita delighted in asking people into her washroom to see the soap stacked against the wall. In the shed built by Cristóbal to Doña Chonita's size (extra short), the foul-smelling soap was displayed like fine china.

On the day my mother sent me to pick up the soap, I would put off the errand as long as possible, fearful of the small grumpy woman with the marble eyes.

"Why haven't you gone for the soap?"

"I was playing."

"Hmmm, well get going before it gets dark."

"Daaaaa."

I walked across the street, dragging my oxfords along a dirt ridge, trying not to get there too soon. I knocked on the kitchen door, avoiding looking toward the shed. Frail Lidia, her eyes blinking, went to get her mother-in-law. Within seconds Doña Chonita came out and in a hissing voice ordered me to the shed.

The shed was dark and gloomy, without a single window. I could make out spiderwebs above the creaky door and against the far corner. The uneven dirt floor was covered here and there with wooden slats. I waited for Doña Chonita to go in first, but she pushed me in, then stood blocking the door. The room was dark and stuffy, I could barely breathe! My face felt hot and sticky. I gaped at the soap bricks that in the dark resembled tiny loaves of brown bread, anxious to be gone from the scary place. I held my nose and waited.

"You likee?"

"Ummm."

"Me salió perfecto!" The marble eyes gleamed as Doña Chonita contemplated the perfection of her soap.

"Ummm."

I oohed and aahed as if smelling French perfume.

"Bueno, here is your mother's soap," she said. "And here's an extra one. De pilón."

I inched my way toward the door, my heart thumping in my chest. As she handed me the soap, Doña Chonita's hand clutched my arm; her nails dug into my soft flesh. She brought her face close to mine, marble eyes glowing like coals, and in a low voice hissed, "Y cuidado con mis chabacanes. And watch it with my apricots."

I grabbed the soap, fearful of the dwarflike creature in her lair, yanked open the door, and bolted for home. I dumped the soap on the kitchen table and petrified of catching a rash from the poison soap, I dashed to the bathroom to wash my hands, then ran to get Concha. Hair ribbons flying in the wind, we ran down the street, straight to the apricot tree. I aimed a rock at the fruit, scooped it off the ground, then hissed to Concha, "be careful of my apricots." We roared with laughter.

Las Ánimas

Each year during the last days of October, I walked to Guardian Angel Church to pick up the black-edged envelopes—usually one per family—distributed to the congregation at that time. These were used to write the names of our dead, our "dearly departed," whom we wished remembered at a special mass. Following a Mexican tradition, we prayed for the dead, or as my mother said, las ánimas, on November second, a Catholic holy day.

As the official church-goer in the family, it was my job to bring home los sobres, making sure I did not tear or stain them. I then sat at the kitchen table to write in pencil the names of our deceased on the allotted lines.

Writing with a pencil was fun and allowed me to erase a letter or word that was not perfect. I rewrote each "mistake" until either I got it right or the paper tore. But I liked best to use the black India ink that came in a tiny bottle and when spilled on clothing could not be removed. The ink produced letters that were bold and graceful, like what the teachers called calligraphy. When it was time to write the names of los muertos on the black-and-white envelopes, though, I chose to begin with pencil, then finish with ink. Mexican names not only sounded funny but were difficult to write.

"How come Mexican names are funny?" I asked Nora, whose real name was María del Socorro.

"Funny?"

"Do you like yours?"

"Why, yes, I like mine, I was named for the Virgin of . . ."

"The Virgin of Nora?"

"No, tonta! Come on, help me with . . ."

My parents had odd Mexican names, or so I thought. When I filled out forms at school it embarrassed me to write their long, awkward names while my friends wrote María, Lucy, or Margarita. I labored over Vicenta and Tranquilino, grateful they had not named me for Saint Policarpio, who according to the Catholic calendar was born on my birthday. What, I wondered, would my nickname have been? Poli? Carpia?

Most of our relatives were in Mexico: grandparents, aunts, uncles, strangers whose names I hardly knew, let alone memorized. Uncle Louie lived in Pacoima, but he was alive and had a nice name. I never knew if my Mexican relatives had pretty names or not. Later, when my father's brothers moved to Pacoima, I was anxious to know their names.

"This is your Tío Domingo."

"My Uncle Sunday?"

"No, Domingo. And this is your Uncle Rómulo."

"Like in Rome?"

When it came time to write the names of our deceased, los difuntos, as Doña Luisa insisted they be called, I prepared well. I cleared the table and ran a dish rag over the worn linoleum to make sure that it was free of food. I arranged the envelopes (having made sure to bring extras in case Duke ate one) on the table, then placed the ink bottle on my right, cleaned the pen on a cloth, and began.

In pencil I wrote the names of my sisters Socorro and Rosalía (whom I had never known), followed by Rito's (whom I barely remembered). I then went looking for my mother or Elizabet so they could once again tell me the correct names of our other muertos. Each year I tried to memorize my deceased grandparents' names, but I invariably had to ask my mother, "es Pedro Solís o Pedro Ponce?" I knew my grandmothers were Martina Vallejo and Manuela Ramírez. It was the Pedros that confused me.

My parents had left Mexico while still young. I had never known my grandparents nor any aunts or uncles. I knew my mother was from a family of eleven; my father from a smaller one. There were no pictures of relatives to compare with the names mentioned on the Day of the Dead. Yet I knew how important it was to remember los muertos.

Of all the names, none evoked the emotion I felt as I wrote Rito's name. My oldest brother died when I was about four. His picture hung in the hallway, so that every morning I looked into his blue-green eyes and smiled. I wished he was alive, knowing he would have spoiled me. Unlike Berney, who chased me across the yard, and Josey, who snitched to our mother, I knew that if Rito were alive, he, like Doña Luisa, would have been on my side.

Rito's name was simple, with only four letters, all of which I knew well. There was no need for caution, no need for pencil first. I first experimented with the letter R. I wrote it in the Palmer Method, in elegant, fancy scrip, then in large block letters, making sure they were each the same size and width. The first three letters were no trouble, but when it came to the O, I found it too square, odd almost. Can there be a square O? I wondered. I settled for a composite version, traced it in ink, and waited for it to dry before moving on to the others. I knew that if what the catechists said was true (that all Catholics went to heaven, where they looked down at us), Rito would be pleased with my handiwork.

After I had written the names of our immediate family, I would concentrate on others: those of friends, neighbors, and celebrities. Abraham Lincoln, los Roosevelts, Joan of Arc. Later I added Bambi and Pinocchio, but was told by Elizabet (who constantly checked my spelling) that these were not real persons. Once I got the family names right and wrote them in pencil, I went over each one with dark ink, my elbow on the table to steady my hand. I dotted the i's with a swift, tiny speck, blew on the ink, fanned the envelope to and fro, then went in search of Doña Luisa.

"I'm ready for los muertos."

"Cómo?"

"The envelopes. Uhhhh, los sobres?"

"Okay."

Doña liked me to write her envelopes inside her house, away from our noisy family. Mostly she liked to have me to herself. She lacked a large table, so I sat on her lumpy bed or on the cold floor of the front room that was her bedroom. I myself preferred to tackle this chore on the porch, from where I could see which of my friends were playing in the street.

It was a challenge to fill in los sobres for Doña Luisa. She could neither read nor write, but knew only how to place an X after her written name. She appeared to know few ánimas; often the names on our envelopes appeared on hers, in addition to those of her former husbands, men whom she alluded to with deep sighs and few words. Her tiny house was bereft of such mementos as wedding pictures, baby shoes, or lace handkerchiefs. Unlike other viejitas on Hoyt Street, Doña Luisa did not hoard faded letters in shoe boxes nor hide jewelry under the mattress. In fact Doña Luisa had few things. Now and then she got letters from a nephew in Mexico, which I read to her and, when I was older, answered in my best Spanish. She had no family and had all but forgotten her relatives in Mexico. In order for her envelope not to appear embarrassingly empty, it was up to me to make up muertos. I attacked this chore with enthusiasm, making up new names for the occasion.

She allowed me to be inventive and to add or delete names at will. One time I saw the movie "Lassie" and cried for weeks at the fate of this poor doggie. Then I saw "My Friend Flicka," about a raven-coated horse that almost died. Not knowing if the two were dead or alive, I wrote their names on Doña Luisa's black-and-white sobre. I knew our pastor would not mind praying for the animals, movie stars really, along with Doña Luisa's relatives.

Finally I licked the envelopes, then hand-carried ours and Doña Luisa's to Thursday's rosary, at least three days before November 2. I wanted to ensure that our difuntos would not be left out. I dropped the envelopes in their designated place, satisfied that come All Souls' Day, neither my relatives nor all the other difuntos would be forgotten.

One year Doña Luisa volunteered my writing services to Doña Remedios, an old woman I disliked. I was infuriated.

"Must I go?"

"Sí."

"But I wanted to play."

"Después."

"Awwwww."

I accompanied Doña Luisa to visit this dreaded lady, trusty pencil in my dress pocket, trying to ignore my friends lining up cans for a game. Doña Remedios greeted me like a long-lost daughter, although she often said that, for a girl, I was much too rowdy. She offered us cookies and lemonade, then brought out a cigar box in which lay a packet of envelopes bound with a rubber band. In Spanish she asked me to read each letter.

"What? Qué?"

"*Sí*, read the letters, then note the names on the envelopes. Los muertos."

"Right now?"

"*Sí*."

I opened a dusty envelope, scanned the letter, wrote the sender's name on the black-and-white envelope, then did the same with the other letters. The afternoon dragged on; I wanted to play with my friends. Doña Luisa, sitting next to me, noted my impatience and quickly gave me her cookies. Still I fumed. When Doña Remedios left the room, I reshuffled the envelopes, then quickly filled the sobres with the names of winos who hung around the alley. Santos, Gabino, Tomás. I licked the envelope with the spit left on my dry tongue, wound the rubber band on the cigar box, my hand working furiously, then handed Doña Remedios the envelope. She smiled, her big yellow goat teeth glowing in the afternoon light. I thanked her for the lemonade and cookies, fluffed my dress in a ladylike fashion, then skipped home, leaving Doña Luisa behind. I felt good, holy almost, knowing the still-living winos would receive a special blessing thanks to Doña Remedios.

On All Souls' Day, the church bulged with gente. It seemed that everyone knew someone who was dead. On this day I dressed carefully in a navy-blue sweater and skirt (laid out the night before). I left for church with Doña Luisa and the Trinidads, all of whom wore black dresses that flapped around their ankles. From their shoulders hung black rebozos brought from Mexico; from afar the women appeared to have long, black wings.

We sat in our accustomed place: third row from the front. A sedate Doña Remedios, face hidden behind a dark veil, sobbed quietly, her thin, skeletal shoulders moving up and down with the Dies Irae. Next to her Doña Chencha dabbed at her eyes as she mumbled words that to my alert ears sounded like "perdónales Señor, perdónales. Forgive them Lord, forgive them."

The catafalque, that eerie wooden structure covered in black, stood in front of the main altar, around which the priest chanted

"Requiem aeternam dona eis Domine," as incense floated upward (like the souls I was sure floated to heaven). I chanted along with the priest, straining to hear the prayers. It was from the liturgy that I first noted the relationship of Latin to Spanish. *Lux, luz.* I spent more time matching words than praying. During the offertory we sang:

> *Salgan, salgan, salgan,*
> *Animas de pena.*
> *Que el santo rosario*
> *Rompe la cadena.*

I disliked this hymn. The images of dead folks strapped in chains and burning in hell were most unpleasant. El himno was from Mexico, the melody repetitious, the words scary. A dead person went either to heaven, hell, or purgatory, our priest intoned. On this day the hymns made note only of those burning in hell or left to await their fate in purgatory.

Later we all surged forward to offer a communion for the dead. To offer the Body of Christ for a muerto counted much more than a high mass and was much cheaper. As I took the host on my tongue, I held it without swallowing. Once back in the pew I shut my eyes tight and chewed slowly.

I chewed for my grandmothers and for the two Pedros, for Socorro, Rosalie, and Flicka. A fast chomp for los Roosevelts. I chewed and rechewed for Rito, the brother whom I loved but never knew. For his soul. I then swallowed the remains of el pan del cielo, satisfied that once again I had complied with the responsibility of remembering our dead. Later as I skipped off to school, a tardy excuse in my dress pocket (written the night before), I hummed a hymn from the liturgy and offered it for the dead. Para los muertos, los difuntos. Las ánimas.

Holy Week

As católicos we strove to do as Father Juanito and later Father Mueller taught us: to observe holy days and attend Sunday mass. During Lent, when Ash Wednesday rolled around (and once more we were told that we were nothing but ashes), we prepared for what the catechists claimed was "the most glorious day in Catholicism," Easter Sunday. Once school was out and the cardboard baskets put away, we played furiously, aware of what the following week would bring. We literally went into deep mourning during Holy Week.

Beginning on Monday of that week, our mother would suggest that, out of respect for Jesus, we not listen to the radio or play in the street. Trina and I hated the restrictions and old-fashioned customs brought from Mexico, ideas no longer in vogue. But we were forced to obey.

"It ain't fair."

"My friends will make fun of me!"

"Tell them the radio broke."

The year I was nine I vowed to attend daily mass during Holy Week. This to me was a great sacrifice; I liked to sleep late during vacation and talk from my bed with Elena, a granddaughter of Doña Nicolasa, the lady who shared Doña Luisa's house. Elena and I would spend the morning shouting back and forth until hunger drove us into the kitchen; we were both chubby and lived to eat. Once the grandmothers had left, we would make toast on Doña Luisa's wood stove, layer it with butter, then down it with quarts of milk. Often we polished off a loaf of bread, a cube of oleo, and a jar of jam at one sitting. This did not bother us in the least; our abuelitas liked to see us eat.

Being stuck in church during Holy Week, however, never bothered me. For one thing I got out of doing housework. I loved everything about church, especially the statues on the altars; I would spend hours gazing at them. The Virgin Mary, called simply la virgen, wore a blue cape over a white dress. From afar her golden hair appeared to glow with a special intensity. The Guardian Angel had wings that sprouted from his shoulders. I often wondered if he was related to the red-winged horse painted in gas stations, but I was afraid to ask.

Our church did not have a statue of the Virgin of Guadalupe. This really bothered me. After all, were we not mejicanos? Father Mueller constantly assured me that the Virgin Mary and Guadalupe were one and the same, but I never believed him. How could they be? One was from Mexico and had appeared to an Indian named Juan Diego. And the other? She was American, with blue eyes and blonde hair. Although I accepted them both as holy women, I actually preferred the Virgin Mary; she at least understood English.

During Holy Week the faithful made offerings and paid mandas to a favorite saint. While Doña Luisa prayed at the main altar, I counted the number of candles in front of each santo; I was curious to see which saint was the most popular, the most sought after. In a small niche near the side door was a small statue of a saint named Atocha. He was short and fat, with stubby fingers, and resembled a dwarf. Still I noticed that he had the most candles!

The figure I most pitied was that of poor Jesus, whose bleeding heart dangled outside his chest. It was impossible to offer him candles, only novenas. Pobrecito, his eyes were full of pain. I just knew it hurt.

During Lent the priest wore purple garments. The red cape worn during Corpus Christi and the one worn during Advent were folded and put away. He chanted prayers not heard during the liturgical year. I found this mumbo jumbo fascinating! I enjoyed the incense, bought from a religious store in Los Angeles, that accompanied the chants and filled the church with a smoky and agreeable aroma. Nonetheless I missed the flowers that graced the altar during the rest of the year.

During Holy Week the altars were swept clean. Gone with the flowers were the pretty candleholders and embroidered altarcloths. Only the plain, white candles, like those sold at the corner store, and white covers resembling sheets, adorned el altar. The idols were swathed from head to toe in purple cloth. Still I knew each statue from memory, each forehead and foot. It pleased me to think that they were resting from being stared at. They too deserved an Easter vacation.

More than anything I enjoyed the church music sung during Holy Week. Although my favorites were: "Bendito, Bendito" and "Pués Concebida," I also liked the liturgical music sung at this time, "Pange Lingua," among them. Some songs were too long. Others sounded like the rancheras sung by Jorge Negrete; they went on forever. I refused to sing those I disliked. I would turn my head so that Doña Luisa would not see my clenched teeth.

During Holy Week I accompanied Doña Luisa to mass every day. I practically *lived* in church, or so my friends teased. I had barely wiped the ashes off my forehead when it was Palm Sunday. Once again it was time to receive a palm frond blessed by our pastor. This was hung on a wall at home and considered a holy relic. I never tired of church, of the quiet; I felt at home among the silent statues.

Except for Holy Thursday, church services during Holy Week were devoid of music. The choir loft remained silent; the bells did not ring. To summon the flock, Father Mueller appointed Don Crispín, an elderly man who worked odd jobs, to bang two wooden boards together in front of the church prior to each service. *Tras, tras, tras.* That was our bell.

On Monday of Holy Week, a low mass was celebrated, followed by mediations either by individuals or by church groups such as the Holy Name and Altar Society. Each group attempted to bring out the most members. The Altar Society always won; most members were women. Tuesday was almost the same.

During the days of lesser importance we cleaned house, washed bedding, and polished the living-room furniture. All was done in preparation for that most holy day: Good Friday.

"You forgot to wash the kitchen windows!"

"I did them for Christmas!"

"This is Easter. Do them again!"

"Awwwwww."

By Wednesday our mother was ready to shop for the lenten foods sold at the Pacoima General Store. She never made a list, but she knew exactly what was needed. Mostly she bought a lot of every-

thing. I trailed behind her as she bought powdered shrimp for camarones, to be mixed with nopalitos, tender cactus pads. This was one
of my favorite dishes, made only during lent. She also bought lentils
and garbanzos, foods to replace meat and stretch a budget. Finally,
she got to the good stuff: almonds, raisins, and piloncillo, brown
sugar sold in chunks, all for the bread pudding we would devour on
Easter Sunday.

By now the house was well cleaned, the curtains crisp, and the
kitchen linoleum shone brightly. My brothers were assigned to clean
the yard. They swept the front and back, gathered dead leaves, then
watered shrubs and trees. My older sisters stayed busy inside, ironing and changing linens. My father sorted wood or changed the oil
in the truck. My mother, with the help of Doña Luisa, cooked and
cooked. I was spared these mundane tasks. I sat in church staring at
poor Jesus, who I knew was about to die.

Lenten services were mysterious, somber. At times what Father
Mueller preached about Jesus Christ confused me. He was already
dead and in heaven, but on Good Friday he would once more be put
on the cross. Although he was only recently born (during Christmas)
and was barely three months old, he grew quite fast (He *was* a God!)
and was now a grown man, destined to die on the cross! Everything
was too confusing! Still Father Mueller stressed that we as Catholics
must believe, have faith, and not ask too many questions.

I never understood how Catholics had allowed Jesus to be cruci-
fied by the Jews. Father Mueller insisted that Jesus was not a Jew,
yet the inscription, "INRI," atop the cross was said in catechism to
mean "Jesus of Nazareth, King of the Jews"! I thought that perhaps
Jesus was Italian; after all, the church was born in Rome! Nothing
was ever made clear.

On Holy Thursday we prepared our Easter clothing. When possible my parents (and later, my older sisters) bought Trina and me
new dresses and Easter bonnets. One year Nora bought me a baby-
blue bonnet with pink rosebuds and flowing blue ribbons. This was
the most beautiful hat I had ever seen. It was of grosgrain, or something similar, soft yet stiff, like the material grown-up hats were
made of. The rosebuds, of pale pink, resembled spun sugar and were
sewn at the front; two pink ribbons fit under the chin. I wore the hat
on Easter Sunday and every Sunday thereafter. Once, in return for

a sucker, I loaned it to Concha. Virgie wanted to borrow it too, but her head was too big; I feared she would tear it. I wore the hat even in the winter and once got caught in a rainstorm. I ran home, dried it with my mother's best towel, then sat down to cry.

"My Easter hat is all ruined."

"Here, give it to me."

Elizabet boiled water, put a cloth across the pan, and then, as the steam came up, reshaped my hat. Still it never fit quite right again.

But our parents could not always afford new Easter clothes. Many times I had to wear a school dress; I hated it. On occasion, however, my sisters would sew me a dress or pinafore trimmed with rick-rack. This was my Easter outfit. If there was extra money, we were bought white shoes, but otherwise I wore school shoes; and hated that. While I was glad to have a new outfit, I prayed no one would look at my feet.

By Thursday afternoon everything was ready. My Easter clothes hung on a wire hanger; my school oxfords were clean and gleaming from a new coat of Shinola. I ate an early supper, gulped down some milk, then left for church to attend the ceremony I found the most entertaining: the washing of the feet.

By Holy Thursday the church was packed. On that day even Mundo, the bully of Hoyt Street, shuffled off to Guardian Angel Church. Nancy attended, mostly to ogle the altar boys now at stage center. Father Mueller emphasized that good Catholics should show respect to God by getting to church on time; I made sure to scurry off before the *tras, tras, tras,* fearful of not getting my usual seat.

One day, in an effort to make it to services on time, I ran across the field bordering Doña Choñita's house, my beanie hanging on for dear life, and found myself heading right for Don Crispín.

"Ay! Cuidado!" he began.

It was too late! I rammed into him at full speed; my knees crushed his scrawny legs. He gasped, tried to move aside, but dropped the wooden boards.

"Gosh Mr. Crispy, I didn't mean to do it!"

I helped to pick up the *tras, tras, tras* boards, but Don Crispín, his face a mottled red, shoved me aside. I picked up my beanie, dusted it off, smoothed my dress, then walked off as Don Crispy went in-side the sacristy. I knew he would be late in banging the boards; our pastor would notice the delay. When within minutes of entering the church I heard the muted sounds of the boards, they sounded just fine. I smiled at Doña Luisa, frowned at Doña Cruzita, then settled down in the pew, full of respect.

During the evening services on Holy Thursday, Father Mueller wore a simple outfit, a garment so plain it could have come from J.C. Penney. While it was said that all priestly garments were made by nuns, I wondered about the chasuble Father now wore. I then decided that he feared getting his fancy clothes wet, and therefore did as I did when cleaning house: wore old rags.

I sat smack in the front row, Doña Luisa behind me. I was anxious to get going with the washing of the feet. The choir, I knew, would sing a few hymns, but the organ would remain silent. And so I sat. Just then I looked up to see Nancy coming my way. She slid into the pew, fluffed her hair, rolled her eyes, then looked expectantly around.

Although Nancy attended catechism and considered herself una católica, she never remembered the order of the mass. While others knelt, she sat; when others sat, she stood. During Holy Week, when forced to attend services, Nancy liked to sit next to me, so I could prompt her.

"Psssst Nancy, you're the only one standing!"

Nancy found it hilarious that we Catholics never stood still. Up and down we went; forward and backward. Now, as I waited for the procession to begin, I tried not to giggle. Doña Luisa was watching from behind. She disliked Nancy, saying that Nancy was too forward for her age. One time she called me aside and said "Pues, esa niña es muy . . ." She pursed her lips and in her hoarse voice began to list Nancy's faults.

"But she's my friend!"

"Hmmmm. Con lipisticki?"

I waited for the show to begin. Most of all I wanted to see Father Mueller's feet. It fascinated me to know he had feet. Mostly I saw him in the long, black dress that swept the floor and hid them. I especially liked to stare at the altar boys' feet. Most were my friends and were ashamed to have us in the front row. I tried not to giggle as they sat awaiting Father Mueller.

The procession began. We stood as the priest approached the main altar, mumbled the prayers, then took his place to the side, where there were three chairs. He sat in the middle one, three altar boys on each side. I spotted Mundo trying to hide behind some palms stuck in a pot. First Father Mueller removed his shoes; then the others followed suit. When Mundo leaned down to take off his shoes and socks, I made a big show of holding my nose. Next to me first Nancy began to giggle, then Virgie and Concha.

"Lookit Mundo's big feet!"

"Ugh."

"And Father Mueller's white ones."

"Shhhhh. That's a sin."

Behind me Doña Luisa gave a nervous cough, her warning to me to be quiet.

The show was getting good. Nancy and I smothered our laughter; Virgie held a hankie to her face. In an effort to get Mundo's attention, I began to cough and cough, then waved my finger at him. Desperate now I craned toward the communion rail that separated the flock from our leader, and was about to tip over when I saw a hole in Mundo's socks!

"Mundo's got a hole en los calcetines," I whispered to Nancy.

"Okay." Nancy answered, then stood up.

I yanked at her dress, but she ignored me. She stood, waiting for the rest of us to do the same. Unable to control himself, Mundo began to snicker. Next to me Virgie keeled over with laughter. I leaned across to whisper to Concha, whose eyes were glued on our pastor and Mundo, then looked up to meet Father Mueller's steely glare.

Holy Thursday signaled the beginning of the more somber services, all of which would lead to the death of Jesus—and his Resurrection. They began with the "Pange Lingua." The priest entered from the rear of the church with the altar boys, swinging incense holders, at his heels. The short procession came to a halt at the main altar, where the priest removed the golden chalice with the sacred Host. He carefully moved the Host to a side altar, as the choir continued with this same hymn. The main tabernacle, its doors ajar, remained empty; Jesus Christ was no longer with us. He was in jail, waiting for the Jews and Italians to get him. I trudged home through the dark streets, my hand clutching Doña Luisa's, thinking of what was still to come.

I never knew who God was. In catechism I learned only that He was our Father and the Father of Jesus. God was a father and a spirit! All three were one, One Holy Trinity. It was common knowledge that Mary was the mother of Jesus, and God was his father. But God was not married to the Virgin Mary, because she was married to Saint Joseph. And although Our Lady of Guadalupe might be the Virgin Mary, she could *not* be the mother of Jesus. Why not? Because both Jesus and the Virgin Mary were white and had blue eyes. Only God knew how all this came about.

Father Mueller preached that God was in the Host inside the tabernacle. I spent hours in front of the main altar hoping to see God come out. Often while waiting for Doña Luisa to finish her petitions, I would sit in the dark, silent church, staring at the little doors.

Our pastor emphasized that within Catholicism many things were sacred, miraculous even. I totally agreed, because had God been a real man, he could not have squeezed inside the tiny altar doors. I kept asking Father for a better explanation, but every time he saw me coming, he went the other way.

On Good Friday, soon after breakfast, we were put to work embroidering fundas (pillowcases) or dish towels. We spoke in hushed tones; the radio remained unplugged. It was almost the time when the Jews killed Jesus.

My mother and Doña Luisa worked silently in the kitchen. They put lentils to soak, whipped dry shrimp with egg white, and cut up bread for capirotada, bread pudding. Elizabet first toasted the bread in the oven, then with swift, precise movements, cut it into tiny, perfect squares. Some women on our street deep fried the bread, saying that this gave the bread added flavor. Not so Elizabet. She brushed the bread with melted oleo, saying that too much fat was bad for us. In a large square pan, slightly greased, the cubed bread was layered with raisins, walnuts, and piloncillo, the hard brown sugar sold in big chunks. It was then set aside, to allow the brown sugar to soak through the bread.

My brothers, all of whom went to church on Good Friday, remained outside to sort wood and clean the yard. One time they had worked their way to the garage; Berney was tinkering with a car motor while Norbert sparred with the black punching bag. When Doña Luisa saw this, she immediately told my father, who, although not overly religious, respected what Good Friday represented. My brothers were told to get out of the garage and keep to los cuartitos. Toward noon, when in catechism it was said that "the skies darkened," my father would stop work. He ate lunch, then sat outside to read *La Opinión*, our dog Duke at his feet. I remember well the silence within—as though no one was about.

As good Catholics we knew well the exact hour at which Jesus Christ died; it was precisely at three o'clock. I found this incredible. There were no clocks at that time!

By midafternoon all was silent; the earth appeared to stand still. The streets were empty of cars; the stores closed. Even street dogs ceased barking. We were in deep mourning.

Good Friday was an especially long day. I bathed and dressed early, then put on a clean, starched dress. My sisters combed out my curls. I gave my shoes a wipe, then sat to wait until I could leave for church, before services began. My mother counseled us to allow time for contemplation and to beg God's forgiveness before He was put on the cross. This appealed to me, impatient as I was. I ran off to be with Doña Luisa.

On Good Friday Doña Luisa remained in church most of the day. She ate nothing, saying she wished to emulate our Lord, who for forty days did not eat. I found it incredible that anyone could live this long without food, even God! I never stopped eating. In her hoarse, scratchy voice, Doña Luisa explained that Jesus could not eat because of fright. He knew the Jews and Italians were after him.

On Palm Sunday, she claimed, her eyes full of tears, they had received him with palms, even a parade, then stuck cactus in his hair, offered him vinegar to drink, and arrested him.

"Lo traicionaron," she whispered.

"Who?" I asked, curious as to who had betrayed Jesus.

"Los judíos y los romanos."

I think that is why I never liked Italians: because they were so mean.

On Friday morning mass was not celebrated. God was no longer in the altar but in the street, lugging the cross, which in reality was our sins. I could not understand how a cross could be made of sins and not of wood, but Father Mueller said that was how it was. I had to believe.

At times I considered Father Mueller a big liar. First he said the Jews killed Jesus, then he said it was our sins. Later he conceded that it was the Romans who did it. I once tried asking the catechists, but they mumbled something and took off.

At exactly two thirty the first *tras, tras, tras* sounded. It was time for the Viá Crucis, the Stations of the Cross, which would culminate at exactly three o'clock. The church immediately filled with people. In the dirt streets, dark-robed women and freshly scrubbed children scurried to reach their seats. In the parking lot next to the church, dusty cars parked at will, some taking more than one space. Inside the corner store, the shades went down.

On this solemn, sad day, when even the pope went into mourning, the congregation sang:

> *Perdón o Dios Mío, perdón e Indulgencia,*
> *Perdón y clemencia, perdón y Piedad.*

I hated this hymn; it was too, too sad. Once Father Mueller disappeared inside the sacristy, Doña Clarissa (the best singer of the Trinidads) took the lead and concluded this desolate hymn. Goose pimples rose on my chubby arms at the thought that I too had killed Jesus. I knelt next to Doña Luisa to ask forgiveness.

The Vía Crucis was short but lively. Unlike regular mass, when we knelt most of the time, during the Stations of the Cross we literally jumped up and down the whole time. This was a challenge to Nancy, who dared not leave my side.

By four o'clock I was home, tired but exhilirated. We ate a simple dinner, then while my sisters washed and dried the dishes, I searched for bottles to take to church the following day: Holy Saturday.

En el sabado de gloria, holy water was blessed, then distributed to the congregation. On that day, too, the Easter candle was blessed. Taking care not to be seen, I locked myself in the bathroom in search of bottles. Once I selected them, I lugged the bottles to the kitchen sink, washed, rinsed, then dried each bottle with a snow-white cloth from the kitchen drawer, wanting to ensure that they would be worthy of the blessed water.

Most of my friends were altar boys who, given the chance, would give me all the water I wanted. Once the water was blessed and ready, it was their job to fill the bottles and then hand out el agua bendita. I took my place in line, pushing aside those trying to cut in and being careful not to step on Doña Chonita. Once Father Mueller turned his back, my friends willingly filled all my bottles.

"This one, too!"

"You already gots three."

"This one's for Doña María. She's blind, you know."

"Oh, okay!"

I tucked the bottles, filled to the brim, into my sweater, taking care not to trip. I walked in the middle of the road, avoiding the rock-strewn path that bordered Hoyt Street. Once at home I handed one jar to my mother; the rest were hidden under Doña Luisa's bed.

The sacred water was potent; it was used to banish evil spirits like Sátanas, who it was said never slept. We also kept it in reserve in case Father Mueller came to administer the last rites. El agua bendita was not to be desecrated nor wasted, we were told in catechism, or we would be punished. But when no one was around, I would take our bottle, lock myself in the bathroom, and drink small sips.

The first time I drank only a small amount; I wanted to experiment. I stood in front of the mirror to await a transformation. I thought I might turn into another person, even an animal, so I watched my face for any change. I stretched my eyelids, rolled my eyes, and bared my teeth, but nothing happened. So I drank an entire glass. I told no one, not even Elena; I feared she would tell my mother, who in turn would tell my father. My father did not condone disrespect for things of the church.

Another time, after drinking two tumblers full of holy water, I got a stomachache. I was petrified, certain I was being punished, just like they said in catechism! I ran outside, yelling for Doña Luisa.

"Ayyyyyy."

"Pero qué te pasa?" She asked, looking annoyed.

"I'm gonna die," I screeched, then started to cry.

For a while I let the water be, but I was still curious. Now and then when no one was looking, I sipped the blessed water. It tasted sweet, pure. It made me feel good and holy, full of the Holy Spirit. Secretly I yearned to be a priest!

I loved to pray in Latin, not always sure of what I was saying. I especially liked the outfits of damask, taffeta, and silk worn by

Father Mueller. The long flowing capes that hung from his shoulders came in lime green, scarlet, white with gold, and the dull purple of Lent. They were like those worn in the movies by magicians; they hung to his feet. Each was lined in a bright color, and all were hand sewn with tiny, tiny stitches. When he turned around at the altar, the cape swung to and fro. It was said that Father's outfits were made with gold thread by nuns in Belgium. I thought they were fantastic.

Once in a weak moment, I asked Father Mueller to let me be an altar boy "Ha, ha, ha," he laughed, his blue eyes crinkling at the corners.

"I'm smarter than Mundo! I can light candles, too!"

"No, no, the Church does not allow this," he said, his face a bright red. "Girls attract the wrong attention." Then he added, with a smugness I sometimes hated, "Women are not allowed at the altar."

This I knew, was a big lie. It was women who swept and cleaned the altar. Women polished the tabernacle, too! And women arranged the church flowers. But Father Mueller only laughed: "Ha, ha, ha." Soon after that he suggested I join the church choir. "You have a fine voice," he said, "and Our Lord is pleased when one prays in song."

He shooed me out the door, then retreated to the sacristy, another place women weren't allowed. Thus instead of becoming an altar boy, I went off to sing in Latin.

On Holy Saturday mass began with a long, flowing Kyrie, sung a capella. At the start of the Gloria, when it was said "the heavens opened," the church was filled with the joyous peal of bells. The large church bell rang out, Don Crispín at the rope. The altar boys, full of religious fervor and enthusiasm, shook the smaller bells as though they would never stop.

Up in the choir loft, the church organ began to peal the Gloria, accelerating to catch up with the runaway singers. At the altar Father Mueller chanted the mass, as around his feet incense rose upward to encircle the statues. Everything was like magic!

The candles flickered, the bells filled the room, the flowers shone bright. Suddenly Don Crispín, dressed in a spotless white shirt, appeared from inside the sacristy; in his hands was a long pole. He approached the Guardian Angel and lifted the purple covering; then he did the same with all the other statues. Last of all he unveiled Jesus Christ and the Virgin Mary. I stared at my friends who had been in hiding, delighted with how refreshed and happy they looked. Even Jesus, his bleeding heart still dangling to the side, appeared less sad.

When mass was over, Father Mueller blessed the Easter candle (which would burn throughout the liturgical year), the water, and the faithful. By this time I was exhausted, yet happy. The Gloria, the bells, and the incense had lifted my spirit. This was a most glorious Saturday!

On Easter Sunday our small church bulged with people dressed in their Easter finery. From my vantage point in the choir loft I would inspect the various outfits and the colorful array of head coverings worn by the women: straw hats, plumed hats, toques, flowered hats, lace veils, and plain black rebozos. Nancy, who insisted on being in the choir loft with me, liked to compare different dress styles and to argue for a favorite.

"Ugh, lookit Lola's ugly dress."

"I think it's pretty!"

"And that hat on Josie sticks out like . . ."

One year I counted twenty outfits in bright pink and six straw hats with cabbage roses. Many of the women wore corsages of orchids or gardenias that their children had given them. The young women looked elegant; the men looked about the same.

Easter Mass began with the "Vidi Aguam." Father Mueller, dressed in all his glory, strode up and down the aisle, his face full of holiness and goodwill. He raised his arms high to bless the congregation with holy water, which felt cool against my heated face. The Mass of the Blessed Virgin Mary, sung only on special occasions, followed. The Kyrie was intricate, demanding; our voices rose in a crescendo, then diminished like that of a choir of angels. During communion we sang:

Regina Coeli, Regina Coeli latarae,
Alleluia, Alleluia, Alleluia.

Most people received communion, if only to show off an outfit. From the choir loft Nancy and I pushed our way to the communion rail. Nancy wanted to ensure that everyone saw her pink outfit; I showed off my beautiful Easter bonnet. Once mass was over, I closed my St. Gregory's Himnal, then scrambled down the stairs to join

Concha. We discussed hats, dresses, and gloves. Satisfied that we had missed nothing, I left for home. I dashed into our kitchen, starved to death, to find that my mother had laid the table with pan dulce and chocolate. To her this day was deserving of more than oatmeal.

Toward afternoon, after a supper of camarones y nopales (dried shrimp patties and cactus), lentils, beans and tortillas, and capirotada served with canned milk, my sisters hid two kinds of Easter eggs: sugar eggs and hard-boiled eggs colored in bright pinks and yellows. Josey and I fought over the sugar ones. I hated the cooked ones; sabían a huevo, they tasted of egg. Once the egg shells were cleaned up and the household quieted down, we once more played in the street with our friends. Toward evening this day became like any other Sunday: my mother in the kitchen and my father with *La Opinión*.

In the evening I left as usual to sleep with Doña Luisa. I slowly undressed, folded my Easter clothes over a chair, placed my new shoes next to the bed (so I could look at them a while longer), then blessed myself and prayed to my Guardian Angel. I lay back against the pillow, content and sleepy. I was happy knowing that Jesus Christ was alive and well, even though come next year, we would again kill him with a cross made of sins. But for the moment I moved closer to Doña Luisa, to feel her bony, dry body—to feel her love.

When My Father Became un Comunista

I was about ten when my father became un comunista. The affair began when Don Samuel, a crusty old gentleman who claimed he had fought in Mexico with the infamous Pancho Villa, paid my father a visit. Called el general by his intimates, Don Samuel was a tall, skinny man with white hair that stuck out like a rooster's feathers. His white eyebrows were a stark contrast to his deep brown eyes. He wore a red kerchief tied around his neck, like the ascot worn by English actors in the movies, except that his was a common handkerchief that sold at the five and dime. Still the kerchief-ascot gave Don Samuel a certain air.

Don Samuel carried a stick, but not a walking stick like that of Don Limón, a man who limped up and down Hoyt Street. His was made of polished wood and resembled riding crop. He walked with it held next to his right leg, and while talking, he would wave it back and forth to make a point. Now and then he wore a white hat, wider than the Panama hat my father wore. For the most part he went around bare-headed, the rooster's crest fluttering in the breeze.

El general wore white shirts (starched stiff by his dutiful wife) buttoned at the cuff and up to the top of his scrawny neck. On the middle finger of his right hand he wore a gold ring said to have been given to him by Villa. His baggy pants were secured at the waist with a leather belt. On his feet he wore high boots like those worn by Teddy Roosevelt and the Rough Riders. I feared el general. When he visited my father, I ran to hide, afraid of his shouts and the whip.

The general was a most excitable man. When he spoke his eyebrows shifted up and down on his craggy face. His eyes blazed with an inner fire; his small mouth spewed profanities never before heard in our yard. He marched like a soldier, his scrawny legs lifted high in a kind of goosestep.

Don Samuel relished giving orders. He would tell his short wife (a woman who rarely ventured out of the kitchen) what to cook and serve for dinner. He screeched, shouted, and stomped his booted feet at his two skinny sons, one of whom stuttered every time his father came near. While it was never clear whether or not el general was really a general, my father accorded him the respect due a Mexican general.

El general liked to squeeze. He squeezed arms, necks, and at times, legs. When I saw him walking up our driveway, I would tear off to the fig tree, then watch him stomp up to my father, greet him in a loud, screechy voice, and squeeze my father's arm. He squeezed and squeezed, his face redder by the minute as my stoic father also turned red. Satisfied that he was still strong and able to paralyze a victim, he stood back and grinned.

"No es que no puedo?"

"Hmmmmm."

My father never flinched while Don Samuel squeezed, nor did he get angry. He merely moved away, then waited to see what orders would issue from the general. My father, I saw, took Don Samuel seriously. He never dared to outstare him, but spoke to him in a most respectful voice.

One day I saw Don Samuel approaching, boots lifted high in the air. He came up Hoyt Street, his stick swaying with the movement of his legs, ascot tight around his neck. When he reached our house, he made a quick right turn, like a real soldier, then marched up to our door in short, precise strides. My father, who was working inside the garage, went out to greet him.

"Adelante las tropas, Ponce," he screeched in Spanish, "prepare the troops." His white crest shimmered in the morning light, his arms quivered at his side.

"How are you, Don Samuel," responded my father, wiping his oily hands on a rag. Seeing the look on the general's face, he quickly added, "mi general."

"Hay que formar las tropas," he repeated. The general was calling the troops to order at eight o'clock in the evening. "A las ocho en punto."

"Cómo?" began my father, then he looked across to where I sat giggling.

"A general never repeats orders," Don Samuel responded in Spanish. He made an about-face and in one swift movement brought the stick to his side. He turned on his heel, bowed to my mother (who was hanging clothes on the line), and marched off, dust swirling around his dark boots.

Don Samuel was forever inviting my father and "the troops" (the men of the neighborhood, that is) to attend meetings of one kind or the other. Since my mother knew his wife, she never minded the time my father spent away from home, but she refused to accompany him.

"Just for a short visit."

"I'd rather not."

"María would like to see you."

"Lo siento."

I never knew why my mother refused, but I think it was because the general's wife (whom it was said he stole from a former suitor) insisted that all guests look through a faded album of sepia-brown pictures of the general in uniform. More than once I had been forced to admire pictures of el general loaded down with medals astride a black horse. She related the general's military exploits and had memorized each battle, each town, and how many Carransistas Don Samuel had killed.

"This was taken in Monterrey."

"Hmmmmm."

"This was taken when he was decorated for bravery under fire. And this . . ."

I liked being inside the general's house, and when I was sent on errands, I lingered in the kitchen, then worked my way to the living room, called la sala by Don Samuel, a room as wide as the church hall and often used for baptisms, wedding receptions, and funerals. The wood floor was kept polished to a bright sheen. The walls were painted a light green and had wide baseboards. At the top of the wall, right before it curved into a round dome, was a narrow strip of decorative wood covered with gold leaf. Along the walls sat sofas, settees, and odd tables of scratched mahogany. The sofas were upholstered in dark maroon and sick green and had feet that looked like bear claws. Most of the furniture was threadbare, but it was made to look elegant by the crocheted doilies put there by the faithful María.

My father attended the meeting. He first put on a clean shirt, cleaned his shoes with a rag, tucked the shirt inside his work pants, then off he went to join the troops.

The meeting had been organized by a man with reddish hair and blue eyes, a stranger dressed in work clothes whom Don Samuel had never questioned about the purpose of the gathering. I had seen this man before. He often passed out leaflets near the corner, in front of a place said to be a labor hall.

That night my father and other señores of the neighborhood, asked by Don Samuel to hacer bulto, make a crowd, attended the meeting. The general wanted to ensure that the invited speaker would not feel embarrassed at the lack of attendance. My father left early, wanting to be on time. He was accompanied by Duke, who turned back home when he reached the corner.

"Buenas noches, general."

"Adelante!"

"Buenas noches, Doña María."

"Tu vieja, a la cocina!"

No introductions were made, or so my father later said, so those in attendance did not know that the speakers, two men in addition to the red-haired one, were comunistas. The main speaker, whom my father took a liking to because he seemed honest and looked directly at him, began to speak to the men. He used Spanish and English, but then gave up and stuck to English. Once the speaker finished his spiel, the general passed around a jug of red wine. Just before the men went out the door, my father and the others were asked to sign un papel, a paper they did not readily understand. The men, few of whom could read or write in Spanish, let alone English, signed their names with the pen proferred by the organizers. They prided themselves on being courteous Mexicans, hombres corteses, who would never embarrass a host.

Soon after my father began to receive letters and flyers from Communist organizations, protesting not only the working conditions of laborers, but also the lynching of "Negroes" taking place in the South. The letters urged all members, all good comunistas, to write the government to demand a halt to the lynchings.

My father, who read little English, did not readily understand the content of the letters. Once he had scanned them, he threw them in the trash bin at the back of the house. He never bothered to tear them into tiny pieces, but merely stuck them next to yellowed copies of La Opinión.

One day my mother was out back hanging up clothes. Just then my father went by on his way to the trash barrel. Once he was out of sight again, my mother asked Elizabet to translate the contents of the letter still warm from my father's hand.

"Que dice?" asked my mother, as she pulled the clothespin bag towards her. "What does the letter say?"

"It's from the comunistas," explained Elizabet. "They want mi papá to send telegrams to Washington. They want all communists, uhhh, my father to protest, uhh lynch Negroes!"

Elizabet read on as my mother wiped her damp hands on her apron, then walked off in search of my father, now busy inside the garage.

"What does this mean?" asked my mother, holding aloft the incriminating letter.

My father, never at a loss for words, mumbled an explanation. "I did sign un papel," he cried, "pero no soy un comunista."

"And the general?" asked my mother, certain that Don Samuel was at the root of the problem.

"El es Villista."

My father, who strove to learn enough English to become an American citizen, turned pale at being mistaken for a dreaded Communist, a Red; they were said to be not only against the American government, but also against the pope.

After that whenever letters addressed to my father arrived, be they from the Communist party or the gas company, my mother, a wide smile on her face, would hand him the letters saying in Spanish, "Here, this is from the Communists asking you to lynch Negroes."

My father took the letters and, head bent in embarrassment, pushed them to the bottom of the trash heap. This threw us into a dither; we would roar with laughter until my mother silenced us with a look that implied that children should never, ever laugh at their parents.

After a time the letters ceased. My father continued to visit el general. He eventually attended a meeting or two, but he never again volunteered to sign un papel, not even out of courtesy. He wanted to be an American, not un communista out to lynch Negroes.

El Mes de Mayo

To the practicing Catholics of our town, the month of May was el mes de María, dedicated to the Blessed Virgin Mary. Starting on the first of May, young girls of Guardian Angel parish (including Concha, Virgie, Nancy, and me) took part in the ofrecimiento, the nightly offering of flowers to Our Lady. This Mexican custom, brought by our parents to this country, was something I enjoyed. Not only was I emulating my Mexican abuelitas, but I was also calling attention to myself. In truth, taking part in el ofrecimiento was like being onstage, with the whole town watching.

During this spring month, the statue of la inmaculada was taken down from her niche in the side altar and placed in front of the communion rail, where a temporary altar was set up. The alabaster statue of Mary, blue-eyes downcast, fair hair covered by a blue vestment, was placed atop an embroidered altar cloth on the middle of a makeshift table. Home-grown flowers were placed on each side of Mary. The space in front was left empty for the flowers we brought to *la sanctísima* as a token of our love and devotion.

The offering took place between the rosary prayers and the Mysteries recited by our pastor and the congregation. Each evening before the last of the three bells that called us to prayer had sounded, my friends and I, all of whom lived on Hoyt Street, were expected to be sitting in the seats reserved for us at the back of the church. We were supposed to bring our own flowers, too, but for those who did not have a garden at home, or were unable to snitch posies from a neighbor, a variety of flowers sat en la tina, the zinc tub beneath the choir loft. During the warm May evenings, the pungent fragrance of roses, carnations, and Shasta daisies filled the church.

We wore white dresses of cotton, plissé or chambray, and white veils of every size, some with lace at the bottom. Nancy, who thought she was "so big," wore a crocheted dress with a separate slip. The dress, made by her grandmother in Mexico and starched stiff as cardboard by her mother, scratched me whenever I walked next to her.

Other girls wore their still-new First Communion dresses and carried the pearl rosaries and prayer books bought for that special occasion. These were called "adornments" by the strict catechists, and although they had been blessed by the priests and thus were somewhat holy, they were supposed to be kept at home. Still the girls carried them, acting holier than ever.

Dressing up to look like the Virgin Mary was fun. Each time I covered my head with a veil I felt holy, special, like a "little bride," or even a child saint. I walked slower, knowing full well that women like Teresa of Avila, Saint Cecelia, and especially the Virgin Mary— which was as high as I could aspire to—walked gracefully. But for girls from poor families, the ofrecimiento often created a problem. Not everyone had white dresses, veils, or shoes.

The older girls, those ready for confirmation, wore white ribbons or a white scarf on their dark heads, thinking perhaps that they should look different. Many were sent home after the first night and returned wearing borrowed veils. Girls who could not afford to buy a velo put one together using a piece of net bought at a yardage store in San Fernando. Others, more inventive, would attach a crocheted or lace cap made by a doting grandmother or tía. When it was starched stiff and attached to the misty veil, the crocheted cap made a pretty contrast to the blue-black hair of las niñas mexicanas.

Some of my friends, including Concha, wore hand-me-downs. Like me, Concha was the youngest girl in her family and was forced to wear old, limp garments passed on by her older sisters. For the ofrecimiento, Concha wore a white dotted-swiss dress, but because she was taller than her siblings, her mother had added a ruffle and lots of rickrack. Concha hated the dress, and each night poked her hand in the pocket to stretch a hole, praying her mother would tire of mending it and buy her a new one. Concha's veil, however, was the envy of all the girls on Hoyt Street. Of pale ivory with a crown of creamy orange blossoms called azahares, the veil was on loan from her sister Celina, who had worn it as a bride. In exchange for a Babe Ruth bar, I sometimes talked Concha into letting me wear her veil.

"Ta, ta, ta, ta."

"Here come the bride."

". . . big, fat, and wide."

I was chubby, so I wore a dress never before worn by my older sisters, all of whom were slender. It was of white chambray with a smocked front, tiny buttons, and short puffed sleeves that cut into my round arms. I was still too young to plan my own clothes, but I already hated dresses that resembled baby clothes. I longed to dress like Nora, who had an assortment of stylish dresses in her closet.

Few of us wore white shoes. We came from large families who could only afford one pair of shoes for each child. I wore school oxfords, Concha wore saddle oxfords, and Nancy wore her favorite brown shoes stained with Shinola, which dribbled down to the heel. If we were bought white patent-leather shoes at Easter, and providing they weren't too scuffed, we wore those instead, delighted at being dressed completely in white, todas en blanco, like the Virgin Mary.

Each afternoon Elizabet or Doña Luisa would check to see that my dress and veil were clean and starched. Doña Luisa liked to hand wash and iron my dress. Often she forgot to iron the inside of the hem, and I wore a dress with a damp bottom edge that felt cool against my legs.

My mother sometimes cut garden flowers for me to take to the offering. She favored the pink rambling roses that grew alongside our white picket fence, but her very favorite was la rosa de Castilla, a stately rose with velvety petals and huge thorns that stood apart from the others. When this flower was in full bloom and my mother was in a generous mood, she fixed me a special bouquet. After she cut the common roses, she added fern, crespón, from a vine that grew along the porch rail. Last of all she would snip one of the pretty roses and toss it smack in the middle of the bunch. She rearranged las flores, then wrapped the stems in waxed paper, to protect my hands. When she wasn't looking, I would crush the delicate rose in my hand, then rub the oily petals on my chest. The fragrance of roses accompanied me to church, where I surrendered all but the Rose of Castile to the communal tub.

At times I played outdoors until past the second bell and arrived late to church. My friends would give me a dirty look, then shove me to the farthest seat, while they adjusted their spotless dresses. Veil askew, knees smeared with dirt, I would fidget in my seat, not accustomed to looking messy, afraid of not being allowed to be at the head of the procession.

To be at the front of the procession was terribly important. People in church, especially the boys, were sure to spot the lucky girl who walked ahead of the pack. Should a girl wear an off-white or pastel dress, even one with a faint design, her chances of being picked for this high honor were minimal. Those selected *had* to be all in white, todas en blanco. More importantly, the girl had to look pious, humble, and pure.

The older girls, those who had already made a confirmation, knew their prayers backwards and forwards, and never talked back to the Saturday catechists, were selected to march at the head of the procession. But not always. At times those chosen were put there by a relative whose job at the ofrecimiento was to line up the girls, and who now played favorites by pushing a niece or sister to the very front.

At times I wished Elizabet still went to the May offerings. She, I knew, would put me in front, or die trying. Unfortunately my older sisters had already lived through this experience and had better things to do on warm May evenings. It was up to me to see that I was picked. At home I locked myself in the bathroom, then stood in front of the mirror, eyes downcast, head lowered. At church, while the others giggled and shoved each other in line, I remained impassive, the epitome of saintliness. I was chosen more than once.

Once the rosary began, we settled down in the pews, straight and stiff in our white dresses, dark heads swathed in veils and bent in prayer, until the Third Mystery, when we were lined up for the first offering. Anxious to get going, I pulled at my veil, smoothed out the wrinkles, then stood around waiting to see what order to follow. At times best friends were allowed to march together, but for the most part we were discouraged from picking a friend as our partner because we tended to giggle when passing by the boys. A giggle in line often mean a good pinch from the ladies in charge.

One of the best pinchers was Lucy, Nancy's older sister. Lucy was rumored to be a pachuca who hung around with zoot suiters (which was the worst thing a girl could do). Lucy was pretty, with olive skin and small, dark eyes that rarely smiled. I found it hard to believe that such a pretty girl could be a zoot suiter who wore a knife stuck in her pompadour and another stuck inside her socks. Jesus, Mary, and Joseph!

One time when she was busy helping line up the girls, Lucy saw someone giggling and acting smart. Without checking to see who it was, she gave the veiled figure a good pinch.

"Babosa! Why did you pinch me?" screeched an outraged Nancy.

"Shut up, hocicona, or I'll slap your face," hissed Lucy.

"Jesús, María, José," sighed Doña Clarissa.

"Dominus vobiscum," sang Father.

Everyone froze: old women, kids, and those of us waiting to march. At the altar our pastor paused, cocked an ear, then continued with the prayers. From the choir loft women leaned over to see the commotion better; in the pews the boys, alerted by the delay, began to turn around and giggle, until Don Serafín cleared his throat in warning. Just then the organ began to play:

> *Venid y vamos todos*
> *Con flores a porfía*
> *Con flores a María, que madre nuestra es*
> *Con flores a María, que madre nuestra es*

I secured my veil, Nancy yanked at hers, and Concha adjusted los azahares. Our attention shifted from el escándalo to the business at hand.

The procession moved up the main aisle. We slowly walked to the front, genuflected (making sure our knee touched the floor, or else it wouldn't count), laid down our flower offerings, genuflected once more, then returned through a side aisle to our seats. We marched in step: walk, pause, walk, the palms of our hands pressed together, eyes down. We dared not look up, let alone smile at the boys. To do so would mean we were sin gracia, lacking in grace.

One time I had been at the head of the procession and had just returned to my seat, when I looked up to see Nancy. Her dark head was held high, defying everyone not to look her way. Her cheeks were rouged, her mouth was a bright red, and the palms of her hands were pressed together. As she went by Chita, her mortal enemy, she stuck out her middle finger and hissed, "Toma." She then straightened out her finger, tossed back her head, and continued as before.

"Gosh! She gave Chita the finger."

"She's going straight to hell."

I was shocked at Nancy! Never had I seen her, or anyone else, do such a thing in church. This, I was certain, was a mortal sin, possibly a sacrilege. I dared not turn around, so I ignored Nancy as she took her seat, fluffed her dress, and pushed back her veil. Secretly I admired her; the boys rarely picked on her. Nancy was not una miedosa, a scaredy-cat. Unlike others; unlike me.

We continued with el rosario until the last mystery, then once more struggled to our feet, ready to march. We sang:

> De nuevo aquí nos tienes,
> Purísima doncella,
> Más que la luna bella,
> Prostrados a tus pies, postrados a tus pies.

The Litany of the Saints, almost a roster of all the santos in heaven, followed. I listened for my favorite, Santa Anastasia, then gave the response: "Ora pro nobis." By the late 1940s my friends and I had picked up pachuco jargon; we loved to use forbidden words like cabrón, simón, órale. During this prayer, providing no adults were nearby, we would respond with "Orale, pro nobis."

Next came the benediction. We bowed our heads for this final blessing, then checked our limp veils and equally limp flowers for the last time. By now the communal flowers were gone, the tub half-empty. Impatient with the delay, we remained in line as the women split up what remained of the flowers, concerned that we not approach Mary's altar empty-handed. We straggled up the aisle, anxious for the offering to end. Then we sang a farewell to Mary, who smiled at us from her perch.

Adiós, Reina del cielo,
Madre del Salvador,
Adiós, o madre mía, adiós, adiós, adiós.

I knew this hymn by heart; I had heard it since infancy and had memorized each stanza. Still it pleased me to sing church songs that were special to my parents and a part of our culture. I felt chills on my arms; the Spanish words filled my eyes with tears. I loved la Sanctísima and wanted to be just like her. Pure, holy. As the candles flickered and the smell of roses filled the air, my heart thumped with joy and happiness. For a ten-year-old, full of fervent faith, it was almost like being in heaven.

An air of excitement now filled the air; soon we would be finished and could start for home. Although I enjoyed el ofrecimiento, by the time it ended my friends and I were bored and tired and wanted to do something else. We hurried to take our places, eager to finish while it was still light, anxious to be with the boys.

Soon it was over. We knelt for the last time, grabbed a sweater, then ran outside, happy to be done for the night. Inside the church the organist closed and locked the organ, as our pastor disappeared into the sacristy. We then dispersed. Some girls dashed across the street, white veils flying, to buy a penny's worth of candy at la tienda de Don Jesús. Others helped clean the mess from the tub. Still other girls hung around playing dumb, or as we said in the barrio, haciéndose mensas, waiting for the altar boys to change clothes and snuff out the altar candles. Then, two by two, they left together.

The men of the Sacred Heart Society carried the tub to the back of the church and dumped the water on the plants that grew next to the fence. Inside the empty church, the women, corn brooms swishing back and forth, swept the greenery dropped by the girls. Soon all was in order for the next day, when once more we would return for el ofrecimiento de las flores.

Walnuts

In the summer many Mexican families in Pacoima harvested crops. Picking fruit entre familia was what folks did come June, July, and August; it was the only way we had to add to the income earned by a parent. My father, however, was adamant that his children not work before their time.

As a child he had been forced to work en el fil; he detested child labor, but did not criticize those who, once school ended, hauled their families off to pick plums, peaches, or grapes. But my mother thought of our "going up north" as an adventure; she rarely went anywhere other than to the grocery store. At the harvest she got to see old friends, relatives too, so she did not mind too much. The times we harvested crops however, were few and far between.

It was not uncommon for families to be gone the entire summer. Some left in late June for the San Joaquin Valley to pick apricots and peaches, then in August made the trip to Reedly or Parlier to pick Thompson and muscatel grapes. By late summer they returned home, rested a while, then in late September packed up again for la nuez.

Few families were assured of a job beforehand. Although some contracted to work a year in advance for a particular ranch boss, others left with no assurance of being hired. They took with them their tiliches (pots, pans, and bedding) and la esperanza, the hope of finding work in that green, fertile valley, where everything grew in abundance.

Mexicans were known to be hard workers, muy trabajadores. At that time few braceros, workers imported from Mexico, lived in the north, although many lived in Pacoima. I had heard that Mexicans were a cheap source of labor. Mostly we were poor folks who welcomed the extra money earned in summer.

Working entre familia was trying for some. Whole families were forced to share a tent or tiny hut. As the summer temperatures rose, tempers flared and children became irritable. Still most families did become accustomed to sleeping 3 to a bed.

One year in late September, my father, coaxed by his compadre Rocky, arranged for us to pick walnuts for a Mister Berenson, a walnut grower from Camarillo, who was kind and considerate of his workers. He paid well, and at the end of the season gave each family a sack of walnuts in addition to a well-earned cash bonus. He never "drove" his workers as did other bosses, but urged everyone to work at his or her own pace. And he advanced wages so that workers could stock up on flour, sugar, and beans. It was clear to see why el Señor Berenson was my father's choice.

The trip to Camarillo was for me one long adventure, from the moment when we awoke to a breakfast of oatmeal and toast. We spent the morning running back and forth among our triquis, our belongings, and giving our mother a bad time.

"Josey hit me."

"She was jumping on the clothes!"

"Liar!"

Our truck, used to haul old wood, sugarcane, and day-old bread, transported us to la nuez. Early on in the week my father gave the truck an overhaul. He checked the oil, tires, and battery, then slid in the side panels that kept us in like cattle.

Packing for the trip began with trips to the grocery store. A few days prior to our departure, I accompanied my mother or Elizabet to stock up on food for the journey. Elizabet filled our shopping basket with canned goods that would keep for months, as well as brown sugar and vanilla for pan. My mother stuck to the usual staples: flour, lard, beans, and coffee for my father.

Once my mother's trunk (brought from Mexico) was hauled onto the truck, it was time to leave. Inside the patequilla lay towels, dishcloths, and garras, rags for any and all emergencies.

My mother, her dress gathered to her knees, her face flushed with excitement (or fatigue), was the first to climb up on the milk crate that served as a stepladder. Her sensible shoes pressed hard on the crate as Berney or one of my sisters gently lifted her up. She squeezed her ample body into the chair off to the side, then collapsed. The rickety chair, like a throne in a kingdom of boxes, was anchored by the truck tailgate. If nothing else, my mother would not fall off.

Berney sat in front with our father, to help drive the sixty-some miles to Camarillo. My sisters and mother had the rear to themselves, except for Josey and me. They immediately began to give orders.

"You sit there!"

"I get this side."

"Amá, Trina's gonna hit me!"

Nora rarely went to la pizca. She was a "career girl" and could not leave her job with the telephone company. Berney helped out by driving, but once we were settled, he returned home to keep an eye on things at 13011 Hoyt Street. Doña Luisa never went to la nuez, but stayed behind to cater to Berney, keep an eye on Nora, and feed Duke, who, when we went away, hid under the house until dark.

Doña Luisa hated for me to leave. She knew I was "on loan" to her, and I was quick to defect when our family was about to do something exciting. The minute I began to pack my favorite books and puzzles, Doña Luisa started to pout; her dark eyes glistened with tears. She liked me to be beside her; I was the reason she trekked to San Fernando for lemon drops. When she saw me atop the truck, Doña Luisa began to whimper like Duke. As my father backed up the truck, she brought her cotton apron to her eyes, then looked straight at me from between the folds; hers was the face I last saw.

My father never deviated from the route he had taken years before. Once past San Fernando and on the road to Chatsworth, Josey and I fell asleep or switched places with Trina. I snuggled down between quilts and pillows to look at clouds, making sure my head didn't bang against my mother's trunk.

I liked September and the feel of the sun warming my face, arms, and legs. The sky, always a clear blue, seemed closer, brighter. More than once I would awaken when my head bumped against a hard edge. Startled for a second, I slept on, the warm California sun on my face.

The fluffy white clouds that in Pacoima appeared to swoop over the open field followed us as we swept through one small town after another: Northridge, Chatsworth, and on to the treacherous hills.

When the truck began to sway from side to side, it became apparent that we were approaching the most dangerous part of the journey.

The road to Camarillo was for the most part a two-lane highway. Past Chatsworth (called Chateeswort by my father), we entered the Santa Susanna Mountains. The road now became a series of sharp curves that our loaded truck, my father at the wheel, approached at a slower pace.

"Are we almost there?"

"I'm scared!"

"Crybaby."

"Amá, Josey's calling me a crybaby!"

Small hills dotted with rocks and brush lined the entrance to the mountains. The rocks looked like red clay; they glistened in the warm sun. Farther up into the hills, the small rocks gave way to huge boulders. Unlike the gray-white rocks of the San Gabriel Mountains that bordered our town, these piedras looked dry and thirsty. They clung to lone trees or scrawny brush, peering down at us.

I feared having a rock fall on me, knowing I would be squashed flat like the sow bugs I stomped on with glee. As we approached the mountain's crest, I shivered, with goose bumps on my arms. I moved close to Elizabet, as my mother took out her black rosary and began to pray.

"Lord we ask you . . . guide us," she prayed in Spanish. The words were comforting, but only for a moment. We clung to each other as the truck grumbled and puffed up and down the mountain road that from afar looked like a dusty ribbon coiled around the hills. The creaking of the truck, the swaying of the boxes and mattresses, and the whimpers from Josey kept me awake and alert. Now and then I peeked through the window of the truck cab to see if my father looked scared. If he looked nervous, I knew we were going to tip over and land on the dirt below. I tapped on the window, but he ignored me, his clear hazel eyes glued to the road. Berney, perhaps aware of the fear I felt, smiled, then turned his curly head toward my father.

After we prayed and sipped water from a jug, my mother, wise in the ways of women, quickly passed out pan, baked the day before. As I munched on the sweet egg bread, it became less frightening to look out at the huge boulders and deep crevices.

Finally the scenery became enjoyable; the green mountains, nourished perhaps by a mountain stream, were full of trees and green bushes. As we approached the outskirts of Camarillo, I craned my neck to see the hospital said to be "para los locos." The building was old, with a tall fence and heavy gates. When we went past it, I kicked Josey in the shin and threatened to leave him there.

"Psssst Josey, we're passing your next home."

"That's not funny." This from Elizabet, who I sometimes thought had eyes and ears in the back of her head.

"Ha, ha. You're gonna get it," hissed Josey, now wide awake. He wanted our mother to scold me for making fun of los locos.

We settled down again, the mentally ill safely behind, to share tacos of beans and fried potatoes. We sipped water from my father's tin canteen; it tasted cool and sweet.

We drove down highways dotted with orange groves on each side and on to Ventura, famous for the oranges that flourished in the cool, damp climate. The road curved inland past walnut trees with painted white trunks (to keep off the bugs); their fragrant branches loomed over houses with dark shutters. With the truck groaning from its heavy load, we climbed the last hill and sped over the long stretch to where adventure, money, and boyfriends for my sisters all awaited us.

"Are we almost there?"

"Pretty soon, I think."

When we finally arrived, my mother pocketed the rosary, as Josey rubbed his eyes and stretched his arms. Ronnie and Trina checked their lipstick and rubbed on rouge, just in case. I slipped on my shoes, which had slid under a box, smoothed my wrinkled dress, and looked around.

The workers' camp was next to the main house, beneath a walnut grove. It consisted of corrugated tin buildings separated into units of two rooms each: a kitchen and a large bedroom. The bathrooms and showers were a short distance from the main building, next to a pretty walnut tree. Everything looked clean, new almost, especially the showers, recently painted a soft yellow. I considered them quite luxurious, with their spigots that spewed hot and cold water at the turn of a hand.

Next to the showers were dressing rooms, small cubicles of the same pale yellow with a seat at one end. Three large dress hooks were nailed to a wall. At one side, high above, was a tiny window like a porthole.

My father parked the truck, flipped open the tailgate so that we could get out, then went to find Mr. Berenson. Within minutes Mr. Berenson, blue eyes twinkling, a white Panama hat atop his white hair, came out to greet my parents and to assign us to our house. He was a small man, shorter than my father, with pink skin and white teeth. He smiled, trying to guess our names and ages.

"I'm in high school now."

"Hmmm."

"I'm Ronnie and she's Trina."

His hat was pulled down low to shield his milk-white skin from the glaring sun; his shirt sleeves, like those of the field hands, came to his wrists. By October his face turned lobster-red, because he was muy güero and sensitive to the sun. His plump wife was also friendly and waved at us from the house porch. Each year, once the workers were accounted for and assigned a housing unit, Mr. Berenson walked around the corrugated huts in the camp to ensure that the hired hands lacked nothing. He took pride in the cleanliness and order of his camp.

My father, Berney, and Norbert unloaded the truck. Elizabet helped our mother arrange the inside of our unit, Trina tore off to inspect the showers (looking forward to some privacy), and Ronnie helped stack canned goods in the tiny pantry. Toward late afternoon the familiar smell of beans, tortillas, and papas fritas, fried potatoes with Spanish onions, permeated the camp. Josey and I waited while the men, then our older sisters ate. When it was our turn I stood in the tiny kitchen, trying not to complain. I missed the roomy cocina at home and the sturdy table and benches.

The year I most remember was when my friend Anita and her sister Lola accompanied us to la nuez. "Nita," as I sometimes called her, was one year older than I, with straight brown hair, freckles, and short, bowed legs. Lola was a close friend of my sisters Ronnie and Trina. She and Anita lived with a brother and his wife in a small white house on Carl Street. They had never picked nuts, but were anxious to make money for school supplies: binders, shoes, gym clothes, and makeup.

I was happy to have a friend my own age at the walnut picking, but Josey was jealous, thinking I would have not time for him. When we assured him he could play with us, he stopped pelting me with dirt clods.

Although one unit was allowed per family, that year we were allocated two: one for my parents, Josey, Nita and me, and the other for the older girls. The minute my father told them, they began to screech and giggle. But when they found out that their unit was next to ours, Trina said it wasn't fair. She and Lola had already picked a section at the far end, near to where some cute guys were living.

My sisters were by then at an age where they wanted to be alone. At home they hid in the bathroom for hours, heedless of others' needs. Trina, especially, would turn the radio on full blast, then experiment with makeup and the latest hair styles. Ronnie did the same, but took less time. At the camp the three quickly hung a mirror above the stove and began to sort their makeup.

"Shucks! I forgot my pink lipstick."

"Is that pancake no. 2?"

"No, it's lighter."

Once settled, with mirrors placed at strategic points, my sisters and Lola arranged their beds and hung up their nicer clothes, aware that once the day's work was done and the evening still young, they would be free to visit other camps, to make new friends. They knew that young men from other towns also came to la nuez to work— and to look for girlfriends.

My brother Norbert befriended those young men without parents, inviting them to our tin home for warm pan. Once satiated with my mother's beans and tortillas, they would go outdoors to plug in a radio and listen to the music. I fell asleep to the sound of trumpets and laughing boys. Within a week Norbert was rooming with them, not wanting to be with either my parents or the girls.

Before our first night was over, my sisters and Lola found some excuse to be outdoors, near the boys. Lola, I recall, took not one, but two showers. Wrapped in a white towel, her hair dripping wet, she stuck her face out the door, then blushed a bright pink as she spotted the boys across the way. Romance was in the air and in the walnut groves, where the fragrant trees, dripping with ripe fruit, waited to be picked.

My sisters dressed for el fil as for a dance. They stayed up until the wee hours to wind aluminum curlers on their hair, then tied a bandana on their heads. Each evening, once they had removed their dusty clothes and mud-caked shoes, they cleaned their faces with Ponds cream, certain that in five days they too would have a wonderful complexion. They plucked their eyebrows into an arch, just like Joan Crawford's, and outlined their lips with red lipstick. In the mornings their curly hair shone squeaky clean, their olive skin glowed with good health and rouge. To their dark eyes they added a layer of the Maybelline that came in little cakes. They would spit on the brush, rub it on the color cake, then put it on their dark lashes. Dressed in work pants cinched tight at the waist, flannel shirts, and old shoes, they would head out the door as my mother scolded:

"No comiste!"

"I'm not hungry!"

"Hmmm. Lipstick won't fill your stomach."

"Gimme a taco, then. Pronto! The truck is coming."

Exasperated at my sisters and Lola, who was as thin as a weed, my mother wrapped tacos of beans and papas for my sisters, who she knew were likely to share their food with the guys.

In the grove the girls took stock of what lay before and around them.

"Did you see the cute guy in the next row?"

"All reet tweet! He looks so fine!"

"Is he looking this way?"

"All reet tweet."

When parents weren't around, even nice girls were prone to sneak off to the wooded groves with boys. Each evening my sisters and Lola took long walks; they would shower, slap on layers of makeup, then go off.

Anita and I spent the day mimicking our sisters. We memorized their conversations, spewing words like "all reet, tweet," "cool cat," "jitterbug," and "chick." Guys who dressed sharp were "cool cats"; everyone else was a "square."

Anita and I spent the afternoons beneath the leafy trees, writing in secret code. The code made us feel grown-up and kept Josey from reading our letters. I would first write a word on paper, assigned it a number, then transfer this to the "key" (a card I hid in my pocket). Then I gave Nita her copy of the key.

"What is number three?"

"Cool cat."

"And eleven?"

"Lookit your card."

We whiled away the warm afternoons writing notes back and forth. That summer we also learned what was then the rage at school, pig Latin.

We added an *f* in the middle of each vowel: Anita became Afanifitafa; I was Mafareefee Hefelefen. It took forever to say what normally took minutes.

"Afanifitafa, whafat afar youfu dofuifing?"

"Nafathifing, afand youfu?"

"Ifay afam gofoifing tofu thefa shafawefers. Dofu youfu wafant tofu gofo?"

"Nofo."

I worked hard to be proficient; each morning I drilled Anita, who kept forgetting how to say my name. We felt full of importance as we walked to and from the walnut grove, until the day Josey asked: "Whafat afar youfu dofuifing?"

My father did not allow our mother to work en el fil. That year, of all the women at la nuez, only she stayed in camp. Nor did he force Josey or me to work, although most kids our age, Nita included, worked alongside the older folks. He had never forgotten the cold and hunger he suffered as a boy and frowned on parents who made their children work like adults, as did his compadre Don Frutos.

Don Frutos was a short, stocky man with a bushy moustache and ears that resembled dried apricots. He was the disappointed father of three daughters, all of whom he treated like men. He worked them from dawn to dusk, a pan y agua, without a break. They were barely allowed to stop for water and at lunchtime, they gobbled their tacos in haste. Don Frutos became angry when the girls stopped work to go to the bathroom.

"Apá, I have to go to the bathroom."

"Finish that row first."

"Apá, I'm gonna do it in my pants!"

"Acaba, te digo, finish first."

My father frowned on his compadre's practice of riding herd on his wife and children, but said nothing. He was un hombre tradicio-

nal, who did not question the head of a family. He merely frowned
at Don Frutos and became more tolerant of Josey and me.

My brother and I roamed the groves. We hid in between the sacks
of walnuts stacked along the road. Up and down we went, making
swirls of dust, happy at being alive and able to play at picking walnuts. When tired of jumping, or if we were told to stop, we walked
back to camp, grabbed a tortilla, then returned to our game. When
we chose to, we helped in las pilitas, the piles of walnuts left to the
women and children.

I remember best the diamond walnuts. They were big and round
and covered with a thick skin that turned dark, then fell off. They
were meaty and tasty and were eaten either raw or roasted in the
oven. La nuez was harvested in September, packed into sacks sten-
ciled with the Berenson name, then trucked to the Los Angeles produce markets.

The "shakers," or as was said in Spanish, "los chesquiadores," held
an important job. They rose at dawn to begin work while we slept.
The men left camp in a group, their muted voices drifting through
the dark trees, on their way to prepare la huerta for the pickers who
soon followed. Their job was to shake down the walnuts with a long,
hooked wooden pole. They would position the hook on a branch,
pull hard, and then stand back while a shower of walnuts pelted the
ground. The ground under the tree was soon covered with the glossy,
dark-skinned walnuts.

Once a grove was done, and the walnuts lay in small piles, they
either joined the pickers or were trucked off to work in other groves.
Mr. Berenson wanted to ensure that all his hired hands, women included, had equal opportunities. Not all the families included able-
bodied men. Women with children trekked to the walnut camps, and
even abuelitas with gray hair, cotton dresses wound around their
tired knees, worked at la nuez.

Once the first round of picking was over, the men and older boys
would rake the left-over nuts into mounds called pilitas between
the trees. Women who sought a "rest" from the continuous bending
welcomed the pilitas, a place where we kids played at work.

We sat on work buckets turned upside down, then dug into the
pile, racing to skin a walnut and dump it into a sack. We elbowed
each other to get at the nuts, grabbed a handful, then peeled them,

until a pile was finished. We giggled and laughed, and when no one was looking, we tossed nueces at each other. The work turned into a shucking contest, as we tried to outdo each other.

The adults, being more experienced, first rubbed the walnuts together with their feet to loosen the skins, then finished the job with their hands. Once the sacks were full, they were placed in the middle of the rows to await the truckers, los troqueros, who took them to be weighed and counted. As we worked and played, the rich smell of la nuez permeated the air; the juice that stained our hands remained much longer.

In Camarillo, it was easy to spot walnut pickers, not only because we shopped in groups and spoke in Spanish, but also because of our stained hands. When we saw others with darkened fingers, we would smile and wave as if they were family. The store clerks, however, grew apprehensive whenever we fingered clothing. They would follow us up and down the store aisles, their suspicious eyes on our backs; yet they accepted our wrinkled dollars, never checking them for stains.

The younger girls hated to have stained hands, so they wore work gloves; but then it was difficult to peel off the walnut skins. Others wound rags around their hands, but this did not help. Still others soaked their hands in lemon juice each evening, then swore their hands looked much lighter the next morning. In time most women became reconciled to their brown hands; the gloves were laid to rest next to rusty buckets and old cans.

In most families the first earnings were paid to el contratista, a man like my father's compadre Rocky, who secured jobs for them. Don Roque, or Rocky, owned a fleet of trucks used to transport laborers to work sites either in the San Fernando Valley or, in the fall, to Camarillo. He himself did not work in the fields, but was in charge of taking families and single men, hombres solteros, to and from camp. His family was left behind in the large house with the bay windows and the modern bathroom. During the week he drove to the camp in a shiny Dodge truck, a white Texan hat atop his head, dark glasses over his beady eyes.

Most workers looked on a contratista with envy. His status was above that of the pickers and shakers. He not only hired people, but was on friendly terms with el patrón. Unlike the common folks dressed in pants and denim shirts, Rocky wore starched shirts and gabardine pants; diamond rings adorned his unstained hands. Never did I see him wear work boots (called "clodhoppers"). Rocky wore the kind of shoes that were worn to church on Sundays and were kept under the bed for special occasions.

Although Rocky was my father's compadre, my father did not approve of how he treated his workers, many of whom were our neighbors. They told of how Don Roque bought work gloves, knives, and buckets for one dollar, then sold them for two dollars. Por el doble.

Not all the men had someone to make them tacos and so were forced to buy food on credit from Rocky—al doble. My father found it difficult to respect him, who he felt was worse than a thief, because he stole from impoverished folks. From his own people.

One time Rocky's largest truck broke down in the Santa Susana Mountains and had to be towed back to Pacoima at great expense. Rocky was forced to pay a competitor to haul the men to camp. They jeered when a local mechanic, an equally dishonest man used to dealing with contratistas, charged Rocky double. They quoted from a dicho popular on Hoyt Street: "he who does wrong should not expect good."

One year during October, as part of a program to provide education to migrant kids (as we were identified), we were enrolled in a school in Camarillo. The program enabled us to continue school while at the harvest, so that once home, we would not be put back a grade. Only kids at the elementary level attended; the others chose to work. We got a ride to school in the morning and were allowed to walk back to camp.

The other students were all blond Anglo's, the children of growers and other local people. They looked at us with childlike curiosity. Josey and I felt ill at ease. Our stained hands betrayed us as migratory workers; our imperfect English told of a lack of education. It was only when we read aloud that I felt I was as smart as the regular students. I *was* bilingual, able to pronounce with ease the names of such early Spanish conquistadores as Cabeza de Baca, Hernán Cortés, and Ponce de León (who I inferred was a relative). When reading a particular passage, I first cleared my throat, then in a clear voice said "Ponce de León," stressing the soft *d*, in *de*. I returned to my seat, face flushed, head held high. If nothing else, I could read with the best of them.

By the time I became comfortable with my new classmates and had memorized their names, the walnut season was over. Soon we would pack our belongings for the trip home to familiar, friendly faces. But for the present I was happy, playing at harvesting walnuts, writing in code, and speaking in pig Latin. My happiness knew no bounds when I met the Berenson's daughter.

Betty Mae Berenson was a schoolteacher. She was in her late twenties, of medium height, with light brown hair, bright blue eyes, and a sweet smile. She taught school in nearby Camarillo, but not at the school we attended. Betty Mae was concerned with children who missed school because of the harvest and had instigated the migrant program. She lived in a small cottage adjacent to her parents' house, a few steps from the workers' showers.

When I first learned that the Berensons' daughter did not live at home, I was somewhat alarmed. What, I wondered, had caused her to leave home? In Mexican families it was not considered proper for "nice" girls to have their own apartments. "Career" girls like Nora worked in offices but lived at home.

As we became fast friends, Betty Mae explained that when she turned twenty-one, her parents gave her the guest cottage as a birthday gift. The small house had a cozy living room with chintz chairs, a braided rug, and sheer curtains. The walls were covered in a bright wallpaper that matched the chairs. I thought of the cottage as a doll house, small and pretty, except for the ugly South American wall hangings that clashed with the furnishings. From the first Betty Mae made us feel welcome; she invited Anita and me to visit "anytime." We soon did.

Each afternoon I checked the kitchen clock, then sat near the showers to await Betty Mae's return at three o'clock. At a few minutes past the hour, she drove up in a blue coupe. I waited a few minutes (to allow her time to remove her jacket), then knocked on the door.

"Hi Betty Mae! Are you home now?"

"My, yes! And how are you?"

"Fine. We were just playing . . ."

"I see! Would you like to . . ."

"Yes!"

She welcomed us with enthusiasm and cookies, then sat to read to us for hours about her favorite country, Argentina, a place that sounded glamorous and exotic. Betty Mae had been spent two years in Argentina. She and a lady friend had traveled to South American to gather material for a textbook and had readily adapted to the language, foods, and customs of Argentina. Betty Mae now spoke Spanish with a slight accent, one I assured her was not noticable. She liked to model a wool garment with a hole called a poncho. As she pirouetted around the small living room, she explained that this was the uniform of the gaucho who lived in the pampas. I tried not to laugh as the heavy wool blanket engulfed her small body.

"How do I look, muchachas?" she'd ask as the poncho dangled at her feet. "How do I look?"

"All reet, tweet," I answered, trying to impress her.

"You mean nice, don't you?"

"No. I mean yes." I feared Betty Mae would find fault with my English.

Once Betty Mae announced she had a treat for us, then served us yerba mate in tall wood tumblers. Mate, Betty Mae explained, her blue eyes misting over at the very word, is a favorite of the gauchos. They begin each day with this drink.

I idolized Betty Mae, and hated to hurt her feelings, but I could barely swallow the bitter drink that looked and tasted like alfalfa juice. I played with the straw, trying to put off the inevitable.

"Hmmm, very good, don't you think?"

"Hmmmm."

Anita looked at me, her eyes raised in alarm, a film of perspiration on her brow. I twitched in my chair, not daring to speak for fear of choking on the green liquid that refused to go down. Pleading a stomach ache, I refused more mate. After that Betty Mae stuck to milk and cookies.

Early on Betty Mae had identified me as a bookworm. She brought home books for me to read, many of which, she explained with a twinkle in her blue eyes, were for older students. "But you can try them," she said, as she handed me a stack of books.

She considered me her prize pupil; I thought of her as a celebrity. After all, had she not written a book! Betty Mae took an interest in my schoolwork and encouraged me to try for good grades. "Someday you can be a teacher." I literally gobbled books on geography, history, and Argentina. I was very grateful that Betty Mae taught social studies and not math!

One day, just before we left for Pacoima, Betty Mae called Anita and me to the doll house. She gave us milk and cookies, then took a brown book down from a bookcase, took a pen from her purse, then wrote on the frontspiece. "Here is a copy of my book," she said. "I hope you like it."

I took the book in my hand and held it tight against my chest. It was a thrill to receive a book autographed by the author! I had few books at home, only those given to me by Elizabet and others overdue at the library. I ran off, the book clutched in my sweaty hand, to sit under a walnut tree. I slowly opened it.

Much to my dismay the inscription read: "To Mary Helen and Anita from Betty Mae Berenson." My eyes began to burn; I knew I would cry. I clutched the book, trying hard not to look at Anita. How I wondered, would we split the book? Would Anita get the first half? Who would read it first?

Suddenly the book was something I wanted even more than Anita's friendship. I smoothed the cover, my hand brushing against the brown grain, then handed the book to Anita. She leaned against the tree trunk, flipped the pages, then thrust it into my eager hands. "You keep it," she said. "It's too long and doesn't have any pitchers." I ran off before she could change her mind.

I read the dedication over and over, then the first part, which was about Argentina and the gauchos who drank yerba mate. Once Anita was asleep, I took my father's flashlight and read Betty Mae Berenson's book until the words blurred. In the morning, book in hand, I crept to the kitchen, wrapped waxed paper around the cover (making sure the corners were straight), then tucked it under my pillow.

Money was spent wisely in our family. Wages earned picking the walnuts belonged to la familia. My older sisters and Norbert were given an allowance; Josey and I received nickels and dimes. But we saved the major part of our earnings. Once back home my parents decided how our communal earnings should be spent. Unlike my friends, who immediately sported new shoes and dresses, we received only necessary clothes: shoes, a winter coat or sweater, and material for skirts. Our first priority was to fix up the house.

My mother made known her needs: new linoleum for the kitchen floor, a bigger pantry shelf, and a new set of dishes. My father rarely bought anything for himself other than a felt hat for winter or a tin of tobacco. One time, however, he bought a new car.

The two-toned 1938 Buick had once belonged to Mr. Berenson, but it was still almost new. There was no other car like it in Pacoima, of that I was sure. During the last weeks of the harvest, my father arranged to buy the car from el patrón. He used the money earned there, together with our savings, to buy the automobile while we were still at camp. I had never seen mi papá so happy.

The car was a shiny mass of steel and chrome, and except for a lack of curtains, resembled a hearse. The headlights, surrounded by bands of steel, were bigger than Josey's head; the smooth fenders were longer than a bench. The seats of brown leather were huge and puffy, like a new mattress. I felt small and insignificant when thrust into the back seat of the square car that was my father's pride and joy.

"Get in the back!"

"No! I can't see nuthin."

When he heard of the car, Berney (who had stayed in Pacoima), immediately came to visit. He parked the Buick underneath a walnut tree to protect it from the sun, then washed and waxed the hearse-like vehicle, hoping to drive it and impress his buddies. As the eldest male, Berney got to drive the car first, much to the Norbert's disappointment. Elizabet, who was older than Berney, began to pout, but once Berney had left, she went to work on my father.

"Papá, I can drive too!"

"Hmmmm."

"Por favor, Daddy. I'll be careful and . . ."

"Bueno . . ."

Elizabet was the most intelligent of my sisters, or so I told her whenever I needed a favor. With our father's permission, she soon learned how to drive the awesome car. At first she was unable to

reach the clutch, so she got a pillow, adjusted it, and was then able
to start the car. Poor Elizabet could barely work the stick shift; the
gears screeched in agony as our father watched anxiously.

Once Elizabet learned to shift without a squeak, my father let her
drive provided she only drove five miles an hour along the roads
lining the groves. Up and down she went, taking care not to raise any
dust. Josey and I, always alert to new adventures, chased the slow-
moving car, hoping to be asked inside, but Elizabet would not be
distracted; she left us behind in a dusty wake.

That Sunday during World War II, Elizabet took us for a ride.
At first only adults were allowed, but when Josey began to howl,
Elizabet changed her mind. In the back Anita and I squeezed between Trina and Lola, who were trying not to wrinkle their tight
skirts. First Elizabet drove around the camp, blowing the horn each
time she went past our smiling parents.

"Bye, Amá."

She turned toward the road, her short legs straining, and off we
went to enjoy a Sunday ride.

The day was warm and the sun bright. Trina quickly turned the
radio up full blast; strains of "A Sunday Kind of Love" filled the
stuffy car. Up and down the dusty lanes we went. Now and then we
stopped to admire the homes of los ricos.

"Gosh, what a pretty lawn."

"I see a chimney!"

"I can't see nuthin."

I looked with envy at the homes with their trim lawns and pretty
flowers. Sheer curtains called "Priscillas" graced the upstairs windows. We drove through streets that looked more and more alike:
dusty, with walnut trees on each side. The afternoon grew long.

"We already went by this ranch, Elizabet."

"Hmmm, let me turn here and . . ."

Elizabet was disoriented—or just plain lost. Ronnie, trying not
to look concerned, lowered the radio, although her favorite singer,
un flaco named Frank Sinatra, was just then crooning. Josey, quick
to smell a crisis, stood on the seat to peek out, but was told to sit
down. We moved aimlessly through unfamiliar groves, the car's tires
crunching dirt roads that took us nowhere.

The afternoon turned into evening; the blue sky above turned a deep grey. Next to me a bored Anita chewed a wad of bubble gum, as Lola readjusted the bobby pins on her dark head. Trina crossed and uncrossed her long legs, angry at her wrinkled skirt.

Just then we heard an air-raid siren. Elizabet stopped the car and shut off the lights. I knew that during an "air alert" all car lights should be put out, so that the enemy above would not send bombs hurtling down.

"What happened?"

"It's an air raid, stuped."

"Are we gonna get bombed?"

"Mensa. They have to spot us first, dummy."

In the back seat I looked out the window at the looming walnut trees. Their white trunks with ringed eyes resembled the Loch Ness monster that I had read about in Betty Mae's books. As the day darkened the monsters appeared more threatening and much closer. I began to cry.

"I wanna go home."

"Be quiet, crybaby!"

"Shut up, shut up," shouted Trina and Lola. Their mouths opened and closed on cue. Like parrots denied a cracker, they screeched in unison at Josey and me. While Elizabet searched the floor of the car for a flashlight, I fidgeted in my seat, trying not look at the walnut branches that stretched above my father's pride and joy. The seats I had found soft were suffocating me. Trina's gabardine skirt grated against my bare legs. Not knowing what else to do, I hitched up my droopy socks, folded tops down, and adjusted my dress. Josey dosed off, his dark head on Ronnie's lap.

We sat and waited. In the dim light Elizabet's face looked pale, drawn. Scared stiff at having gone too far, she now fiddled with the steering wheel. I moved close to Anita, but she pushed me aside, then opened the car window to look out. The trees stared at us with their white eyes; their branches swayed in the evening breeze.

Finally Elizabet, scared of what our father might say, started the car. Just then a dark shadow appeared in front of us. I held my breath, then almost jumped off the seat when I recognized my brother Berney, sent by our father to find us. Elizabet breathed a sigh of relief, shut off the engine, then scooted across the seat. Without a word of reproach, Berney started the car. Just then we heard the "all clear." Berney turned on the lights; Trina and Ronnie began to hum "A Sunday Kind of Love." Anita closed the window and moved over, closer to me. I dared to look at the trees again.

We found the road that led to the Berenson ranch, and to our house of corrugated tin beneath the walnut trees.

Catechism

Catechism was what we went to on Saturdays. Cada sabado before ten o'clock, Concha, Mundo, Virgie and I would trot up the street, across the lane that bordered Doña Chonita's yard, and on to the churchyard, where we waited for the black-robed nuns who taught el catecismo at Guardian Angel Church.

Ours was a poor parish, with neither a Catholic school, convent, nor nuns to call our own; we imported catechists, as we did missionaries. The church was adequate but simple, with a hand-carved altar hewn by Don Anselmo, a wood carver who learned his trade in Mexico. The church rectory too was shabby, which suited Father Juanito, our dowdy pastor who wore the same outfit year in and year out. But what our parish lacked in fancy altars we had in an abundance of snot-nosed kids who drove our pastor crazy, and, who, given the chance, would do in the catechism teachers.

The nuns, or monjas, I best remember taught el catecismo while Father Juanito was our pastor. They were of all ages, sizes, and shapes. They wore black outfits of serge, a material that shone with wear and picked up chalk marks quite easily. Their tunics had a small cape of the same material; when the nuns moved, it would flare out like bat's wings. Their drab dresses hung to their tired ankles; those of the shorter sisters swept the floor and picked up the street dust we brought with us. Across her waist each sister wore a black band in which was tucked a large rosary with a cross that hung past her hidden knees. Atop their heads rode a black-and-white headpiece. The outer fold was black, while a white lining framed their serious faces. Others wore a pleated brim with a thin band around their heads. It puzzled me that they did not dress the same.

"How come your hats are different?"

"We're from different orders."

"Orders?"

"Yes, different, uhhhh, schools . . ."

They wore sturdy black shoes with small heels and laces, like those worn by Doña Chonita. I assumed the nuns wore stockings too, not coarse cotton hose like those of Doña Luisa, but fine, woven stockings blessed, perhaps, by the bishop. I rarely saw their ankles (they were quite modest), but noticed that they walked with short, bird-like steps. From afar the monjitas resembled penguins, except for their eyes. Even I knew that penguins did not have blue eyes.

The older nuns had lined, sallow faces; they rarely smiled. They reminded me of black crows, their voices cackling like those of the birds perched on our eucalyptus trees. "Yaaaack, yaaaack." Most of the monjas wore glasses, bifocals even, with wire frames that clung to their beaks. They peered at us from behind the thick glasses, alert for mischief of any kind.

I hated most to be taught by Sister John Laetare. She had bad breath and yellow teeth. She often complained of a sour stomach, then belched twice in a row. When I saw her coming I pulled back, wary of her foul-smelling mouth.

The holy women, especially the older ones, had funny names, none of which made sense to me: Sister John Laetare, Sister Pius, Sister Hippolitus, and Sister Gregorius. These were not their real names, they explained, but those taken with their final vows, vows that could not be repudiated. They had started out with sensible names like Jane or Betty, I knew, then traded them in for ugly, churchy names.

"Is there a Saint Gregory?"

"No, no, I took Pope Gregory's name . . . I got a special dispensation and . . ."

"What's a dispensashen?"

"It's when . . . Oh, there goes the bell. Time for class."

It bothered me that these religious women chose to be known by a man's name, even an important one like Pope Gregory, who it was said had made up the church calendar and composed new masses. What, I wondered was wrong with Sister Agatha? Teresa? Agnes?

"I would never want a man's name," argued Nancy, tossing back her head.

"Ugh," responded Concha, rolling her eyes. "Me neither."

"Sister Virginius sounds okay," added Virgie, piling her thick braids atop her head. "I kinda like it."

"That's 'cause you're stupid," hissed Nancy, sticking her nose up in the air.

"Well, it's better than Sister Hippolatus."

"Hippolita, stupid. Like a hippopotamus."

"Gosh Nancy, you know everything!"

From reading the lives of the saints, I knew that some had pronounceable names, except for Saint Scholastica whom I knew loved books.

One Christmas Elizabet gave me a book entitled 'The Lives of the Saints.' On the shiny cover was a picture of Saint Teresa of Avila, holding a flower in her delicate white hands. I immediately read the entire book from cover to cover and memorized each story, including those of Saints Agatha, Clare (mother to Saint Francis), Anastasia, and Cecilia.

Saint Teresa, called "The Little Flower," was my favorite. She had creamy white skin, blue eyes, and rich auburn hair that fell below her slender shoulders in long, thick waves. She wore a pretty blue robe, which I knew was made of silk, over what resembled a white nightgown like that worn by Doña Luisa on cold nights. On her delicate feet were tiny slippers, which must have been of silk too. What I most liked about Saint Teresa was how she lived: She read books all day long! Never did the story show her wearing an apron or peeling potatoes in the kitchen. Nor did she sweep and mop floors. Her delicate hands never raked leaves. She had talked back to the pope (or some lesser prelate), then had established a new religious order. I liked best that she kept her own name.

I also liked the story of Saint Clare, mother to the sinner Augustine, a woman who spent her time not in reading, but in praying. An illustration showed her on bended knee, her pretty head bent in prayer for the conversion of her son, who "wasted his life on debauchery." I was curious to know the meaning of "debauchery." Was it a country? A disease? Since we had no dictionary, I never did find out. But Augustine should have been an obedient son, I felt, and not have spent his life in a strange town.

Las santas, I saw, were born to rich families: kings, princes, and counts. In fact the women all resembled each other. Each wore a long, flowing robe; each wore tiny blue slippers. Circling their heads were what looked like crowns of sparklers, like that of Cinderella at the ball. I was most impressed by the crowns that resembled one worn by Nora when she was crowned Queen of the sixteenth of September fiesta. It bothered me that none of the women were poor or Mexican. It was certain I could not aspire to be una santa. Still had Elizabeth not given me a book of saints, I never would have known of such important women. After that I read everything about saints and pestered the nuns to tell me more.

"Sister Gregorius, did you know Saint Cecilia?"

"No. She lived in the twelfth century."

"Yes, but did you know her?"

In the Catholic church, I saw, all the important people were men. God the Father, Jesus Christ, Saint Joseph, Moses, Adam. Even the dreaded Lucifer! I was never sure about the Holy Ghost, as we didn't have a book on ghosts, but I assumed that it too was male. The popes, men with funny Latin names of Pius, Innocent, and Urban, were hombres. Our church altars were also filled with statues of men: St. Anthony, St. Francis, the Guardian Angel, and near a small altar, el Santo Niño de Atocha, who resembled a dwarf, a male dwarf. With so many men running the church, it was no wonder the nuns chose male names.

Each September, right after school started, we began catechism. Eager to know which nun would be assigned to our class, we lined up in front of the church hall. I carried pencil and paper in my dress pocket, anxious to begin learning and writing.

"All nuns shave their heads," Nancy whispered as we lined up that first day. "They have to, or they can't be monjas."

"No they don't," interjected Virgie, hands on hips, "they just cut it in half and . . ."

"But I saw hair on Sister Michael!"

"So? Maybe it grew back."

I believed what Nancy said about the nuns' shaved heads. Nancy knew more than anyone else on Hoyt Street. Still I wondered, did nuns really shave their hair? I had to know. One day at catechism I chased Concha; round and round we went, circling around a distracted monjita. While pretending to strike at Concha, I yanked at the nun's headpiece, then murmured an apology as I stared at my empty hand. Try as I might, I could never dislodge one.

The first day of catechism we were assigned by grade and age to a room and a nun, depending on whether we were preparing for First Communion or Confirmation. Those studying for their Confirmation acted as though they owned the world; they got the best room, the one next to the trees, and the better chairs.

During his tenure Father Juanito visited each room to stress that any girl wishing to discuss a religious vocation should consult with las monjas. He droned on and on about the nuns, their virtues, gifts, saintliness, and dedication to the Holy Mother Church. He mentioned that most nuns went to heaven. "Nuns should go straight to heaven," I hissed upon hearing this. "After all, their whole lives are spent praying."

I hated being assigned an old, grumpy nun. The younger ones had clear skin, good teeth, and were pleasant to be around. Their fresh-looking faces and clear eyes complemented their good dispositions. They fluttered around the room, eager to set up lesson materials, while the older nuns gave orders in clipped tones.

The young, energetic catechists spoke mostly English, good English, yet they understood some Spanish. As did our teachers at Pacoima Elementary, they wanted us Mexican-Americans to learn perfect English, to lose our accent and follow their lead. They made an effort to speak loudly and clearly; each word was pronounced with care.

The nuns taught us prayers that in our missalettes were also printed in Latin; their Latin too was perfect. The Latin c was often pronounced like the Spanish che. Saint Cecilia became "Santa Chechelia"; coeli, cielo in Spanish, was heaven; mater and pater were mother and father. It was much easier to learn Latin than English. When we answered in Spanish, the nuns appeared not to mind.

Sister Mary Michael had a sweet, melodious voice that complimented her pretty, round face. She rarely raised it; she tapped on the desk with a ruler to get our attention. When she prayed before each lesson, her dark eyelashes brushed her pale cheeks; her soft voice filled the room.

Each Saturday I stared in awe at the women said to be married to the Church. Not to God the Father or Jesus, nor to another priest. Not even to St. Joseph, who was good and kind, but to a building! How, I wondered, could someone marry a church? Father Juanito never explained this; I feared asking the good women, each of whom wore a gold wedding ring. My friends and I puzzled over this.

"I'd rather get married to a man than a building," Nancy offered, smoothing her hair.

"Me too!" cried Virgie, squinting into the sun.

"I'd rather just get engaged," said Concha, the most practical of the bunch.

"Nuns don't get engaged, stupid!" hissed Nancy. She took off in a huff, exasperated at Concha.

One hot Saturday in June, a substitute catechist was assigned to our room. Her name was Sister Michael the Archangel. Father Juanito walked her to Room 3, introduced her, then left, his black skirt brushing against the floor. I stared at the catechist, as did Nancy and Concha, wondering why we had to have *her* as teacher.

Sister Michael the Archangel did not look like any angel. She looked like a man, and like the old woman she was. She had bleary eyes and long hairs on her chin that flew back and forth when she spoke. Her voice was low and hoarse. When she was angry, she snorted, just like a horse. Sister Michael's hands were huge, with long bony fingers that could snap a ruler faster than anything. She wore ugly, pointy shoes like those worn by Cinderella's wicked stepsisters.

"If Sister Michael is married to a church," I hissed to Nancy, "I'll bet the church is ugly!"

"Shhh, here she comes."

Sister Michael was most serious when teaching us about sin. Venial and mortal sin; small and big. At times it was difficult to determine which was which—everything was a sin! Exasperated with so much sin, Concha and I made a list of the really big pecados: stealing, smoking, and kissing boys. These we knew were mortal sins; all else was a venial sin. It was comforting to know that yanking a nun's hat was a venial sin. Eating meat on Friday, though, meant we were destined for hell.

One time Concha bought a book in which to record her sins. She flipped the blue book back and forth, proud of her work.

"These are mortal sins, see? And over here are . . ."

"Venial?"

"Yeah. Remember last week when I cheated at kickball? Well, I put an X there."

"What about the marbles you stole from . . ."

"Uh . . ."

As First Communion day approached, my friends and I discussed what most concerned us: dresses and veils. The nuns took pains to say that it mattered not what we wore, but what was in our hearts. A long dress was a luxury few families could afford, as were new shoes, slips, and a pretty veil, which is why the nuns suggested we wear simple dresses. Their suggestion, which I assumed was a command, was hard to swallow.

"I want a long dress."

"Me too, but my mother says . . ."

"I have to wear my older sister's . . ."

"Gosh!"

My First Communion took place on a sunny day in May. I wore a short white dress and a simple veil, as did Concha and Nancy. We walked to church in a group, lined up, and were about to enter the vestibule when I spotted Fat Lupe walking up Carl Street. She wore a long white dress of ruffles and lace with long sleeves and tiny buttons down the front. As she walked, Fat Lupe kicked at the dress hem, making sure we all saw her pretty white shoes. Just then a monja spotted her. Lips pursed in disapproval, black habit flying, she went up to Lupe and began to scold.

"All girls were instructed to wear short dresses."

"My papa said I could . . ."

"Hmmm, and is your heart pure, ready to receive . . . ?"

"Yes, and did you see my new shoes?"

The nun was no match for Fat Lupe's father, a man who liked to give orders and who doted on his daughter. He quickly put the nun in her place and Lupe in hers—right at the head of the procession.

When my friends and I lined up for catechism the following year, we were told that the monjitas who had first instructed us were now assigned to another parish. Concha and I pretended to miss them; Nancy said what we all felt.

"I'm glad they're gone."

I felt guilty for having made fun of the holy women, but only for a short time.

The arrival of Father Mueller to Guardian Angel parish changed absolutely everything. He wanted us to be "All American" and do fun things. He banished the old for the new; he replaced the church organ and missalettes and brought in a new order of catechists.

The Sisters of Social Service, as the catechists were called, were based in San Fernando and were almost like nuns, but not quite. They wore crisp grey cotton jumpers with wide pockets and snowy white shirts. On their heads sat grey cotton hats with a rear flap, which resembled baseball caps.

Unlike the earlier catechists, whose skirts skimmed the floor, the skirts these new Sisters wore ended at their shapely ankles. Their shoes were of navy blue leather, with small heels and a square buckle, and they were visible below the soft gray of their skirts. From afar their light-colored stockings also looked gray, but they were in fact white, like those worn by nurses. Their hair, of various shades and textures, was visible underneath the funny-looking caps.

The Sisters spoke both English and Spanish; they were considered muy modernas by our parents, and clearly of a different order. They giggled, moved with energetic steps, and even joked with Father Mueller. On Hoyt Street the Trinidads were appalled at these young women in short skirts, but dared not criticize our pastor, who was out to change the world. And us. Besides religion, the Sisters taught us personal hygiene and nutrition. They extolled cleanliness and cautioned us to brush our teeth each day. In between these lessons they instructed us to be good Catholics.

They also organized Girl Scout troops throughout the San Fernando Valley. They were concerned that girls from the barrio be exposed to camping, marshmallow roasts, and horseback riding. They taught us fun songs and games and took us to visit other troops. I remember best a visit to Santa Rosa Parish, where I met other Mexican Girl Scouts. And they were patient with our incessant questions.

"How come you don't shave your head?"

"Can you get married?"

"My granma says your dress is too short."

Our new catechists had pretty names too: Celina, Teresa, Margaret. Some were Mexican, with names like Guadalupe, Mercedes, and Antonia.

Sister Antonia was my favorite. She looked not a day older than my sister Ronnie, with dark olive skin, light brown eyes, and thick hair worn in a long braid. She often wound the braid around her head, which made her cap stand up like a woodpecker's crest. At other times her braid wound around the nape of her neck; it reminded me of a comotose snake. Best of all, Sister Antonia spoke Spanish and cared not a whit if the others heard her speaking en español.

Promptly at nine each Saturday morning, the gray-frocked Sisters arrived at the church hall. Wide skirts flapping, eyes smiling, they alighted from a cream-colored station wagon, calling to us by name.

"Good morning, Teresa."

"Good morning Sister Mary."

"Sister Mary Maureen, please."

Eager to be of help, I carried supplies inside the church hall, then set up chairs in a straight row for the Sisters. In front they set up an easel with drawings of Jesus, Mary, and Joseph, Gabriel the Archangel, the Garden of Eden, and our "first parents," Adam and Eve.

While the Sisters sorted out catechism pamphlets and sharpened pencils, I would help clean the blackboard. One day I decided to draw a picture of our priest on the blackboard. I was alone, so I felt free to experiment. I drew a face, arms, two sharp horns, and a long tail. Father Mueller looked ugly, with beady eyes, a long hook nose, and a tail that curled up toward heaven. I was about to scribble his name on the board, when in walked Sister Drusilla.

"Hmmmmm, is that Satan you're drawing?"

"Daaaaaaa."

"And what begins with *M?*"

"Meat," I answered, wiping chalk off my sweaty brow. "The Red Devil meat, you know, the can of . . ."

"Ah! Well just make sure Father Mueller doesn't see it."

The Saturday lessons always began the same way. Once attendance was taken and prayers said, we settled down to be instructed. We read the lesson of the day, filled in the missing word in our booklets, recited our prayers individually (so the Sisters could tell who were doing their homework), then discussed the importance of confession and how, when cleansed of sin—and after communion—we could be pure once more. We progressed at a good clip, memorizing Latin responses and new hymns. The Sisters worked hard to implant within us the love of God and church. Now and then they retold the story of Adam and Eve, expounding on the sins of the flesh and the many temptations in the world.

The monjas who had prepared us for First Communion made sure we knew the Catholic version of the earth's creation: the biblical Genesis, the beginning of the world. And since nothing had changed, the new catechists also delighted in retelling this story, their clear voices echoing in the quiet room. I sat enthralled as they flipped the pretty pictures back and forth.

I knew the story of Adam and Eve by heart; it had been my favorite for years, ever since first grade, when the nuns began our indoctrination. Still the Sisters of Social Service wanted to ensure that we knew our Catholic "beginnings." There was nothing to do but sit quietly and listen as they retold my favorite Bible story.

The drawings of "our first earthly parents" were the most beautiful of the entire set. The first illustration was of a garden with green trees, grass, and creepy vines. At the bottom of the picture lay a small snake. Adam, a handsome, muscular man with dark hair, wore something akin to a grass skirt, slit up the side. Eve had dark hair, too; her eyes shone a pretty blue. She was tall and slender, with nice legs. Her dark dress was like the sarong worn by Dorothy Lamour in the movies. In the first illustration, Adam and Eve looked young and healthy on their tropical island. In the second picture, Eve ate an apple, while Adam hid behind a branch; at her feet was the slimy snake. Next we saw Eve crying, while a troubled Adam held her hand; in a corner the sly snake smiled. The lesson ended with Eve clinging to Adam, her blue eyes full of fear and her dark hair flying, as they fled the Garden of Eden.

I often confused Adam and Eve with Tarzan and Jane of the movies; their coloring and clothes were almost identical. Eden was exactly like the African jungle, and the vines that encircled the Garden were just like those Tarzan swung on.

But unlike Adam and Eve, Tarzan and Jane were best friends; they teased and smiled at each other, swam together in the African river, and chased after each other from vine to vine. And they ate everything in sight. Some other important distinctions were that Eve looked sad, Adam guilty, and the snake satisfied. Also missing was the chimp.

I found it difficult to believe everything the Sisters taught. God was "merciful and just," yet He banished Adam and Eve from Eden for having eaten one little apple! It was much safer to steal apricots from Doña Chonita, I confided to my friends; at least we would not be sent to suffer in a world of sin.

After catechism I would walk home with Nancy and Concha. Often we stopped to buy candy at the corner store, where Don Jesús kept hard candy in glass jars. From there we cut through the alley to our houses. Sometimes we dawdled and reviewed the catechism lesson.

"Gosh, God sure is mean! He chased Adam and Eve from the pretty garden for nothing!"

"Yeah."

"Do you think they were kissing?"

"Hmmmm, maybe . . ."

Years later Nancy alluded to what Adam and Eve had *really* done, but I never believed her.

Las Misiones

Making fun of people kept most kids on our street alert, inventive, and mean. Folks with visible defects were rarely spared a harsh epithet. Unlike my brother Norbert, who befriended everyone, we rarely differentiated between los pobres (the poor), los pobrecitos (the blind or infirm), and los mensos (kids who were cross-eyed or overweight— "the dummies"). From catechism we knew that it was a sin to make fun of the unfortunate; had not Jesus consorted with lepers and thieves? Still we cried over a lost pet, while poking fun at others.

Not all nicknames were based on defects. Often they were earned because of a scrape or a bad habit. Nita was "la mocosa," because she refused to wipe her nose. Rojelio became "Tojo" (after the Japanese emperor) and also "el Bugs Bunny," because of his buckteeth. Poor Rojelio; he answered to everything but his given name.

Not even girls with husky brothers were immune from cruel kids or nicknames. Virgie, who once peed in her pants, was called "la miona" until, during baseball, she became invaluable. Nancy, labeled "la volada" by Mundo, just giggled, knowing full well he too was a flirt. Most pet names were given with love and affection, con cariño, and forgotten or replaced with the years.

We feared few things in the barrio. We knew everyone; everyone knew us. We belonged. We had family: parents, sisters, brothers, tías, tíos, abuelos, and godparents. Ours was a secure world. We were free to play in the streets, climb trees, and snitch fruit off a neighbor's tree without fear. The poverty of our homes and the lack of education and jobs was something our parents and older siblings worried over. For us there was only the security of community, school, church, and the corner store.

Now and then this security was threatened by a natural disaster, such as the flood that in 1938 almost caused the Tujunga Dam to overflow and inundate our town. Doña Luisa never forgot that the flood was caused by a series of rainstorms, and brought it up each time it rained. My older siblings remembered the flood as "scary." Some families were forced to flee their homes. Others, such as my parents, who had nowhere else to go, braved the floodwaters that made a muddy stream of Hoyt Street, praying all the while.

Much to the chagrin of sus padres, none of my friends remembered the flood; they felt that a good scare, un susto, would help keep us in line. Our concern was with our own world, one dominated by games of baseball, "kick the can," and hide-and-seek, as well as poking fun at others. For a time one of our victims was el Pancho, a man we knew little about, except that now and then he "threw fits."

El Pancho lived with his widowed mother and two sisters on the far side of Pacoima, in what was called el Rancho de Olivos. He attended church regularly, dressed in a pin-striped suit that had seen better days. He wore glasses with thick frames, which made him resemble an owl.

He suffered from epilepsy and often had what we kids called "fits." Frequently they occured during Sunday mass, when the church was hot and stuffy. Folks sitting next to el Pancho didn't know how to help him, so they avoided him like the plague. I feared el Pancho more than I did the winos that hung around the alley; the drunks might call out to me, but they never approached me.

Years back, right before the war, lone men roamed the streets of our town in search of work, often sleeping in the abandoned railroad cars lined up along San Fernando Road; many were said to be Okies. They were of undiscernible ages and dressed in dark-stained pants, thin jackets, and tired-looking shoes. Most had honest faces and were willing to clean up a backyard or help put up a fence in return for a hot meal and a place to sleep. These were los pobres, men without homes, called "trampas" by Mundo and his friends. Although at first they appeared menacing, I neither laughed at them nor feared them as much as I did Pancho. Their eyes did not cross, nor did they throw fits. Mostly they stared at me with kind, hungry eyes.

I first saw el Pancho have a seizure during las misiones, held each year at Guardian Angel Church. Each fall, soon after school started, our parish held a revival of sorts. La misión was conducted by visiting missionaries, pale-looking men who preached to us in loud, whiny voices during the rosary. Their real mission, I often thought, was not to collect money for darkest Africa, but to save our town from hell, el infierno.

One balmy Sunday in mid-October, a missionary, dressed in a brown robe that resembled a flannel nightgown and with rope sandals on his feet, blessed himself, adjusted the rope at his waist, cleared his throat, and began his mission. He proceeded to preach not of sin, as had the missionary of the previous year, but of el diablo, said to be lurking around the corner to make us sin! He ranted about Satanás and warned the astounded congregation that only through prayer (and confession and communion) could one be saved. He took forever to finish.

"Sal de aquí, Satanás," he shouted, his voice hoarse and pained. "Begone Satan."

I felt terribly sleepy and wanted nothing more than to be at home. Often I fell asleep, only to wake up when everyone sang "Tu Reinarás," a hymn like a march, which always woke us up. I took a deep breath, adjusted my beanie, and looked around. Most of my friends, bored with the misión and the missionary, now down on his knees, had left. But Doña Luisa and the Trinidads remained in their favorite pew.

That night as the missionary droned on about Lucifer, I once again grew sleepy, and with the approval of Doña Luisa, leaned back in the pew and dozed off. I was half-asleep when I heard a commotion toward the back of the church. I sat up, rubbed my eyes, then stood on the bench to get a better look. I saw two men trying to restrain a third, who was thrashing out with his arms as he groaned aloud.

It was el Pancho; he was having an epileptic attack. I stretched as far as I could without tipping over, but I still couldn't see. Everyone in church turned to stare. From the choir loft, the organist peeked over the music on the organ, then she continued to play. I remained standing. Just then Doña Luisa yanked me down, her eyes suddenly angry. I tried to disengage myself from her legs, but she stood firm. At the altar the priest whispered to the puzzled missionary, who quickly concluded the sermon. Soon the church was quiet again. The priest gave the benediction; we sang the last hymn. I dashed outside, but el Pancho was not to be seen. I called to Virgie and Concha, who had seen the whole thing. Concha was feeling important, having just witnessed such an important event. She now smoothed her dress and dark braids and prepared to tell Mundo and Beto her tale. Next to her stood Virgie, tapping her foot, waiting to tell her version.

"Éjole! He almost died!"

"He was having a feets."

We walked off together, whispering among ourselves, scared stiff of Pancho, who was nowhere in sight. Next to me Mundo crossed his eyes and groaned aloud.

"Gosh, you're so mean!" scolded Virgie. "God's gonna punish you, just wait."

"Yeah," squealed Mundo, twisting his head to and fro. "And the devil's gonna get me. Ha, ha, ha."

The next night, on the way to church and the continuation of the mission, I begged Doña Luisa to let me sit in the back with Virgie and Concha, but she refused. I was furious and wanted to kick her in the shin. This might be my only chance to see Pancho in action! But she would not listen. I sat in my seat, angry and defiant, but alert. When the priest came out of the sacristy and was about to begin the rosary, I leaned over and whispered:

"Tengo que hacer chi, I gotta pee."

"Tienes que esperar," she responded.

"No! I'll pee in my pants!" I responded firmly, then crossed my legs tight for emphasis. "If I wait I'll do it in my pants."

"Anda pués," she hissed, giving in to my plea. I climbed over the mute form of Doña Cruzita (who had by mistake sat in our pew). "But hurry, el rosario is about to begin."

I tore off down the middle aisle to the front door, then out and around to the girl's bathroom. I waited until I heard singing from inside the church, then skipped back inside. I took my place beside Concha and Virgie, daring not to look toward the front. Once settled, I scouted around for a pin-striped suit.

"Psssst, Concha. Where is . . ."

"Shhhh, your granma's looking."

During a pause in the sermon, Concha leaned over to say that Pancho was often late; the ranch was somewhat far away. Not to be outdone, Virgie swore she earlier saw him coming down the road.

We sat and waited. Each time I heard footsteps, I turned around, only to be disappointed. By the Third Mystery I knew he was not going to show. I was doubly upset; not only had I disobeyed Doña Luisa, who was sure to tell my mother, but I had also missed Pancho! During the especially boring sermon, my eyes began to close, right on schedule. I yearned to lean back and sleep, but behind me Don Serafín, surrogate father to the neighborhood kids, fixed me with a stern look. I managed to sit up and stay awake.

The next two nights of the missions I sat with Doña Luisa, secure in the familiar pew, where I could sleep if and when I chose. Other than the same sermon, with a few directed jabs at lax Catholics, nothing much took place.

On the last night of the misiones, I played outdoors past the third and final bell; along with other stragglers, I was forced to sit in the choir loft, where it was hot and stuffy. I pushed my way to the front and was about to sit down, when I spotted Concha and Virgie. Behind them sat el Pancho in the pin-striped suit. I waved frantically, nearly tipping over from the effort, but they did not look up. I then realized they were engrossed in comparing the sizes of the candles being passed around.

The last night of the missions was special. The church bulged with católicos eager to participate in the final, spectacular ceremony. None of us kids dared to miss the highlight of the mission. Out of respect we now wore our Sunday clothes.

This night was also the scariest. Right after the final benediction, it was customary for all catholics to reaffirm their baptismal vows. First the church was darkened, then the ushers, each with a lit candle in his hand, walked up and down the aisle until each vela was lit.

"Pssst, over here."

"Mine went out again!"

"Mensa."

That night as we held aloft the burning candles, the missionary, still in the same faded outfit, began to rant again about Satanás, his face flushed and agitated, as though *he* had been possessed by the devil. He stood at the foot of the altar and in a loud voice asked:

"Renuncias a Satanas? Do you renounce Satan?"

"Sí!"

"Renuncias sus ejemplos? And all his examples?"

"Sí!"

At first the congregation, forgetful perhaps of this yearly ritual, responded with a timid "sí," followed by a louder one, until the whole church resonated with a thunderous "*sí, sí.*" I stood on tiptoe, as beside me Mundo laughed and shoved other boys. When once more the missionary asked if we renounced Satan, Mundo hissed "no," until he spotted Don Serafín.

By now the entire church was in a frenzy, the smell of incense permeated the air, and the crowd surged and swayed to shouts of "sí, sí." I felt hot, exhausted, but could not stop shouting. I had almost finished denouncing the devil and all his works when I looked down and saw el Pancho.

He was completely turned around, his head thrown back, his eyes rolling in their sockets. From his mouth came a loud groan that filled the church, a groan that almost drowned out the shouts of "sí." I stood there in a trance; the hot wax from my candle dripped onto my dress. Next to me Mundo gaped down at the man who from all appearances was seriously ill.

It was an eerie sight, almost like a horror movie. Below me Pancho thrashed and groaned, the pin-striped suit rumpled around his thin shoulders, as the crowd screamed "sí, sí." In the darkened church, the candles, like a hundred shining stars, continued to burn. At the altar the two priests waited for the crowd to quiet down. At the back, Pancho stopped thrashing, calmed by the presence of two women, relatives perhaps, who now flanked him. Then the lights came back on; the candles sputtered and died. The choir began a familiar hymn, but few other than Doña Cruzita (who sang the same words to each hymn) joined in. We stood for the benediction as Pancho, calmed by the presence of his mother and sister (as Concha identified them), slumped in the pew, head on his chest.

We filed out of church as the choir sang "Adiós Reina del Cielo," a pretty hymn that bids the Virgin goodbye. Pancho, I saw, walked unassisted. As luck would have it, he reached the last row just as I came down the stairs and fell into line. I held back, but was unable to fight the crowd that surged forward. I was carried along, my shoulder rubbing against Pancho's slender arm. As we neared the door, his mother and sister moved close, then each gently put an arm through his and guided him down the church steps.

Their eyes never left his face, a face now composed and to my surprize quite handsome, with expressive dark eyes, aquiline nose, and gentle mouth.

"Cuidado, hijo mío," I heard his mother say.

"This way, Francisco," whispered his sister. They disappeared down the street, the three shadows merging into one.

I walked home in a daze, my mind awhirl. Francisco. *Francisco!* He had a name! Pancho had a name. An identity! And he was handsome, far better looking than my brother Berney, who folks said was bien parecido.

At home I undressed slowly. I felt tired, drained. The last misión had been more than I had expected. I could not forget the sight of Pancho, nor the sound of his groans amid the shouts of "sí, sí." The smell of hot wax lingered on my dress. Images of the dark church, flickering candles, and the shadows cast on Pancho's face, were still fresh.

I felt different, older. I had so yearned to see el Pancho throw a fit, and he had. He had suffered a serious attack, but I had not been amused. Making fun of this man, who now had a name and an identity, was no longer funny. Francisco was a person. He had a family that loved him and who braved the jeers and snickers of mean kids like me. His mother, una viejita, still guided his steps; his sister had the dignity to call him Francisco.

In the following years I saw el Pancho often, both at church and at the corner store, where he ran errands for his family. I no longer called out "Hey Pancho," but the name Francisco caught on my tongue.

Years later I saw him at a baseball game. He was still handsome, with smooth skin and a full head of hair. His gentle eyes seemed untroubled. He sat alone in the bleachers, his slender body thrust forward, feet firmly planted on the ground. I was shocked to see how young he looked. Not much older than Berney!

At first I thought he might be waiting for a son, then remembered that he had never married. At that time the law did not allow epileptics to marry. I was filled with sadness for Pancho, who had suffered the insults of rowdies like me, and who because of an illness thought uncurable, was denied a normal life with a wife and children.

I felt full of remorse and shame and wanted at least to say "hi." But when next I looked, he was gone.

The Day World War II Ended

 World War II ended on a hot summer day. My friends and I were almost teenagers, at least eleven and twelve years old, and thought of playing in the street as something only little kids did. But now and then, when there was nothing else to do, we joined in the fun taking place on Hoyt Street.

On this day Concha was having trouble staying up on the stilts borrowed from Beto, when the bell began ringing at Guardian Angel Church. The constant peal was puzzling; no one I knew had died, nor was a wedding taking place.

"How come the bell is ringing?" cried Virgie, tugging at her new belt. "Did somebody die?"

"It's scary," Concha said, jumping off the stilts. "Maybe I better go home."

"Me too," added Virgie, heading toward her house. "I'll be back if it's nothing."

Alone in the street, I decided to try the stilts, but try as I might, I couldn't stay on the sancos that shifed to and fro in the dirt. With my hands firmly on the stilts, I poised my right leg over the can nailed to the wood and was about to jump up, when I heard cars on Van Nuys Boulevard.

Pacoima's main street was jammed with loudly honking cars. Honk, honk, honk. Round and round the block they went as both driver and passengers waved to each other. I watched the slow parade of cars, alarmed at the noise and the constant ringing of the church bell. I jumped off the sancos and ran home, dragging them with me. Why are folks honking their horns? I wondered. What's going on?

I dashed into the kitchen, grabbed a glass from the sink, and gulped down some tap water. I gazed out the window at Doña Luisa's house and across to the Morenos', but nothing seemed amiss. Within our house a radio was blaring; the sound of voices filled the air. I sauntered into the living room, where the noise was coming from, and was surprized to see my sisters and their friends huddled around el radio.

"What happened?"

"They dropped a bomb somewhere in Japan!"

"The war's over," said Jenny, a friend of Ronnie's. She fiddled with the radio dial, her dark eyes troubled. On the floor next to her sat Ronnie, biting her nails.

Bored with how my sisters and their friends were acting, and raring to be with my own friends, I ignored their account of the details of the atomic bomb that ended la guerra. I grabbed a tortilla from the kitchen counter, smeared it with oleo, then went to sit beneath the pepper tree, anxious to finish the most recent book I had sneaked from Nora. I feared she would send back the latest Book of the Month Club selection before I had read it. The street noise and the incessant ringing of the bell were irritating. I wanted nothing more than to sit and read in a cool place. It was hot, very hot, but excitement was in the air.

On this historic day, as the church bells tolled, folks on Hoyt Street called to each other from their front porches, their voices happy and excited.

"Did you hear?"

"Sí. Now my sweetheart can come home!"

"My brothers too!"

Across the way Doña Caridad, a light shawl draped over her shoulders, appeared to be crying. Next to her Doña Magda kept blowing her nose, while Doña Clarissa, dark skirt straddling her ankles, appeared to be in a trance. Santos, Doña Cari's grandson, and Esteban, Doña Magda's nephew, were in the service; the women had good reason to be so moved. I stood on our porch, looking out at the street and at people running about, then walked off toward the pepper tree. After a time I was joined by Concha. She was relieved to know the world was not about to end. We munched on candy and talked.

"Now we can get butter."

"And Tudi can come home."

"Wanna play sancos?"

"No. That's baby stuff. Let's go to the store."

The war was no longer interesting. Few kids who lived on Hoyt Street had discussed what was going on between our country and the enemy. We were now interested in other things. Few kids played war; not even Mundo, who daily instigated fights for any and all reasons, fought mock battles. The war was not something we talked about except on the way home from the "show," where the newsreels screened were just another black and white movie.

From translating the English newspaper for Doña Luisa and the Three Trinidads, however, I knew something of the war. The Pacific Theatre was not a movie house but the place where battles were taking place. Still the war overseas was something remote. I was intrigued by names like Corregidor and "the Aleutians," said to be islands. The Americans and their "allies" were beating the Japs, Germans, and Italians; the Russians were now on our side. It was still patriotic to mimic Hitler and Mussolini.

The thing is, I liked Musolini! His name evoked images of my favorite Italian foods: mostaciolli, rigatoni, and spaghettini. He was the enemy and by rights should be hated almost as much as Hitler. But I liked him, especially because his nickname, "Il Duce" was identical to our dog's name.

Mussolini was short, fat, and tough. He wore polished black boots, a dark olive uniform, and a square helmet that came down to his dark, sparkling eyes. He screeched orders in a commanding voice and rode in a motorcycle with a side seat. Mussolini exuded power.

During the early war years, kids on our street, especially rowdy boys like Mundo, admired the tough leaders on the opposing side. They liked Hirohito (called Tojo in the movies) and Adolph Hitler. Mundo would kick up his heels in the street in something called a "goose step," similar to the way the Italian soldiers marched, "Il Duce" in the lead. Mundo, who could kick the ball way out to Carl Street, painted a short moustache on his face, then paraded around Hoyt Street, kicking up his heels and giving the Hitler salute.

"Heil Hitler."

"Heil your nalgas!"

"I'm gonna tell . . ."

Many families on our street were affected by the war. Those who could afford to, bought war bonds; others stuck gold and silver stars on the front door, anxious for neighbors to know that someone in their family was fighting or had died for his country. Young girls with boyfriends in the army and navy sold war bonds as part of the war effort.

Our family was not directly affected by the war. Rito had died before Pearl Harbor, Berney sat out the war, Norbert was still in high school, and Josey was in elementary school. But many of Berney's friends were drafted. When home on leave, or "furlough," as they called a short visit, they came by our house, strutting around in their snappy uniforms.

Concha's brother Tudi, a round-faced guy with brown eyes that crinkled at the corners, joined the army, which in my opinion had the ugliest uniform. Right before he was shipped overseas, he came home wearing the ugly khaki outfit and a neat cap. Concha's mother made chicken mole and pumpkin turnovers (his favorites). Since Concha and I were best friends and always in each other's houses, I got to eat the special treats.

One of many obedient sons on our street, Tudi sent his mother an allotment each month. From a place named Corregidor he sent letters sealed in envelopes of a double thickness (so that the "enemy" could not glean information from them). Called V-letters, they were treasured by most parents, who read them with great interest. It *was* exciting to have a relative in the armed services. Often I envied Concha, who bragged about Tudi every chance she got.

"My brother's in the army!"

"We buy war bonds."

"So what?"

Often Concha shared Tudi's letters. It was fun to learn of the exotic names of places where men like Tudi now fought. He was somewhere in the Pacific, although his letters went to a postal box number in San Francisco. He later admitted he was in the Phillipine and Marshall islands but was unable to say this in his V-letters. When her mother wasn't looking, Concha and I stole the V-letters from her purse and paraded them around, pretending they were written to us by our boyfriends in the military service. Afterward we folded the letters with care and returned them to her purse.

The García boys, two green-eyed, lanky brothers who also lived on Hoyt Street had signed up together and were now in Italy, fighting the dreaded Mussolini. In their letters home they described the many villages they marched through and told of eating bread made in outdoor ovens. Italian bread, they wrote, tasted just like the pan baked by their Mexican mothers.

I was jealous of girls with a boyfriend in uniform. Most uniforms were striking, except for the army's. The marines' dress uniform, complete with white gloves, was my favorite. Sailors had two distinct uniforms: blue and white. The navy uniform was of wool with a wide, square collar that flapped in the wind. The pants had a string waist and fit close to the hips. The white outfit was identical, but was made of cotton. Now at Sunday mass, rather than scrutinize the clothes worn by women, I would scour the packed church in search of a uniform.

My friends and I yearned for the war to last longer. Until we were old enough to date, that is. Nancy and I constantly talked about the boyfriends (handsome soldiers and sailors) we would never have and the secret V-letters (with a snapshot of our novios against an aircraft carrier) we would never answer. Concha too felt cheated, but said nothing. She knew that once the war ended and Tudi came home, her mother would no longer mope.

My sister Ronnie liked a boy named Baldomero. Although he had a funny name, Baldy, as he was called, was quite handsome. He joined the U.S. Navy along with Bartolo, his twin brother, and was somewhere in the Mariana Islands. Baldy was tall and slender with huge brown eyes, curly hair, and two dimples! He wore funny pants called bell-bottoms and a snappy white hat. Ronnie never confided to me about Baldy, but I knew they were going steady. She kept a picture of him on top of her dresser and carried a snapshot of him in her wallet. In the snapshot a bare-headed Baldy, curly hair askew, dark eyes crinkling, smiled for the camera.

On the day the war ended, Concha and Nancy found me reading underneath the pepper tree.

"Gosh, the war is over!"

"The one in the movies?"

"No, stupid, the one in the Alushens."

Once the town settled down, Concha and I decided to walk to the store for a popsickle. We were walking out the back gate toward the alley when I distinctly heard my name called.

"Mary Helen!"

"What?"

"Come here!"

"I'm busy!"

"You'd better come right now or . . ."

Concha left, promising to return, as I stomped into the kitchen, angry at the church bell, the incessant honking of cars, and being taken from my friends. Just then my mother walked into the kitchen and told me to change clothes. It seems I was to accompany Ronnie to church.

"I don't wanna . . ."

"Sí."

"No, I want to finish my book and . . ."

I began to protest, saying I went to church more than anyone else in our family. Enough was enough! I ran off to find Ronnie, furious at her too. How dare she force me to go with her to church? Couldn't she walk the one block by herself? Normally I didn't mind being around Ronnie. It was fun to be with someone the boys liked. Not only was Ronnie pretty, she was also muy graciosa, friendly and nice, as was said in the barrio.

I barged into the bathroom, where Ronnie was dabbing her cheeks with rouge, and began to whine. Ronnie fixed me with a look from her pretty brown eyes and said, "Don't you want to go pray for our brave soldiers?"

"I wanted to . . ."

"It would be nice if you . . ."

"I go to church more than you!"

"I think you should . . ."

I began to stamp my feet, which usually worked, but I was overruled by my mother, who said, "Acompaña a tú hermana." She commanded me to go with my sister to church, then fixed me with a stern look.

I threw off my wrinkled dress, splashed cold water on my angry face, then grabbed a clean dress and my faithful beanie from a drawer, and off I went, running to catch up with Ronnie, who appeared anxious to be in church.

Ronnie wore a two-piece dress of a linenlike material. The skirt was black, the top a creamy white, with wide shoulder pads. On her head was a straw hat with a pink cabbage rose. She looked prettier than ever; her eyes were bright and teary at the thought of Baldomero's return. As we walked the short block to Guardian Angel church, Ronnie merely smiled at the "wolf whistles" directed at her. At home we were taught to be modest and, when complimented, to smile sweetly and murmur a "thank you." I trudged along, fighting to keep my hat from falling, bored with the war, and angry at Ronnie.

The church, normally empty in midafternoon, was full of people: old women dressed in black shuffled to the altar, young mothers with children clutched rosaries in their hands. Scattered here and there were younger girls, their dark eyes swollen and red.

The inside of the church was cool; the hot sun that earlier had scorched my face had given way to a fresh breeze. On the main altar stood large vases with pink roses and white lilies of the valley surrounded by green fern. On one side stood the ever-faithful Saint Joseph, looking down at the men and women who slowly drifted in.

Once in church Ronnie blessed herself with holy water then walked off, leaving me at the door. The tap, tap, tap of her high heels resonated throughout the church, as she turned left at the main altar toward where the red votive candles were kept. She knelt at the altar then prayed for a time, as I remained in the back, still angry at being ordered to church.

From afar I saw Ronnie reach into her purse, then I heard the clatter of nickles and dimes dropping into the money slot. I was terribly impressed by this display of money and piety. She then struck a match and lit the red votive candles; one, two, three, four, five! Ronnie lit all of five candles!

I stood and watched, unable to believe such extravagance. Most people lit only one candle! But Baldy *was* special. Ronnie stood at the altar, lips moving in prayer, eyes glistening with tears. I moved up to where she was and put my hand in hers.

A year later, dressed in a white brocade dress, creamy gladiolas in her hand, Ronnie stood at this same altar as the bride of Baldomero, the sailor for whom she had prayed on the day the war ended.

The Funeral of Daniel Torres

During World War II many young men from the barrio of Pacoima joined the armed forces not because it was patriotic, but because for some of them there was nothing else to do. Still others joined because they wanted to show they were not cowards but had guts, huevos, and could fight and kill with the best of them. In time many of them came home in a coffin or as a memory, as did Daniel Torres, posthumously awarded the nation's highest award for valor while under enemy fire: the Congressional Medal of Honor.

I first heard of Daniel Torres when Father Mueller announced in church that the government was planning a special mass and ceremonies for the war hero of our town (whom few could remember). He outlined the program for the astounded congregation, which would begin in Guardian Angel Church, then terminate at Valhalla Cemetery in nearby Burbank. He excitedly told of the many dignitaries and officials who would attend (none of whom we knew), and of the men's choir that, much to my dismay, would sing part of the mass. He emphasized the importance of this event, which was somewhat perplexing because no one could place Daniel, nor understand the sudden interest in our little town.

Father Mueller further explained that all the ceremonies would be recorded. In addition to the dignitaries, a film crew would document the event. I was awed by all this information. Very little happened in our sleepy, dusty town. Even a funeral, I thought, is better than nothing. But to me it was important to know about Daniel. Who was he? Where had he lived? Was he cute?

Most of the kids who lived on Hoyt Street had older brothers who knew of a Danny Torres (or several, as the name was not uncommon). However, Daniel-the-hero could not be placed. Concha immediately said he might be her cousin. Not to be outdone, Virgie insisted she had once said "hi" to him at the corner store, while Mundo grumbled that he didn't care to know un pendejo who got himself shot. Shy Beto twisted his cap back and forth, trying to decide whether or not he knew Daniel, then admitted the only Daniel he knew of was a much older man who currently was en el bote, in jail. The rumors flew as the funeral day approached.

People said Daniel had only lived for a short time in Pacoima. It was also rumored that Daniel had been a pachuco. Then someone discovered that Daniel had once been in juvenile hall. This was not unheard of in the barrio, where distraught parents of vagrant teenagers often placed their kin en la juvy. Upon his release, Daniel Torres had joined the army. This story appeared to have a ring of truth to it. During wartime young men who volunteered for duty could have their criminal record expunged; it was an opportunity for guys from our town to clean up their records while playing war games. More than one man used the war to leave a barrio that offered nothing more than a place to hang out. Unfortunately more than one also came back in a pine box.

The weeks before the funeral were quite busy for Father Mueller, who was assigned to coordinate the whole affair. Altar cloths were selected with care, flowers ordered from Mr. Flores (who owned a nursery), the dying shrubs along the church walls replaced, and the church floors scrubbed and waxed. The choir was instructed to learn a new mass for this occasion; the music was selected by Father Mueller, a trained musician, who wanted something dignified yet not too elaborate. He did not want us to compete with the men's seminarian choir that was to participate.

The men's choir was recruited from St. John's Seminary in nearby San Fernando. These would-be priests, who daily sang Gregorian chants, would be hard to compete with. During choir rehearsal the choirmistress drilled us over and over until we sounded just right. Aware of our consternation (and fear of Father Mueller's criticism), she tried to pacify us by saying that we sounded very professional. Father Mueller said nothing.

The local newspaper, *The Pacoima Post,* soon got into the act, too. A bevy of articles about the brave Mexican-American boy who had died fighting for his country soon appeared on the front page alongside articles about zoot-suit gangs. It was never mentioned that Daniel had lived in Pacoima for only a short time and, worse, that he had never set a foot in church! No one dared tell Father Mueller the truth (although we suspected he knew). He was caught up in the excitement; no one dared to spoil his day.

The day of the funeral dawned bright and clear. The entire town came out to watch the parade of limousines lined up outside church all the way to Pierce Street. At la tienda de Don Jesús, business picked up as boisterous kids ran in to buy a penny's worth of candy to eat while waiting for the funeral to begin. From her front porch, Doña Remedios, busy watering her droopy geraniums, tried to appear uninterested in the commotion near the church, in the men in uniform beginning to form a line, or in those in white naval caps alighting from shiny black cars. The marines in full-dress uniform stood at attention, holding high the American flag. In the choir loft, the singers squeezed together to one side to make room for the camera crew and the seminarians, all Anglo-blond with ruddy cheeks, who in the somber black cassocks, looked just like choir boys.

Soon the townspeople began to emerge, like ants long dormant but now excited by the funeral. The short, stumpy figure of Doña Chonita merged with the thin, skeletal form of Doña Zenaida (dressed completely in black), then quickly disappeared toward the front of the church, where the three Trinidads were firmly ensconced in the third row. Outside the church door, Don Cresencio and Don Serafín stomped out Lucky Strikes, then spat into colored handkerchiefs before removing their hats to enter the crowded church. In the sacristy Father Mueller nervously paced back and forth, adjusting his new surplice, while the altar boys kept a vigilant eye on the flickering candles. In the front pew, la Lulu whispered to other pachucas wearing elaborate pompadours and dark jackets with huge shoulder pads, their eyes thick with Maybelline, bright red lips set in expectant smiles.

In the crowded choir loft, much to the concern of Doña Martita, an elderly lady who monitored and sometimes pinched rowdy kids, we took turns peeking out the small window toward the entrance; but it was impossible to recognize either friends or relatives, due to the array of uniforms and flags.

I had expected to see only representatives from the army (in which

Daniel had served). However, there were from thirty to forty men in navy dress uniforms with gold braid on their shoulders, snow-white hats on their heads and spotless white gloves on their hands. In addition to the military, various community members (none of whom we knew) sat in the places of honor in the front pews. There were few occasions for Anglos to venture into the barrio (aside from the cops who now and then chased a stray pachuco), let alone attend our church. However, Father Mueller had stressed the importance of the funeral to the community; we welcomed the white strangers, those in uniform and those in civilian dress.

During the funeral mass, it was customary for the deceased's family to be escorted to the front pew prior to the mass. But no one knew what to expect. We knew nothing of la viuda, the widow. It was whispered that Daniel's parents were dead; he had no other family. But much of this was just gossip that fueled our anticipation.

Soon a group of women moved toward the church's entrance. All wore black except for a slight, young woman with a sallow complexion and yellow peroxided hair, dressed in slacks and a dark jacket. Murmurs of disapproval at the young widow's clothing were heard throughout the church.

"Gosh, she's wearing pants!"

"Que vergüenza!"

"Pobrecita."

At that time few women wore pants in public, let alone to church. I thought perhaps la viuda had not been told what one wears to church; still we felt disappointed. Much to our relief, the day was saved by a relative who accompanied the young widow, a tall, well-formed lady with light brown hair, appropriately dressed. She wore a black polka-dot dress, black patent leather pumps, a black straw hat, and spotless white gloves that held a handkerchief to her eyes. We stood and gaped at the crowd, which was now immense and included even the rowdies who *never* went to church.

The procession began suddenly, when the honor guard marched up the aisle, their polished boots tapping out a cacaphony of precise, staccato notes on the hard floor. One, two, one, two, one, halt. In the choir loft I ran a sweaty hand over my hair, adjusted my hat, and looked expectantly toward the movie camera.

The high requiem mass followed. At the altar presided a pale Father Mueller, light eyes gleaming, hair shiny clean. The marines held their bayonets at attention; the men in navy hats stood straight and stiff. Although the choir had agreed to learn a new mass, we had not been able to satisfy Father Mueller, who liked precision and was most impatient with a choir that dragged the music. After numerous discussions the choirmistress (with Father Mueller's approval) had decided that we should stay with the Mass of the Dead. We knew it.

We began with the "Liberame Domine." We sang ever so carefully, aware we were being watched (and rated) by experts, experts who stood waiting their turn. When it was time for the Sequence, the young seminarians sang the Dies Irae, an eerie, somber hymn written in Gregorian style. This monastic chant sung a capella was most demanding, but the seminarians rose to the occasion; their voices swelled and diminished as one, their breathing staggered to avoid an abrupt break.

I stood mesmerized as the camera trained its eye on us and on the seminarians, as well as on Father Mueller, arrayed in all his glory: a gold-colored chasuble and stole no one had ever seen before. His Sunday best. He looked quite elegant, only his protruding ears— now a bright red—betrayed his excitement. The altar boys, dark hair slicked in place and wearing starched white surplices, looked nervous. The candles flickered, flags swayed, and the cameras whirred as the organ pealed out the rich music of the requiem. In the front the widow appeared to sway. Next to her the fashionable relative dabbed at her eyes. In the back of the church, the men readied the collection baskets.

Prior to the start of mass, the members of the Holy Name Society, which was in charge of the collection baskets, had decided to forgo la colección, because it would only add to the confusion. Nonetheless Don Crescencio, head of the organization, argued that this was an opportunity for the Anglos, including government officials, to give of their bounty. Surely the elegant crowd would make the church's coffers swell. Much to our chagrin, when the men with the baskets swept down the aisle, none of the dignitaries reached for their wallets; the basket jangled as before, with only the offerings of the poor. The vergüenza, the shame, was felt by all. Just then the priest raised his hands for the benediction. Our attention shifted to the business at hand and to the cameras that luckily had failed to record this incident.

When mass finally ended, I pushed my way downstairs through the throng of dignitaries and visitors to find a ride to the funeral. I had not asked my mother's permission, but was willing to go without it. This, I told myself, is perhaps the most important funeral I will ever attend (other than my own!). I scouted around the parked cars sporting funeral stickers until I spotted Concha's cousin Richie sitting alone in his '47 Ford. When he agreed to take us to the cemetery, I ran to find Concha. We then settled down to wait for the funeral to begin.

But the funeral was delayed by the widow, who evidently had decided she was too sick to go to the cemetery. The fashionable relative had finally persuaded her: "You must be present to receive the American flag." "Mejor me debían de dar otra cosa, they should give me something else instead," the widow was said to have responded, then got into a car.

The rowdies within earshot began to giggle; her retort, they said, had a sexual connotation. Some women whispered that la viuda, devastated by her loss, had lacked words to express her sorrow. To us kids this was typical of a young woman recently widowed, ignorant of what she was expected to do or say.

Once the officials and dignitaries were ensconced in the shiny black cars, the procession began. Much to my dismay the cars did not turn toward San Fernando Road and the cemetery in Burbank, but toward the barrio and the house where the local hero was said to have lived: a small clapboard house in a weed-covered lot. I slumped down in my seat, mortified to know that these fine gentlemen in military hats and white gloves would be subjected to our poverty.

The procession must have been five blocks long. We went down Bradley to la Pinney, left on Ralston, then down Filmore Street and back. The homes we passed were not pretty, nor modern, but like those in most local barrios: of wood, with odd-shaped windows, the yards full of fruit trees and assorted pieces of junk. Barefoot kids ran out to call to us, others stopped to stare at the line of black cars. In the dusty, rocky streets, dogs competed for space with the parade of dark cars that slowly inched across our town.

I sat in the back of Richie's car, my face flushed with shame at what these men had seen. I was just a kid and wanted people to know only the good things about us, about our barrio.

Finally the procession reached Van Nuys Boulevard and turned left at San Fernando Road, toward Burbank and the final ceremonies for Daniel Torres, native son of Pacas, who because he was brave, died a hero's death. Daniel Torres, a hero unknown to most of the people who attended his funeral; a man who brought honor and glory to our town—for one day.

Los Novios

When I was eleven I had a crush on a boy named Santos, or Sandy, as everyone on Hoyt Street called him. He was a grade ahead of me in Pacoima Elementary, highly intelligent, and a regular speaker at school assemblies. He was of medium height, with dark eyes and hair and a row of freckles on his pert nose. He had beautiful white teeth that shone every time he smiled, which was often. I thought him very handsome, except for his hair; it was cut by his father and stuck out where either the bowl or the scissors had slipped.

One reason Sandy was so well liked was because he had lovely manners; Old World manners, Mexican manners. He rose when a teacher entered the classroom, stood at attention during the flag salute, and sang the national anthem in a loud clear voice. He never talked back to his elders as did other boys, nor did he cheat on exams. He respected authority, which is why the teachers and our kind principal, Mrs. Goodsome, all loved him. Even Father Mueller knew he could count on Sandy to be on time for Sunday mass. Everyone smiled when Sandy was around.

Sandy had one sister, Ana Teresa, a pretty girl with a round face, big eyes, and an old-fashioned hair style that set her apart from the rest of us girls, who doted on Shirley Temple curls and French braids. Ana Teresa's hair was pulled back into what resembled my mother's chongo. She insisted on being called by her full Spanish name, although the name "Terry" was then the current rage. (My good friend Teresa López went from "Teresa" to "Tére" to "Terry" in one week!).

During the late 1940s, it seemed that kids in the barrio disliked their Spanish names. Not so Ana Teresa; she liked her name! She and Sandy were born in Mexico; they disdained American names and customs and took pride in everything to do with their native language. I thought of Ana Teresa as a little old lady. She neither joined in our games nor came by to watch, but sat quietly to embroider. Still we tolerated her, mostly because she was related to Sandy, whom everyone liked.

Sandy spoke English with an accent more pronounced than that of other kids whose primary language was Spanish and who were now forced to speak el inglés. At school we were constantly told to speak English; the teachers would chant: "English, English, you're Americans now." This was difficult for Sandy.

Sandy pronounced "comfortable" as "comfort-table," "establish" as "establich," and "ships" as "cheeps." He was good at math and science, though, and was a superb athlete. The teachers forgave his lack of inglés.

He lived in a white clapboard house surrounded by fruit trees. Each morning on the way to school, I saw his mother hosing down the yard and watering geraniums. She was a hard-working woman seldom seen in public. The family kept a pen of chickens and goats en el llano, the open field we crossed to get to school; Sandy was in charge of the goats.

One day on the way to school, I saw Sandy near the goat pen. I stopped to admire the goats—and Sandy. After that I waved at him at school and began to think of him as my boyfriend, mi novio. Often he waited for me near the goat pen. Once school was over I would dash to the girls' bathroom to wash and pinch my cheeks; I scrubbed and pinched until they shone pink, as if I wore rouge! Unlike my sister Trina and her friends, I was not allowed to wear any makeup. Once satisfied that my face had a rosy glow, I dashed off to the goat pen, to Sandy. While the goats bleated and nibbled grass, Sandy and I talked.

"How come you can't play."

"I have to feed the shickens."

He then excused himself to go indoors, change his clothes, and return to change the goats' water and feed the chickens.

He began to come by my house, whether by accident or on his way to the store, I don't remember. Then he joined us at baseball and hide-and-seek. Soon Sandy and I were on the same team! It made me happy to see him at play. He had so little time for fun and rarely could play in the street until dinner, occupied as he was with the countless chores that befell the eldest son. As was the custom, he was expected to help at home and then have fun, unlike the rest of us whose older siblings did our chores while we played in the street.

Sandy never picked a fight. He did, however, have one enemy: Mundo, whom everyone on our street disliked. Mundo was mean, loud, and the street bully. He was jealous of Sandy, too.

Once in sixth grade, Mundo asked Sandy to help him cheat on a test.

"*Pssst* Santos. What's the answer to number three?"

"I can't tell you."

"Yeah, you can. Come on, or else . . ."

"I can't help you sheet, Mundo."

"I'll get you for this."

"Shhhhhh. Here comes the teacher."

When school let out, we ran outside in time to see Mundo push Sandy against the fence and pull at his shirt sleeve. He kept hitting Sandy, who appeared not to want to fight. Mundo's face turned a deep red; he pushed and shoved at the pale-faced Sandy, while we formed a circle. Suddenly Mundo stepped back and with the same ferocity (and meanness) he showed when he played kickball or beat up on stray dogs, Mundo kicked Sandy in the shin. Still Sandy resisted.

"Stupid wetback. Pendejo."

Silence.

"Pendejo chivero."

This time Mundo went too far. Sandy could take an insult, but did not allow anyone to call him a stupid goatherd or demean his goats. Suddenly he turned, raised his right arm, then gave Mundo a swift uppercut, just like Joe Louis! Mundo was sent reeling to the ground; the fight began in earnest. No one took Mundo's side. We rooted for our favorite, for Sandy, especially Virgie, who more than once had been socked by Mundo. We cheered for Sandy to win, as from nearby homes women and children emerged to watch el faite.

"Jesús, María, y José," screeched Doña Juanita from her porch. "Those boys are fighting again!"

"Que vergüenza," lamented Doña Remedios, for whom everything we kids did was a shame.

We ignored the women watching from the safety of their front doors. We knew this was going to be a good fight. We rated fights as we did movies: good or bad.

Sandy and Mundo continued to fight. Sandy was clearly winning, while Mundo, out of breath and bleeding from the nose, kept missing punches. Suddenly Mundo stepped back, put down his hands, and mumbled, "I quit." We stared, our mouths wide open. The street bully was giving up!

"So? Now whose stupeed?" asked Sandy.

"Yo," answered Mundo, grinning broadly, "Me." He brushed the dirt off his pants, wiped his nose, then, still grinning, took off for home. We stood there smiling at Sandy, who now sprouted a black eye, then left, since nothing else was about to happen. After that no one ever dared to use the word *chivero* around Sandy.

Most of us kids liked to ride bikes and to race against our friends on Carl Street, yet few of us had bikes. Sandy didn't. When I borrowed my brother Josey's bike I would loan it to Sandy, then climb onto Concha's handlebars. We would fly up Hoyt Street, turn right toward Carl, then come back around to Hoyt. We rode in the dirt streets, careful to stay clear of the pepper trees, los pirules, that lined the street on the next block.

They were huge. They met high up overhead, obscuring the light, and even in the daytime they gave the street an eerie, haunted look. The street is haunted, it was said. Allí asustan. We avoided that area; rather than walk through the scary trees, we circled the block and ran home.

One summer day Concha suggested to Beto and Sandy, whom we considered our novios, that we go riding. I ran to tell Sandy, who agreed, providing I got the bike; Concha cornered Beto. We made plans to meet on Carl Street, near the church, so as not to arouse suspicion. In those days girls were not supposed to play alone with boys, but only in groups. I ran to get my brother's bike, anxious to get going.

Josey had a Frankenstein bike. It was made from leftover bike parts: tires, handlebars, and rims he had taken from our older brothers. I constantly rode the bike without his permission. After all, I reasoned, I was older—and much bigger. I neither needed nor wanted his permission.

That day Concha and I "borrowed" bikes, then rode off to meet Sandy and Beto, nuestros novios. The boys were first to ride around the quiet streets. They rode like the wind, their backs hunched over the handlebars. They made crazy, daring turns and jumped over bumps. They whizzed by, hands off the handlebars until a car approached, then they quickly grabbed them again. Concha and I were most impressed, but said nothing. We were biding our time until we too could show off.

When it was our turn, Concha and I went wild. We rode around, getting a feel for the bikes, making sure we did not show our calzones. Girls did not wear jeans then, nor were we allowed to borrow our brothers' pantalones. As we pedaled, Concha and I kept our dresses down and our legs close together.

Then we asked the boys to ride us on the handlebars. This was considered daring and somewhat romantic. While Sandy and Beto held the bikes steady, we climbed onto the bars, adjusted our dresses, then hunched our bodies forward while the boys pushed off. Then off we went. We rode down Carl Street, by the church, as kids played tag and hide-and-seek. We rode by . . . and away.

Concha and Beto set the pace. With them in the lead, we rode until early evening, as shadows came and went; lights came on inside warm kitchens. Then, unbeknownst to Sandy and me, Concha (who sometimes appeared timid) asked Beto to ride towards los pirules, or the ghost trees, as I called them. Sandy and I followed, laughing aloud in the early evening light, eager to catch up with them. I was scared but determined not to show it. I hunched forward as we sped down the dark road.

I noticed that Sandy was huffing and puffing; I knew it was because of my weight. I was chubby. Very chubby. I weighed much more than Concha and most of my other friends. I ignored Sandy's gasps for air, but shifted my weight. We rode after Concha and Beto, and had just entered the ghost trees, when suddenly Sandy stopped the bike and jumped off. He said nothing, only stood gasping for air. He took a deep breath, then walked alongside me, pushing the bike as I sat quietly on the handlebars. Concha and Beto were nowhere to be seen. Sandy and I were alone in the middle of los pirules!

My skin began to crawl. I could hear funny noises. I was scared but did not volunteer to jump off the bike. The ride, with Sanndy pumping furiously to keep us moving, *had* been romantic! I liked the feel of his strong arms as they brushed against me. I wanted him to *ride,* not push me. And so I sat.

Sandy stood alongside the bike; I sat deathly still. Suddenly from the pepper tree behind us came an eeerie wail: "Eeeeeee. Wooooooo." It was a ghost! The monster that lived in the ghost trees! My heart thumped; my hands felt clammy. I knew we were about to die. Sandy said nothing. He stood still, hands tight on the handlebars.

"Eeeeee. Eeeeee." The sound came closer.

"I'm scaaaaaared."

"Shhhhhhh."

"It's gonna get us!"

"Nehhhhh."

I was scared stiff. The trees seemed to come closer and closer. I was about to scream for my mother, when a cat jumped from behind a tree and scooted across the street. Faint with fear I remained on the handlebars. Sandy tried to push the bike forward. He grabbed the pedals with his hand and pushed with all his might, but they would not budge.

"Your dress is stuck on the chain!"

"Gosh! What are we gonna do?"

"I dunno."

Sandy pulled at the material, but it would not come loose. He turned the pedals back and forth, trying to release my dress, but the chain seemed to eat up the cloth. He grappled with the bike chain as I shivered atop the handlebars, my eyes on the menacing ghost trees.

High above, the tree branches, like long hairy arms, swooped down on us. I was sure they would carry us off; This was the end. The end of carefree rides, of Josey's Frankenstein bike, and of mi novio. Just then Sandy gave my dress a tug; the ruffle came off. Without a word he shoved the torn cloth into my hand, pushed off, jumped onto the bike, and pedaled home. When we neared my house, Sandy jumped off. Then slowly and reluctantly, I got off too. I put the ruffle in my pocket, then turned to bid Sandy goodbye, but he had already disappeared down the dark street.

Early the next morning, I awoke to hear Josey screaming. He had discovered the damaged bike chain and wanted to hit me. My mother, however, intervened. As he went toward the garage, Josey screamed at me: "Fat cow. Fat stupid." I was itching to chase him, but had lately noticed that Josey was almost as tall as I was.

I never went riding with Sandy again. He moved away soon after; rumor had it that his family returned to Mexico. I later heard that Mrs. Goodsome, the school principal, had tried to dissuade them from moving. She feared that Sandy would not complete his education. She admired his leadership qualities and the straight-A report cards. But Sandy did not have a choice. As was the custom, his father decided for him. I never got to say goodbye. They left before the new school year started, while our family was away picking walnuts.

Years later, when I no longer feared los pirules and often walked through the ghost trees on my way to the store, I thought of Sandy and the romantic and scary bike ride. The sweeping branches no longer appeared menacing. No longer did I perceive of the trees as a home to monsters, but as a meeting place for novios. Boys who walked a sweetheart home from a party appeared to stray toward the pepper trees, where the low branches shielded them from prying eyes.

I thought of Sandy. Gallant Sandy, who while riding through the scary trees had not panicked nor insisted that I get off the bike. I wondered if at that moment he had vowed never, ever to ride with a girl who weighed more than he did.

. . . .

Concha was sweet on Beto, but like most girls with a crush on a boy, she didn't know what to do about it. At age eleven we were still considered niñas and were discouraged from thinking about boyfriends. In fact, boys were our friends in the truest sense of the word; we played kickball with boys, climbed trees with boys, and walked home from catechism with boys. Of all the girls on Hoyt Street, only

Nancy liked being alone with a boy. Virgie and I preferred to play in groups.

I dared not walk home from school with any one boy for fear of being teased about "going steady." If on my way to the corner store I accidently met up with Jesús, a short, pudgy boy who smelled of pee, I quickly went the other way, afraid my friends would mistake him for mi novio. On days I stayed after school, I made sure Mundo wasn't around. To have the street bully think I liked him even a little was utterly repugnant to me.

Concha was rarely alone with Beto. The only time she could be with Beto without her mother noticing was when we went bike riding or during the church bazaars, las jamaicas, when everyone came together to help with the booths. During a fiesta it was not uncommon to share popcorn and cotton candy with a blushing boy, nor for un jovencito to put his arm around a girl's shoulders. When Concha and I discussed our boyfriends, we knew they were really just friends who happened to be boys.

Although she denied it, Concha had always liked Beto. In kindergarten they had sat together on the braided rug to hear all about Mother Goose. In first grade they sat next to each other, desks touching, sharing pencils and erasers. He was her novio, or so we inferred.

"Ha, ha, Concha loves Beto."

"Who is CG loves BT?"

Beto was a thin, long-legged boy with a broken tooth that showed every time he laughed, which was often. He laughed instead of talking, perhaps because of his poor English. My mother would say, "Beto parece un hazme reír," because he never appeared serious. Concha's mother called him un payaso, but Concha told her she liked clowns—and Beto. When he joined us for a fast game of kickball, Concha smiled even more than Beto.

Mundo called Beto "el cepillo," "the brush," because his hair, hidden beneath the cap he always wore, was stiff and wiry. He daily saturated his hair with Three Flowers brilliantine or hair pomade swiped from his older brothers, but it refused to stay down. He slept with a stocking cap, having heard that this would tame it, but even that didn't work. His mother, I heard, offered to put lard on it, but Beto refused. I liked Beto, hairbrush and all.

He wore pants held up by wide suspenders bought at J.C. Penny. The long-sleeved shirts he wore were handed down from his older brothers. Beto wore funny-looking shoes, too. His "clod-hoppers," as we kids called men's work boots, had high tops and thick heels and soles. We tried not to stare at them; like most of us, Beto wore what he had.

"El cepillo" was one of eight children, all boys, whose names each began with an *R*. Rojelio, Ramiro, Rigoberto, Raimundo, Rafael, Reyes, Rubén, and Roberto (Beto). Their father had died some years back, so they all lived with their widowed mother. La viuda Torres felt fortunate in having a family of males.

"Las mujeres sólo nacen para sufrir," she often said. While I did not think women were born to suffer, I dared not contradict her. Our family was predominantly girls, and from what I saw, none of us suffered for anything, except Trina, who wanted her own radio. Nonetheless Señora Torres was especially happy with her family of men.

Beto's brothers, all older, had dropped out of school after completing the eighth grade. They worked en el fil, thinning tomatoes and harvesting beets, except for Ramiro, who worked in a shoe shop; like Beto, he had black, wiry hair.

The widow Torres was thin, with dark eyes and stringy hair. Nurse Smithers (and some teachers) at Pacoima Elementary thought Beto was tubercular, un tísico. They assumed that all Mexicans were either fat or tubercular. When he was called to the nurse's office to have his chest examined, they would comment:

"Hummmm, you weigh the same, Rigoberto."

"Roberto."

"But you have grown one inch! Tell me, what do you eat at home?"

"Beans, tortillas, and papas fritas."

"Hmmm. You people should eat vegetables, too. Too much starch is . . ."

"But my mother . . ."

"Well, yes. But make sure to take your cod-liver oil. You need some color in your cheeks!"

Once the nurse realized that the entire Torres family was thin and healthy, they all quit bothering Beto.

Beto was rarely sick or absent from school; he was the first to arrive, after the janitor, that is. He could ride a bike for hours without getting tired, his skinny legs pumping the pedals up and down. During kickball Beto outran all the other players; he would run back and forth across the playground at top speed, never once tripping on the clod-hoppers. He even outran Mundo, who, when he didn't win, tripped those who went past him.

Beto also worked hard at home. His mother, as did many women on Hoyt Street, took in boarders to make ends meet. Beto helped with the household chores before and after school. Each morning Beto and his mother packed lonche for the boarders, most of who were braceros from Mexico. And when his mother washed the clothes that filled six long clotheslines, Beto was there to help.

Early Monday morning, before the school bell rang, Beto would pile wood around a huge zinc-plated tub perched on blocks. He filled the tubs with water, lit the fire, and then his mother would throw in the boarders' shirts. The two scrubbed clothes on the washboards, then tossed them in another tub. To give his mother a rest, Beto often scrubbed the heavier clothes such as cotton pants and denim shirts, a job he attacked with his usual cheer. While Beto got ready for school, his mother hung the clothes out to dry. After school was over, Beto ran home to empty the tubs.

The boarders admired how the widow laundered and ironed their clothes. The word soon got around; business picked up. Young men looking for novias liked the way she did their clothes: pants with razor-sharp creases, dress shirts lightly starched, and handkerchiefs white and fresh. The widow's reputation as a hard-working woman, una mujer trabajadora, grew, as did her clotheslines.

When Beto's mother was not boiling clothes, she was in the kitchen, cooking for the workers. The evening meal was especially hearty, with beans earlier soaked in a blue enamel pot and the fried potatoes peeled by Beto, stationed near the potato sack. When the food was almost ready, the widow wiped clean el comal and began to make tortillas for her boarders.

Beto's mother made tortillas with whole-wheat flour. They were much heavier and tastier. The boarders, she hoped, would fill up on the thick tortillas and not ask for seconds. As it happened the men thoroughly enjoyed the whole-wheat tortillas and began to eat more. The overworked woman went back to cooking regular flour tortillas.

With the same ease with which he rode a bike backwards, Beto rolled tortillas on the kitchen table. He told Concha (his most trusted friend) that his first tortilla looked like a map of Africa; the rest resembled Australia. One day as Beto was making tortillas, Mundo stopped by and saw him in the kitchen. He snitched to the kids on our street about Beto. They began to tease him.

"Hey Beto, you gonna make cookies?"

"Where's your apron, Beto?"

"I always knew you was a vieja, Beto!"

Thereafter Beto refused to help his mother cook. "No soy vieja," he said, "I ain't no woman." To which his mother replied, "Thank God."

Of all the neighborhood kids, "el cepillo" was a whiz at making money. Often he asked my father for two-by-fours to make stilts. He nailed empty cans to each board, sanded and painted them, then sold them for a quarter. Concha provided the cans; she got free stilts, while I got a nickel discount because my father gave him the wood. Beto also made scooters from crates found behind the grocery store. He added tiny wheels to the bottoms, a handle, then greased the wheels and off we went.

Beto was always on the alert for empty bottles left by winos who slept near the alley. They meant money: pennies, nickels, even a dime! When Beto found a bottle, he quickly washed and dried it, then dashed off to Don Jesús, who accepted bottles as he did kids, with a smile. The refund was of benefit to all.

El Circo Talamante

El Circo Talamante was a small, family-owned circus that played the Los Angeles area in the 1940s. The owner and most of the performers were mejicanos, with dark hair and eyes. They spoke fluent Spanish and broken English, but they made themselves understood. Folks claimed the circus originated in Mexico and was based in Los Angeles, but no one really cared. What mattered was that they performed in Pacoima; when the circus was in town, our town really came alive.

El circo arrived overnight. The caravan of trucks, trailers, and cars entered through Van Nuys Boulevard during the late, late hours, after a performance in San Fernando. By the next morning, the empty lot behind our house was full of tents, trailers, and people.

Our family was among the first to know about el circo. Once the trucks and trailers had found a spot, Señor Talamante, a handsome man with a dark mustache, would come to ask my father's permission to connect the electricity and water from our house to the circus trailers and tent. In return we got free circus passes.

Once the tent was set up and an agreement reached on the utilities, Señor Talamante would assign two big, burly men to string the heavy wires from our garage to the trailers and the big tent.

The men looped wires over tall wooden poles with a notch at the top, checked the slack, poked a hole through a window screen, and in went the electric wire. My mother, afraid of un choque, cautioned us not to touch the switch. When the lights worked, she would give up her vigil by the switch box.

Next the men hooked up a much-patched hose. The faucet was connected to a tee, which allowed for more than one hose. Once everything was secure, the circus men retired to their trailers, assured of water and light.

The circus came in the early fall, while the weather was still warm and the evenings long. Most people were unaware that the circus had arrived, until a rickety Ford truck began to drive up and down the streets. In the middle of the flatbed, a man with a megaphone announced the forthcoming program:

Señores y señoras, el circo Talamante está hoy aquí en el lindo pueblo de Pacoima! No falten de pasar al circo esta noche. Esta noche los esperamos con los elefantes, los títeres, los caballitos. No falten de ver el gran espectaculo de la bella Jasmín! A las siete en punto los esperamos.

Ladies and gentlemen, the Talamante circus is here today in the lovely town of Pacoima! Plan to attend the circus this evening. The elephants, the clowns, and the horses await you. Make sure to see the grand spectacular performance by the beautiful Jasmín. We hope to see you at seven o'clock sharp!

The kids who lived on Hoyt Street would chase after the truck as it went up and down the street. We hung on to the tailgate, daring each other to hold on for an entire block.

"I'm the winner!"

"Ha, ha. Girls can't . . ."

"Ayyyyyy! Me caigo."

"Jump! My father's coming."

We rode only for a short distance; the rocks and potholes on the streets would shake the truck, forcing us to jump off. Up and down went the truck, kids and dogs right behind. Up Hoyt, right on Norris, down Carl, past Guardian Angel Church and la tienda de Don Jesús, and on to the temporary home of the circus behind our house.

The best things in Pacoima take place on our side of town, Josey and I agreed. The church bazaars, catechism, vistas—cowboy movies —shown at the church hall, and the circus! I felt that el circo belonged to me. Were it not for our water and electricity, the clowns would not be able to see, nor could the elephants perform in a circle. Yes, Hoyt Street was the best place in town!

The circus offered something for everyone. To kids it meant fun and excitement. For our older siblings, el circo was almost like being in the movies: the men were handsome, the women slim and beautiful, and the acts all breathtaking. In truth our Mexican-American community had little to offer in the way of fun. Other than church activities, weddings, and sixteenth of September fiestas, the circus was it. It revived everyone and everything: the kids, the adults, and in a small way, even the economy.

Few of us went on vacation; even fewer went to the movies. When the circus hit town, kids went wild, parents smiled, dogs took to the streets, and older boys looked for work under the big top.

One year when I was about ten, Mr. Talamante came to see my father, Norbert (then about fourteen), hung around. While the men talked, Norbert stroked Fawn, his dog. When my father finally left, Norbert, with a determined look on his face, went up to el Señor Talamante.

"*Señor*. Uhh, Mr., Sir. My friends and I want to help with the animals. Uhhhh, if we could."

"Hmmmm, sí, pués. Ever taken care of ponies?"

"No sir, just dogs," answered Norbert, as he pushed back his curly hair.

"Tell you what. Come over in a while, and we'll see what we can find ter ya, okay?"

"How about my friends?"

"Bring 'em too. We'll find sumthin. Can't pay much, but you'll get free passes. That okay?"

"Sure! Thanks a lot!"

Josey and I watched as Norbert ran to find Tito and Chuy, but they were gone. Only los mensos, the dummies, were to be found.

Norbert, the kindest of my brothers, befriended kids like "el Brains," a mentally retarded boy who could only count to ten, and Cosme, called "Tuerto" because his eyes met in the middle. We lumped all kids that were different into one group: los mensos, the dummies. They were neither mean nor clever, but kids who because of a birth defect, illness, or lack of money, were left to their kinfolk to raise as best they could. La familia served as caretaker and provided the "grown-up babies" with love that insulated them from kids like us, who out of ignorance and meanness, or both, made fun of them. Only Norbert treated these kids as equals.

Once they were hired, Norbert and the dummies were put to work clearing a lot to be used for parking. Josey and I, envious at being supplanted by los mensos, watched as they moved rocks and raked the dirt. They were then shown how to clean a pony's rectum, to ensure that los caballitos would not have an accident during the show. Of the three only Norbert learned how; the dummies were too smart to go near the animals' rumps.

That first night of the circus, soon after supper, Norbert put on a clean shirt and pants. His curly hair, parted to the side, shone with brilliantine. His kind brown eyes looked happy and expectant.

"Bueno hijo, cuidado con los animales. Be careful of the animals, son."

"Sí, Señor."

"Que Dios te bendiga. God be with you."

"Sí, Mama."

"Get us some passes."

"Yeah, sure."

Josey and I chased after Norbert. Out the kitchen door we flew, to the alley and across the open field. The tent teemed with workers and performers, as dusty cars pulled into the side street. Inside dented trailers the circus folks sat smoking, waiting for the night to begin.

When it was time for us to get ready, I needed little prodding, but Josey hated to wash and change clothes. "I'm clean," he insisted, rubbing a washcloth over his grimy face. "No lo estás," my mother countered, guiding him toward the tub.

What Josey most hated was having to empty his pockets, those dark, secret places from which poured marbles, slingshots, pebbles, and sometimes an item or two of mine.

"It's mine! I found it in the open field."

"Liar! You stole it. Give it to me!"

"Shut up."

"You shut up."

"Pero ya es bastante," my mother would interject. "I don't like this charape!" We ended the fight, then scampered across the alley to meet our friends.

At the corner of Hoyt Street stood the gang. Virgie was dressed in a plaid jumper and white blouse. She wore French braids with a bright ribbon. Beto, who normally walked with Concha, wore his clodhoppers, a blue shirt, and a beanie studded with bottle caps. Concha, who was color blind and always cold, wore a pink sweater over a yellow dress, an orange ribbon in her hair, and bright green socks. Josey's face was squeaky clean from our mother's scrubbing; he followed, hot on our heels.

"Gosh, I can hardly wait."

"I want to touch the elephants!"

"You can't, stupid! They'll stomp on you, and you'll die."

The first night we got in with the free passes. We sat awhile to see who else came in the tent door, then walked around to look at everything: at the crowd that swelled and swayed atop the bleachers, at los músicos now warming up, at the tent that soared as high as the eucalyptus trees in our yard, and at the performers, in costume, selling popcorn, peanuts, and cotton candy.

Like most kids, I believed that circus people lived exotic, glamorous lives. The daily work that was part of circus life was not always visible, although I had seen Mr. Talamantes carry a bucket of water to the ponies.

"Circus people ain't supposed to work," insisted Concha. "Just do tricks."

"They live in old trailers," she concluded, always practical, as she smoothed her dress.

We stopped to listen to the organ-grinder, a dark man dressed in wide purple pants, with a matching vest trimmed in silver braid. A lively monkey on a leather leash begged for un penny, then scuttled back to his owner. We sneaked a peek at the ponies, their hair braided for the show, then splurged on popcorn, cotton candy, and cacahuates, peanuts in the shell, which sold for a nickel. Our curiosity satisfied, we returned to the bleachers. Just then a man in a tuxedo walked to the front and bowed to the audience.

I recognized him immediately. El Señor Talamante was decked out in a shiny black coat and pants. A black top hat perched on his slick head. He looked terribly handsome, with his dark moustache and deep eyes. In his hand he held a long, black whip, which he curled in the air with a precise, practiced flick. Now and then he glanced at the gold watch on his wrist, frowned, then assessed the crowd.

"Éjole! He sure looks mean," gasped Virgie through mouthfuls of cotton candy.

"The popcorn sure is good!"

"I wanna go home!"

Although the circus remained for a week, Josey and I felt entitled to see not one, but all the performances. After all the performers changed outfits and hairdos every day! I liked to examine the clothes worn by the women: skimpy garments that skimmed over their lithe bodies. Except for the glitter of sequins, they resembled bathing suits.

Within days Josey and I had used up the passes given to my father. I begged my older siblings for theirs, implying that the circus was really for kids, but they refused. Everyone wanted to see el circo; even my mother, who rarely went anywhere, put on her one good dress and walked off with my father. I scrounged around the circus tent for torn tickets to paste together; Beto led the search for empty bottles. Tired of my daily whining, Doña Luisa, her eyes brimming with love, finally handed me her ticket.

"Tenga, y ya no llore." She wiped my nose and smoothed my hair. Josey, fit to be tied, chased me across the street and back, furious at Doña Luisa.

Earlier that week, I discovered that if my friends and I sat near the back of the tent, we were less likely to attract the attention of Mr. Talamante, who frowned on loud, noisy kids, kids likely to start trouble. Kids like us.

While I munched on peanuts, I inspected the tent for spots that would make good peepholes. By the time the pony show began, I had found the perfect hole, midway along the lower part of the tent. I told Concha; she told Virgie and the rest. Assured of the next night's performance, we were ready to enjoy the show.

The circus tent was of blue-green canvas with faded stripes that had once been a bright red. It sported numerous patches, most of them at eye level. The bottom straps were tied to iron stakes. The tent resembled a huge umbrella; it must have been awfully pretty when it was new.

I loved the smells and all the other sensations associated with this spectacle. Nowhere else were peanuts as tasty nor cotton candy as sticky. The smell of buttered popcorn permeated the tent; the sawdust trampled by the animals settled on our clothes.

I liked the trapeze artists the best. Concha adored the ponies but was afraid of the elephants. Mundo ogled the women; he made fun of their skinny legs or fat bottoms. Nancy, thinking I would not notice, sighed over the guys who rode the palomino ponies. Beto, who laughed at everything, almost died laughing at the clowns; when Mundo wasn't looking, he mimicked them. All he lacked was the red nose and costumes.

Circus week passed quickly. By Friday night most folks on Hoyt Street had seen not one, but two performances. Father Juanito was seen without his pom-poms. Both he and the members of the Holy Name Society were given discount tickets, but not so las mujeres of the Altar Society. Elizabet, Ronnie, and their friends, decked out in pretty dresses, sauntered off to the big tent. Berney, having heard, I suppose, that Jasmín, the trapeze artist was pretty and wore a bathing suit, whistled as he left for el circo with other young blades. Nora stayed home to read a good book.

On the very last night, a warm Saturday, Virgie, Beto, and Mundo knocked on our door. Josey, eager to take over my friends, told them I was busy. I was trying to get out of washing the supper dishes so as to join the gang, but my sisters, alert to an impending stomachache or bandaged finger, refused to budge.

"I don't feel so good."

"Where does it hurt this time?"

"Right here, see?"

"Hmmm, sound like your appendix. People die from . . ."

"I feel better now."

Once finished with this despicable chore, I joined the others huddled near the back alley.

"We can't go to the circus no more," sighed Virgie, wiping her nose with a hanky.

"We ain't gots no money," blurted Beto, adjusting his beanie.

"Jando," corrected Mundo, who as leader of the pack parroted the dreaded pachucos. He flexed his fingers, waiting for us to let him decide.

"We gotta get in tonight," cried Concha as she licked a popsickle. "My sister says they're gonna do new tricks."

"They're gonna do the Ring of Fire," exclaimed Virgie, her eyes wide. "It's real scary."

"But we ain't got money," echoed Mundo, yanking Beto's cap. "So, what we gonna do?"

"We can watch from the outside or sneak in," I cried. "I saw a big hole. Come on! I'll show you."

Mundo grumbled as he followed me across the alley; he hated to give in to girls. "I'm not afraid," said Virgie, close behind. She pulled up her socks as if to lift her courage.

"All for one and one for all," cried Beto, his eyes wide as saucers. "All for one," smiled Concha, not wanting to be left out. We scampered off to the tent, now filling up with people.

"This is the spot," I assured my friends. "I saw it from inside." Using Mundo's pocketknife, we slashed the tent to accommodate two pairs of eyes. As Mundo held the tent down, I pulled at the canvas.

"It ain't gonna work," said Beto. "You gotta sneak in."

"Ya chicken, Beto?" mocked Mundo, sticking out his chest.

"Don't call him names!"

"Who's talking to you, Concha?"

Before we left them we agreed to meet later that night. We would either work on the peep hole, or find a loose stake.

Toward evening we met near the alley. Mundo, the most experienced of the gang (he was always in trouble), began to give orders. "When the circus starts,' he began, 'me, Beto, and Virgie will find a stake and yank it up, okay? Concha and you can be the lookouts." He jabbed me in the chest and said "And ya better look out!" I winced but said nothing, determined not to act like a baby.

Josey was the youngest and most pliable of the gang. He was dispatched to get my father's lug wrench in the garage. As Josey ran off, the others disappeared behind the tent. Concha and I waited for what seemed to be hours, fearful that Don Crispín, the watchman, would make the rounds and catch us red-handed. Concerned about Josey, I dashed across the darkened alley and bumped into him.

"What happened?"

"He heard me!" Josey gulped. "My father was en el excusado. He came out of the toilet and almost saw me. I hid in the nopales and now I'm full of stickers." Josey rubbed his rear end and started to cry.

"What about the wrench?" I hissed. "Did you get it or not?" I shook Josey, angry at him for being so stupid and for wanting more attention than he deserved.

"I almost got caught," he whined, the wrench clutched in his small hand. His frightened eyes and the stain between his pant legs were proof enough of how scared he really was.

"Gimme the wrench," hissed Mundo, coming around the tent.

"But I almost gots caught," shouted Josey, wanting Mundo to credit him with something. "I almost . . ."

"That's 'cause you're stuped," retorted Mundo. "I never gets caught!"

"You're mean," cried a brave Virgie. "You're so mean . . ."

"Says who?" Mundo moved in close, his eyes squinting in the evening light.

Josey slipped the wrench from under his pant leg and handed it to Mundo, then put his hand in mine. Mundo, Beto, and Virgie then took off. From afar I saw them tip-toe around the tent, taking care to avoid un hoyo; more than once a mudhole had been my undoing.

I knew every inch of the field. I had played there from infancy, and even in the dark I knew where the soft dirt lay. I tried to take the lead, but Mundo pushed me back. Josey, still wet in the pants, hid behind my dress. Concha clung to Beto; Virgie yanked at her socks. Just then the music from the tent became louder.

"Here." Mundo had found the loose stake and wanted us to know it. He pulled on the bent stake as he dug the point of his shoe into the dirt. Concha bent over to help.

"That it, Mundo?"

"Shhh. You want the old man to hear us?"

Virgie's nose was smudged with dirt, her hair, freed from the French braid, hung across her sweaty face. Mundo pulled and pulled at the stake, then beckoned to Beto.

"Girls don't know how to do nuthin. Come on, Beto, pull when I count to three. One, two, . . ."

"I gotta pee," cried Josey, clutching his crotch.

"You scared, Josey?" asked Concha, holding out her hand.

"Ujule," hissed Mundo, "you acting just like a girl. Always having to go . . ."

"I gotta make chi," wailed Josey, heading for the bushes.

"Chi, pee. Whatcha come for if all you wanna do is piss?"

Mundo was furious at us and at the stuck stake. By the time Josey returned, the loose stake was marked by a circle of rocks. Josey ran to return the wrench, alert for any noise near the outhouse. We held one last huddle. Josey and I still had our tickets (Doña Luisa, moved to tears by Josey's cries had bought him one). We went into the big top, while our friends bided their time.

Once the music began, I scrambled toward the bottom row, ready for the gang. I felt nervous and tense, alert for any movement from the tent flap. I pretended to listen as Mr. Talamante flipped the whip to and fro, then smoothed his pretty moustache. I kept one eye on him, the other on the tent bottom. Afterward Virgie told me what had happened.

When the trumpeter announced the beginning of the show, Concha was put on guard. Virgie and Mundo moved aside the rocks and loosened the tent stake. "Mundo and I couldn't find the pile," Virgie said. "Beto was gone and Concha went to get a sweater."

"It's up to us," Mundo grumbled to Virgie, angry at having to depend on a girl. They found the rock pile but were so preoccupied with the stake that they forgot to watch for Don Crispín. Just as he rounded the tent, Mundo saw the glow of his lantern. He pulled Virgie behind a pile of alfalfa; they waited until it was safe again.

Don Crispín was an expert at this cat-and-mouse game, which is why he was hired for the job. But Mundo knew his adversary quite well; more than once he had outguessed and outrun him. He now vowed to outwit Don Crispín again.

Like most men of his generation, Don Crispín could not understand why Mundo was allowed to roam the streets at will. Once at las fiestas patrias, the sixteenth of September celebrations, Don Crispín caught Mundo stealing candy. He marched Mundo, his face smeared with chocolate, straight to his grandmother, who looked at Don Crispín with irritation and at Mundo with wonder.

"Ay, no! Not my grandson!"

"Doña Chepa, es verdad! It's the truth!"

"But he was here the whole time, no Mundito?"

"Sí granma. I was here all the time."

The minute Don Crispín stalked off, Mundo's grandmother handed him a shiny quarter with which to buy more dulces.

That fateful night, while Virgie kept an eye out for the watchman, Mundo scurried back to the tent. By now Concha and Beto had returned and had heard the story of Don Crispín. Time was running out; if they were to catch the show, they would have to act now! Just then the tent stake came out.

"We did it!"

"*I* did it, stuped. Come on, let's . . ."

Mundo insisted on being first. "I'm faster," he bragged, a thing no one could refute (his own father, it was said, could never catch him). That's why he was our leader.

"You follow," he hissed at Virgie. "And don't make no noise."

"I won't," promised Virgie, shaking dust from her dress.

"Me neither," whispered Concha, her face white with worry.

Mundo hunched down, lifted the tent stake, and with a swift, practiced movement went under and into the tent full of screaming spectators.

When it was her turn, Concha began to sniffle. "I'm gonna get caught," she cried to Virgie, "I'm gonna get caught." The minute Mundo left, everyone lost courage. Cheered on by Beto, who promised to meet her on the other side, Concha scooped up the flap—and was startled to find herself instantly on the other side. Only Virgie and Beto were left.

Once Virgie had disappeared under the tent, Beto prepared to do the same. He was about to crawl under, when he saw Don Crispín coming toward him at a fast trot. In desperation he yanked the tent and was halfway under, when he felt a hand pulling at his belt.

"Well, son, what do you think you're doing?"

"Nuthin."

"Andale. Out of here!"

Don Crispín walked Beto to the open field, then went in search of Mundo. Beto was embarrassed and frightened. The watchman, he was certain, had taken out his anger toward Mundo on him. He pretended to leave, then returned to alert Mundo with a shrill whistle, but the music drowned him out.

I sat inside the big top, twitching nervously in my seat. It was disappointing not to be with everyone else. I made an effort to concentrate on the music and tapped my foot to the beat. Just then up went the tent flap—and in popped Mundo. Right behind him came a grinning Concha. I quickly made room for them on the bench. They looked relieved to be on the other side. In the confusion that was part of this last performance, Virgie's appearance a short time later went unnoticed. I wondered about Beto's whereabouts, but only for a short time. There was little to harm him in our small town. My attention shifted to los músicos: a trumpeter, a drummer, and a saxaphone player, all in faded tuxedos.

Among the musicians was Don Rojelio R. During the day he worked as a butcher; on weekends he played the tuba at weddings and *jamaicas,* and in September, at las fiestas patrias. As a trained musician, he fit in with most groups.

When Don Rogelio played, his cheeks puffed in and out, as sweat poured down his round face. When he sat down, he practically disappeared behind the large tuba but his loud grunts could still be heard. The grunts I noticed, in between giggles, blended with the music that poured out of the huge shiny instrument; it was hard to tell where one began and the other left off!

"Hí jo 'mano! He sure looks funny!"

"Shhhh. He's looking this way!"

"So what?"

"He might tell my father!"

Suddenly the music changed tempo; the performers entered from the left. Dressed in bright red and yellow, the clowns led the parade. They turned somersaults and kicked at each other. They were followed by the three trapeze artists: Rocco, Farita, and Jasmín. All wore costumes topped with a long, flowing cape. The women wore strapless outfits splattered with shiny sequins, their faces encrusted with mascara, rouge, and lipstick. They twisted and turned every which way, smiled at the gaping crowd, and joined the parade.

Las trapecistas resembled Mexican women, with their dark hair and dark eyes fringed with thick lashes. I thought them most exotic. They were from Arabia. Up until that time I had thought that only Mexicans lived in Mexico, until someone told me the two clowns were polacos. Of the two women, Jasmín was younger and the most friendly. As she went by, she grinned and waved enthusiastically at us. Farita smiled at the men.

I knew Jasmín slightly. One day while the circus was still in town, I was sent to the store to buy French bread. I was in a hurry, so I cut across the alley, forgetting that the circus was encamped in the back lot. I was about to turn around when Jasmín came out of a trailer, smiled, and beckoned to me. I walked over, eager to be seen with the star of the circus. We talked for a time, or rather, Jasmín talked while I stared at her face, which without makeup looked pale, lined. She sensed my astonishment and quickly rubbed on rouge.

"I like to let my skin breathe," she explained. "I never wear makeup during the day, only at night." She was very friendly and invited me to come again. I was in such a dither that I forgot about the bread.

A few days later I crossed the open field and ended up in what appeared to be the kitchen area. Jasmín and Farita, both in costume, sat around a table, finishing up the dinner dishes. Farita washed while Jasmín rinsed. They greeted me cordially, asked me to stay, and offered me a peppermint candy. We sat down to talk; I tried to make polite conversation. Mostly, though, I watched Jasmín as she attempted to mend a hole in a purple costume. She neither knew how to hold the material nor the needle and kept pricking her fingers and mumbling: "Ay sonavavichi!"

I feared that Jasmín might hurt her fingers and miss the trapeze, so I offered to mend it for her.

All the women in my family sewed; Elizabet even made her own patterns! Now and then I would mend a torn slip and hem a pinafore. Anxious to please Jasmín, I adjusted my dress, then took the glittery costume and turned it inside out. I was appalled to see the row of safety pins that held it together. I was not allowed to use seguros on my clothes, but sewed all tears with matching thread. I looked around for purple thread, but all I saw was a spool of black. Ugly black. I took a deep breath, pinned the rip together, threaded a small needle (a large one would have made a bigger stitch), tied a short knot at one end, and stitched away. Jasmín stood over me, delighted at the way I worked the needle. She smelled of verbena; her perfume floated above my head. I inhaled, giddy with happiness. Jasmín and I were now good friends. When it was finished, I handed the purple outfit (mended in black) to Jasmín, who thanked me in a soft, melodious voice. As I neared the alley on my way home, I looked back to see the two trapecistas drying the dinner dishes.

Soon I began to drop by Jasmín's trailer after school. Concha and Beto, curious to know her, came too. One day Mundo slithered along, as if by mistake. He was there to stare at Jasmín and to make nasty remarks.

"Ujule, casi asustan sin la mascara," he snickered, thinking I could not hear. "They sure look scary without their masks." Then looking directly at Jasmín, he added: "And she ain't got no chichis!"

"Uhh," muttered a blushing Beto, staring at his feet.

"She is too pretty!" countered Concha.

"Yeah, but she ain't got no titties. She needs Kleenex. Ha, ha, ha."

"No she doesn't," I interjected. "Jasmín is perfect!" I was embarrassed by Mundo's remarks, but suspected that what he said was true. During a performance Jasmín looked curvaceous, but she was less so out of costume. Sometimes in fact she looked as flat as a pancake. Girls on Hoyt Street stuffed Kleenex in a bra to make them look bustier. Still I was content to admire Jasmín and ready to dislike those who did not. That night when Jasmín drew near, I took a big breath and yelled, "Hooray for Jasmín." I clapped for the dark-eyed trapecista in admiration and in gratitude for her friendship.

The circus continued. "Everything is so perfect," grinned Virgie, once Beto had surprised us with his belated appearance (he had pretended to go home). "And here come the ponies!"

The bareback riders were also said to be árabes. Slender, with black hair and deep, dark eyes, they were most handsome! Their white outfits resembled the long johns worn by my father in cold weather. Astride the long-haired white ponies, dark hair flying, the Arabs flew by. They looked calm and secure, with not a care in the world.

Although the entrance parade was only to introduce all performers to el público, the two were intent on charming the crowd. In time with the music, they alternated between the ponies with precise, calculated jumps. One rode between the two ponies, one of his long legs on each horse's rump. He rode around the tent as the crowd went wild, then joined his partner and left the ring.

The one elephant came next, a lone rider seated on the gray, wrinkled neck. The elephant, I decided, was not all that exciting, but Virgie clapped loudly. The organ-grinder and his monkey followed, as did the hangers-on, people who did nothing important, including "el pavo," "the peacock," an elderly man who brought up the rear. He carried a pail and shovel with which to pick up any excrement dropped by the excited animals. The circus workers, whose job it was to clean each animal's rectum, often forgot.

The jugglers, two chunky men with curly hair, were the opening act. Their one-piece outfits were like those worn by the clowns, except for the black and white harlequin checks; all they lacked was a red nose. They stood until certain of the crowd's attention, then bowed and began to juggle large bowling pins. The crowd applauded politely. They juggled what looked like large tennis balls, keeping them in the air for a long time. Up and down went the balls, as the jugglers bent their checkered bodies to catch them; they were quite good. Whenever one dropped a ball, however, the crowd screamed:

"Pendejo!"

"Do it again!"

"Butterfingers."

Our section was filled with the loudest and rowdiest kids, all of whom lived on Hoyt Street. We roared with laughter while screaming insults, a winning combination, learned from experience. Our leader Mundo yelled louder than anyone else. He was quite inventive and original.

"Mentolato."

"Surumato."

We rocked with laughter until we ran out of names. The jugglers were a mere diversion from the most important acts; we applauded, then waited for the next performers.

Los títeres worked the crowds in between the various acts. While they were funny, the three clowns were also clever. They told corny jokes, usually in Spanish, and pretended to fart.

They pinched each other on the bottom, or as Mundo pointed out, en las de Bugs Bunny. They were funny, very funny. They played to older people, those who appreciated their stale jokes. Everyone laughed at the big-nosed, apple-cheeked clowns jumping about the brightly lit tent. As he had with the jugglers, Mundo called out in his best Spanish:

Péquele en las nalgas!"

"Hit 'im again, hit 'im again!"

Each time they smacked one another on the head, the drummer would hit the cymbals: *clang, clang, boom!* They exited the tent as the tired drummer echoed their antics.

When the trapeze artists, Jasmín in the lead, came into view, the crowd went wild. Once I caught sight of her pretty face, I jabbed Concha in the ribs, then jumped to my feet, screaming at full volume. They were my favorite act and the most dangerous. Rocco wore a sky-blue outfit that I had not seen before. Jasmín was in fuschia; Farita wore chartreuese, with a rhinestone tiara on her dark head. Jasmín, I saw, wore a creamy gardenia. Both women looked beautiful, exotic, just like árabes were supposed to. Heads held high, shoulders straight, they glided to the center of the tent and bowed. I clapped and clapped, unable to contain myself. Virgie felt she would pee; Concha said she might throw up. Behind me people yelled "sit down." I reluctantly hit the bench.

All eyes were on the women, whose dresses had short, short skirts and low-cut bodices. We could see their sweaty, round breasts, augmented, I suspected, by Kleenex.

"Casi enseñan las nalgas! They're showing their asses," the rowdies cried. Next to them old women, many of them ardent churchgoers and aghast at the skimpy outfits, crossed themselves and murmured, "Jesús, María, y José!"

The men, all of whom knew a good thing when they saw it, craned their heads to get a better look. Doña Susana pinched her husband, angry at him for staring at Jasmín. Next to her Don Cartucho blushed a deep red, certain that Farita was looking straight at him.

Los trapecistas circled the tent and smiled, assured of the crowd's devotion. Then they sauntered to the middle of the tent, bowed to the audience, and with practiced grace removed their satin capes and handed them to a pale assistant, who in turn bowed to them as if to royalty.

As the musicians played a waltz, the three quickly climbed the rope ladders that rose above the crowd, then stood on a small platform. They tested the swings, setting the correct rhythm, then off they flew.

Rocco remained on the perch, while Jasmín and Farita flew to and fro, legs swinging through the air. This was repeated several times, until at a given signal, Farita remained on the swing. The tiara glittered on her dark head.

Now the real fun began. Rocco poised a muscular blue leg to test the swing. Satisfied he jumped onto it and swung toward Jasmín.

I held my breath, Virgie dropped her snowcone, Concha began to whine. Above us Jasmín turned a full circle. She clasped hands with

Rocco, who was swinging in the middle, then with Farita, and finally returned to the tiny perch, her face flushed a deep pink. Against the blue of the canvas that resembled a summer sky, Jasmín passed back and forth above the cheering throng.

"Hijo 'mano! She's gonna fall," gasped Virgie, as syrup ran down her arm.

"She's too dumb to fall."

"Shut up Mundo!"

Los trapecistas twirled in midair. Once more Jasmín broke away to swing back and forth. Like a bright pink bird, she flew from one ledge to the other, as the crowd below held its collective breath. Then it was Farita's turn. She smiled, kicked the trapeze free, then executed a double flip almost as effortlessly as Jasmín. She repeated this, smiling all the while, her hair as bright as a Fourth-of-July sparkler. Finally she finished, then slithered down the ropes. Round breasts bobbing, she jumped to the ground, the chartreuese costume hanging on for dear life.

The three bowed to the crowd, donned their capes, then exited the tent, as the crowd thundered its approval.

The bareback riders were next. They entered the arena at a fast trot, eyes riveted on the ponies, white outfits clinging to their firm, trim bodies. They were tall and graceful, and moved in concert with the music, a lively Viennese waltz. These skillful horsemen always gave a good performance; on this last night, they literally stopped the show.

I gave my full attention to them as they circled the wide tent in perfect rhythm. They switched horses with ease, their feet firmly planted on the ponies' backs. Round and round they went, two magnificent árabes astride two lively ponies. Each held in his hand a whip, which he twirled, then flipped at a pony.

I sat enthralled as they rounded the corner at full speed. Suddenly the taller of the two lost his footing and fell to the ground. The crowd fell silent. He got up, brushed the dirt off his white pants, then ran after the animal. Face flushed a deep red, dark hair in disarray, he muttered curses at the horse. He caught up with it, but the animal, eyes bulging and nostrils flaring, took off at a fast trot. Once more the rider chased the pony. This continued for some time, with the crowd cheering for horse and for rider.

The furious rider made one last attempt to catch the frightened animal. He slid forward, whip in hand, raised one leg as if to mount, but the horse neighed and ran off again.

Once more the crowd, including the rowdies now clogging the aisles, jeered and made catcalls at the bareback rider. "He'll never catch him!" said a smug Mundo, while Virgie pitied the frightened pony.

White suit streaked with dirt, dark eyes wide and wild, the rider chased after the horse. Finally he increased his speed and caught up with the sweating pony.

He began to whip the pony. The long black whip rose and fell with great ferocity. The outraged crowd gaped; the beating of animals was not tolerated in the barrio. The white horse came to a complete stop. The fallen rider was exhausted from the beating, but kept trying to mount el caballito. Just then the horse let go a spray of excrement, saturating the pale rider.

The crowd screamed its approval; I jumped up and down. The tent was a mass of jeering spectators. Parents held children on their shoulders to see the spectacle. Doña Susana fanned her agitated face; Don Cartucho grinned and wiped his brow. The fallen rider, covered from head to toe with cagada, headed out a side exit.

We screamed our delight. This was more than I had expected. The crowd began to chant: "Quieremos 'el cagado,'" we want 'el cagado'!" Our bench was by far the loudest. Mundo yelled at the top of his lungs; Beto, beanie dangling across his face, jumped up and down. Concha appeared to gag on her popcorn; Virgie pounded her back. It was a real circus!

As if by magic, el pavo appeared with the pail and shovel, as the band struck up el barrilito, the "Beer Barrel Polka." But the crowd would not be appeased. The lone rider attempted to continue with the performance, but the ponies ran around without direction. The rowdies, led by Mundo, kept shouting: "Quiremos 'el cagado.' Que salga 'el cagado.'"

His face a sickly gray, el Señor Talamante tried to control the mob. He adjusted his jacket, smoothed his pretty moustache, then strode to the microphone.

"Ladies and gentlemens, we beg your indulgence for . . ." But his voice was lost in the crowd. He announced the next act, then signaled to the musicians. The crowd, however, was still savoring the last act; we would not be silenced. Finally the clamor subsided; the show continued to its conclusion. We rose to cheer the artists: clowns, tumblers, Farita, Jasmín, and Rocco. 'El cagado,' who had given an extraordinary performance, was nowhere to be seen.

As we left the tent, we discussed the night's events. Mundo was still making up names, but couldn't improve on "el cagado." Virgie ran to the bathroom, while Concha took off with Beto. I searched the crowd for Jasmín and pulled away from Josey. At the tent door, Don Crispín smiled.

The story of "el cagado" would be repeated for a long, long, time; at least until the next year, when once more we would welcome el Circo Talamante to town.

KNOWLEDGE

El Padre Mickey

When I was about eleven, the Reverend Richard S. Mueller, O.M.I., was assigned to Guardian Angel Church. His arrival was an exciting event, for although we loved our old pastor, Father Juanito, he had old-fashioned ideas about everything. The coming of this new priest, a young and energetic man, greatly influenced my life. While I loved everything connected with church, from singing in the choir to catechism, I now was eager to join one of the many youth clubs proposed by our new pastor.

Father Mueller was in his early thirties, about six feet tall, and slender, with bright blue eyes and sandy brown hair. He came to us straight from a Mexican parish in Texas, where he had perfected the fluent Spanish he now spoke. He had nice white teeth, a ruddy complexion, and big ears that stuck out; they turned a bright pink when he was angry or upset. I tried not to stare at them, but did anyway.

I don't recall exactly when he arrived, but I was terribly happy when one warm Sunday he prayed mass, his voice loud and clear. When afterward he asked to meet the parishoners, I elbowed my way to the front of the line, nearly squashing Doña Chonita, and coyly introduced myself.

"Hmmmm, in French your name would be Marie Hélène," he smiled, his kind eyes crinkling at the corners, "but in Spanish you are María Elena."

"Gosh," I whispered to Concha. "He can talk in French, too!"

"He's cute," giggled Nancy, hiking up her socks.

"But he's a priest," explained Virgie, giving Nancy a fixed look.

Father Mueller played the piano! A priest who played piano was a real novelty in the parish. On Hoyt Street most folks strummed tinny-sounding guitars while singing rancheras or boleros, except for Don Rojelio, who played the tuba. I was fascinated by this gringo priest who not only spoke our language but played a mean boogie-woogie. Wow! Our former padre, slightly deaf in one ear, rarely rang the church bell on time, let alone played jazz. Father Mueller was a dream come true: young, idealistic, and full of innovative ideas. The perfect parish priest.

Among the first things he did was replace the church organ, said to be as old as the church. He personally selected an instrument replete with pedals, switches, and two separate keyboards. As a trained musician, Father Mueller delighted in playing the shiny, elegant organ, and could make it sound like a cello or violin. His long tapered fingers slid over the keys, then thumped up and down as he played the boogie-woogie. I thought it scandalous for jazz to resonate inside a church, but Father Mueller only laughed aloud and kept on playing.

Music was important to our young pastor. He once explained that priests studied not only theology, but other subjects as well. At the seminary he had minored in music—not classical music, but jazz! He also had a special interest in Gregorian chants and music by Palestrina. I was not surprised when soon after installing the fancy organ in the choir loft, our pastor announced that he had hired an organist-choirmistress. Because of the new organ, and with the addition of a choirmistress, membership in the church choir quickly increased.

Jenny G., as the choirmistress was named, was a short, motherly Italian woman with dark hair and brown eyes, who smiled alot. She immediately fit in and became fast friends with the female singers, most of whom thought she was una mejicana. With Father Mueller's approval, she ordered new St. Gregory Himnals (which the choir members bought for five dollars each), and attempted to teach us the rudiments of music. Each Thursday evening, right before el rosario, the church resonated with voices: male, female, old, young. All of us were eager to please our leader.

Prior to this Father Mueller had attempted to teach us to read music. He soon gave up. Jennie would not. She bravely guided us through the musical scale and urged us to memorize signature notes and musical terms: *staccato, legato, forté, pianissimo*. Musical notes,

Jennie explained, brown eyes crinkling, are like money; each has a certain value. This made sense to me, but the older women, such as Doña Martita, found it too difficult to memorize whole notes, half notes. She then tried a different approach. She first played the music as written, then explained how she would like it to sound. Finally (in desperation) she waited to hear our interpretation.

We rose to the occasion. Young voices rose on cue; elderly viejitas gasped for air. During Lent we learned "Adoramuste Christe" (page 204A), "Vidi Aquam," and my favorite: "Regina Coeli." We practiced diligently. That first year we sang the Easter Sunday mass as it had never been heard in our church before. The choir grew as did our repertoire, partly as a token of goodwill toward the choirmistress, but more out of love and respect for our pastor.

Father Mueller settled into our parish with ease. He took over the small rectory attached to the church and fixed it up. The rectory was most unattractive, with dark mahogany furniture, dank smelly wallpaper, a worn rug spread over the wood floor, and a dim lamp that shone upward, toward God. Within weeks Father Mueller had spruced up the house; in the main room he installed an important-looking desk, plump chairs, and a small sofa.

"This," Father Mueller announced, his blue eyes aglow, "will be the reception area. From here," pointing to his desk, "I will greet parishoners and visitors alike." He let us try out the chairs, dial the new phone (with the eraser end of a pencil, so as not to scratch), ring the new doorbell, and even sit behind his desk! When it was my turn, I felt terribly important and refused to get off the chair until Father Mueller fixed me with his steely eyes.

The renovation of the rectory ended with the front room; little or nothing was done to the rest of the house, certainly nothing that I could tell. Father Mueller was evidently on a budget; the other rooms would have to wait. Next to the reception room was a small hallway, a tiny bathroom, and an adjoining room with a solitary bed. This was Father Mueller's bedroom, a place we were not allowed to enter. I peeked inside when he wasn't looking, and was surprised to see atop a bureau, a framed picture *not* of Jesus or the Virgin Mary, but of Duke Ellington! Jesus, Mary, and Joseph! Much later Father Mueller told us that "the Duke," was his hero. He didn't use the word *idol,* because to idolize anyone other than Jesus was a mortal sin! But I think that was what he meant.

I don't recall a rectory kitchen. After all, a priest was not expected to cook or wash dishes. His job was to preach about hell and damnation, hear confessions, give communion, ring the church bell, and recite the prayers for the dead. As had his predecessor, Father Mueller took his meals with Doña María, an elderly widow who lived in a clean, stucco house across from the church. My friends and I agreed that this was the right thing for a young priest to do: take meals with a clean, orderly woman like Doña María, who it was said never wore an apron more than once.

Father Mueller was so different from padre Juanito. For one thing he did not wear a hearing aid, nor was he French (although he knew the language). He was German-American and spoke Spanish by choice. He smiled a lot and never stopped working.

He drove a black 1946 Ford with shiny chrome rims. The car was said to be a gift from his dear mother. He drove like a teenager, turning corners on two wheels. Some of the "fuddy-duddies" who lived on our street felt that the car was not appropriate for a Catholic priest. It was too new, too sharp, too fast! But the car suited Father Mueller to a T. It was modern; he was modern, hep to the jive! In it he dashed around our dusty streets to visit the sick, to Los Angeles to rent cowboy movies (shown at the church hall), and, on his day off, to go to the beach.

Father Mueller never discussed his trips to the beach, but kids on Hoyt Street did. We thrived on gossip. Secrets were hard to keep or hide. Everyone knew what days our pastor had free, the time at which he drove up, and even when the rectory lights went off. When they spotted his sunburn, folks concluded he had been at the beach. Father Mueller's burnt face and ears gave him away, as did his freckled arms. The idea of our priest sunning in Malibu left us kids reeling.

"Isn't that a mortal sin?"

"Gosh, I hope they don't send him back to Texas."

I had never known a priest who went to the beach. Certainly not Father Juanito nor the brown-robed missionaries who each year came to preach. It meant that Father Mueller went in the water.

Which meant he had to remove his clothes and put on swimming trunks! Ave María Purísima! But when parishoners (and critics) began to see the results of our young pastor's hard work, they chose to disregard his outings to the beach.

Although Father Mueller was not truly handsome, he had a friendly smile. His huge ears, ears that stuck out from his thin, ascetic face, fascinated me. When he caught me staring, he would explain, in a bantering but embarrassed tone, that they stuck out because when he was in Texas (where he trained at a seminary), he wore a cowboy hat every day. The hat, he insisted, blushing somewhat, had permanently altered his ears, which is why they now stuck out. I chose to believe him. Each time he told this story, his ears turned a rosy pink.

Not everyone liked our new pastor. The pachucos, tough guys who constantly beat each other up, swore to get him. Young women thought him cute but distant. Teenagers like my sister Trina thought him stuck up; Josey liked his neat car. The old ladies, including the Trinidads, adored him and each evening vied at sending him bocaditos wrapped in snowy dish towels: tortillas, tacos, and warm bread.

I thought he was hep! Nancy liked his blue eyes, while Concha liked his light hair. Yet we were all in awe of the big ears. Within weeks the rowdies took to calling Father Mueller "el Mickey Mouse." Even my brother Norbert, who acted tough when our father was not present, snickered and called him "el padre Mickey."

"I think it's funny."

"You're gonna go to hell!"

Our energetic, innovative pastor was committed to change, both inside the church and throughout the parish. Once the rectory was to his liking, he focused on reorganizing the existing church clubs. The Holy Name Society continued as before; once a month the body of elderly men marched into church behind a white banner to receive holy communion. The women of the Altar Society remained in charge of the church altars, all of which were periodically dusted and polished to a bright sheen. Older boys, even rowdies like Mundo, who hated going to church but feared being left out of things, volunteered as altar boys. Virgie, Concha, and I joined the newly formed Stella Maris Club.

The SM Club (as we soon called it) was an offshoot of an older organization, the JCFM (Juventud Católica Feminina Mexicana), affiliated with chapter groups throughout southern California. Its purpose was to bring together "nice" Mexican girls under the auspices of la santa madre iglesia. The JCFM held a yearly conference in Los Angeles, which we attended in a body. What I liked most about this group was the club uniform.

The uniform consisted of a white blouse, navy skirt, navy and white cape, and a matching beanie. I was lucky to have my sister Elizabet sew both my cape and beanie on her sewing machine; she lined each in white! Girls who lacked a uniform wore their best clothes: starched cotton dresses and large ribbons or bright scarves on their heads. We wore snowy white anklets and polished oxfords on our feet.

My older sisters had, at one time or another, belonged to the JCFM, so I got to borrow their hats. Elizabet once was president; Nora only made it to vice-president. It seems that Nora, the prettiest of all my pretty sisters, was outvoted by homlier club members. Although the JCFM was at that time the only club of its kind on the Mexican side of Pacoima, some teenagers, Trina among them, refused to join, saying it was only for "squares."

The JCFM began to fall apart during Father Juanito's tenure. Young women had other things to do, many of which were part of the "war effort." They took part in "canteens" sponsored by local organizations, for instance, where they got to flirt and dance with lonely soldiers. Rather than join the JCFM and sit in a stuffy church hall while an elderly priest espoused the virtues a pure life, they went off to have fun! It was not surprising that the original girl's club disintegrated. Thus, when Father Mueller proposed an organization for the younger girls, we were ripe and ready.

Father Mueller suggested both the club and the club name. Young girls should in all things emulate the Virgin Mary, he often said. He took special pride in his credentials, explaining that O.M.I. stood for Oblates of Mary Immaculate, a select order based in Texas. He alluded to the Virgin Mary as the Star of the Sea, Stella Maris. The natural choice for followers of Mary Immaculate was to name the club in her honor. We readily agreed.

While I considered a uniform to be the first order of business,

Father Mueller felt otherwise; the clubmembers wore what they had: school clothes or Sunday dresses. Nancy, always different, insisted on wearing the JCFM cape over her starched dress. She would waltz into church, swirling the cape to and fro, just like a bullfighter.

A meeting day was selected; elections were held. We learned parliamentary procedure and were given a bound blue book in which to record the club minutes. Dues were set at 25 cents a week. By the second meeting, it was clear that ours was not to be a service club. We would not have to visit the poor, nor collect clothes for the naked children in Africa. Our most important function, we soon learned, was not unlike that of the JCFM: to attend mass and take Holy Communion as a group each first Sunday of the month.

"I wanted to do something different."

"Shhhh, we have to obey!"

Thereafter each first Sunday of the month I woke up early, gulped down my oatmeal, dressed in my best clothes, then went off to be with the other members of the Stella Maris Club. We formed a line at the church entrance, fighting to be at the front of the procession. As we did not have a club standard, we walked up the aisle with the palms of our hands together, looking neither right nor left. Once we reached the front, we sat in the pews reserved for us, proud to have everyone know we belonged to such a select club. At the main altar, dressed in his Sunday best, ears a bright pink, Father Mueller beamed his approval. We were the first fruits of his labor; the future of the parish.

The Stella Maris Club met Wednesday evenings at the church hall. The meetings began promptly at 7:30 with a solemn prayer, in which we implored the Virgin Mary to be our guide in all things. After mumbling the prayer, heads bowed, eyes downcast, the president convened the meeting. That first year Emily Lopez was elected president. She was sort of stuck up; she planned to be a nun. Virgie was elected secretary. But when it became clear that she could barely spell, she was replaced by Elvira, who got straight As at Pacoima Elementary. Concha, who was good at numbers, was elected treasurer. I felt that she was the right choice for that position. When we traded bottles at the corner store, Concha knew to the penny how much we were owed. I was made sargeant at arms because I was tall and strong. Hefty, in fact. I took my job seriously and did not allow too much levity (a new word I had just learned) or horsing around. I paid dearly for this attitude during street games.

Throughout the year Stella Maris Club members took part in numerous events and many boring jobs. We dusted the church, sorted and filed dusty sheet music in the choir loft, and did other minuscule jobs of little importance to us but of great importance to Father Mueller.

"Our Blessed Mother appreciates any and all efforts," he often remarked. "Nothing is too small when done for Our Lady."

"Amen!"

While I helped dust the church, I counted the days until summer and the church bazaars, las jamaicas, when the entire town celebrated.

The church bazaars were important to our parish and had been held even in the old days, during Father Juanito's era. They were a Mexican tradition and rarely varied. But the best jamaicas took place while Father Mueller was our pastor. He had great intuition about what items sold best, what booths most attracted a crowd, and best of all, how to make money. He assigned each parish organization to certain booths and tasks.

The elderly women who lived on Hoyt Street, such as Doña Luisa and the three Trinidads did not belong to any particular organization; they didn't have to! They practically lived in church! But during Father Juanito's time, they were given specific jobs and made to feel important, part of the community: they were in charge of making and selling tamales. Each Saturday morning, while pork and red chile simmered on the stove, the viejitas mixed the ground corn meal called nixtamal on the huge kitchen tables. They spread masa on corn husks, filled them with meat and chile, then steam-cooked the tamales in time for the evening meal. They took pride in being able to contribute to the success of the bazaars, although they often squabbled among themselves.

"Not so much salt."

"Do we have anise?"

"Sí!"

Then one day, without flinching, Father Mueller announced that the elderly women would no longer make tamales. From now on, he intoned, avoiding Doña Luisa's eyes, the tamales would be made under the direction of Doña Gertrudis. He did not elaborate, but it was inferred that the viejitas were too old and slow to respond to customers. I was outraged at this insult to Doña Luisa and her friends, many of whom had worked in the bazaars for years. Our cost-conscious pastor then reassigned the women to sweep and dust the church!

Doña Gertrudis, an old busybody, had snitched to Father Mueller that the women were wasting meat. They refused to make skimpy tamales, so they generously filled each corn husk with un buen pedazo de carne. A good chunk of meat, the women knew, ensured a good tamale.

Another reason for the women's fall from grace, one never spoken aloud, was that the senoras were generous to hungry kids who hung around the kitchen during the bazaars. More than once Doña Luisa had slipped me a sugar tamale. If the women saw someone looking hungry, they gave them the tamales that had come apart in the pot and could not be sold as whole. When she heard the announcement, Doña Luisa said not a word, but her dark eyes spoke volumes. She so delighted in giving me free tamales; it was her happiness—and mine.

The women survived la vergüenza and in time forgave Doña Gertrudis, all except Doña Caridad, who never spoke to her again. I swore to trip Doña Gertrudis in church, knock her to the ground! But I never did. Mostly I glared at her while paying for a sugar tamale.

Everyone worked during the bazaars. The men were in charge of las sodas, card games, and the chipping of ice for snowcones. They arrived at the churchgrounds dressed in cotton pants and work shirts, ready to work. On their feet were the everyday boots, now brushed clean. They hauled two-by-fours from a nearby pile and constructed the bazaar booths. All were the same size, except the goldfish throw, which was wide enough to accommodate the kids who each wanted an orange fish in a bowl. Once finished with the booths, the men took the wood, hammer, and nails to build la cárcel, the "jail" booth that was the number one money-maker.

Throughout the evening of a bazaar, men were jokingly "abducted," then locked inside the "jail" until they paid a fine. Much to the delight of the kids, those without funds were forced to languish inside the booth until someone, usually a relative, paid the small fine. The pachucos, who during the jamaicas dressed to kill, were familiar with el bote; they stayed clear of this booth. But the cárcel was only for men. No women were ever abducted, although I would gladly have pushed Doña Gertrudis inside and locked the door tight.

By noon the men had lugged crates of sodas to the food booths and had hauled blocks of ice from the icehouse in San Fernando. The ice, wrapped in burlap, was trucked home in a dusty old pickup, dumped into a zinc tub, arranged around the soda cans, then shaved for the snowcones.

The older boys helped set up too; even the rowdies forgot to make fun of "el Padre Mickey." Eager to attract the giggling girls who went by every five minutes, they swept, then hosed down the booth and patio next to the kitchen, where people would eat warm tamales and enchiladas. Once the churchgrounds were spotless, the boys attached palm fronds to the roof and sides of the game booths. From afar, each booth looked like a tropical paradise, or so Father Mueller implied. The booth name was written in dark pencil, then secured to the top of the structure, where it could be seen by one and all. DARTS. GOLDFISH. They made sure to spell each name correctly. At one time Beto wrote *sudas* rather than *sodas;* the kids from Hoyt Street never let him forget it.

Mundo and Beto blew up balloons, cut up miles of crepe paper, then hung the colored streamers across the booths. In between they punched each other, at first in fun, then in earnest, until someone called, "Here comes Father Mueller!"

At first the bazaars were held only on Sundays. But Father Mueller, being a man of vision and tremendous energy, was easily talked into extending the jamaicas. His enthusiasm for getting things done was contagious; everyone wanted the jamaicas to go on and on. He decided to hold the bazaars on both Saturday and Sunday because, he explained (his ears a bright red), he needed to raise money for the parish school he envisioned. We pitched in, unmindful of the work, to ensure that dream. The Stella Maris Club, determined to do our part, decided to have a cake booth.

The selling of cake slices was my idea. I had recently learned how to bake the first prepackaged cakes on the market. Cinch Cakes, the box read, are easy and inexpensive to make. Add eggs and water, mix for three minutes, pour the mix into a cake pan, then bake at 325 degrees in the oven and presto: a cake! It *was* a cinch! This was a project I felt our club could tackle, although the cakes I baked for my family always seemed to burn. I was forced to cut off the burnt sides, level off the lopsided layers with a sharp knife, then put the cake back together with toothpicks. Still when smothered with frosting, they were edible.

I soon came to regret this suggestion, as I was put in charge of buying the cake mix, eggs, and so forth. Lucky for me, my mother had credit at the grocery store. One problem was where would we bake the cakes? Our kitchen was too inconvenient; there were too many of us and meals would have to be interrupted. I appealed to Elizabet (now married and living nearby) to allow us to use her kitchen; she agreed. Thereafter, on the mornings of the jamaicas, the SM Club members baked and decorated cinch cakes.

After a time this baking became a chore. It took forever to clean up bowls, sifters, spatulas, and pans. The floor had to be swept, mopped, and everything put away. I soon tired of all this work, although we made a lot of money. At our club meeting I complained to Father Mueller; as our spiritual advisor, he insisted that I not give up on this noble cause, but get help. When several girls volunteered, I was made responsible for them, too!

From the first the baking of Cinch cakes was a contest of wills. Each of us wanted something different.

"You dummy, the box says only one egg!"

"Put in lots of vanilla."

"It's not your cake, stupid!"

"But it's my vanilla!"

We went wild and splashed food coloring on the frosting. Blue cakes, pink cakes, and one slimy green cake (Virgie's favorite color). We sprinkled on gumdrops and with tiny rolls of frosting, spelled out a boy's name. Much to our surprise, the cakes sold like hotcakes, even Virgie's green one. Once the bazaars ended and our pastor felt we had made enough money, I felt free to say "ya no!" I wanted to have fun too!

The bazaars were a time for fun and allowed familias to spend their hard-earned money for a good cause. My brother Josey and I made good use of these occasions. We stalked our brother Berney

until he was surrounded by girls, then sidled up to ask for un cinco.
He never dared refuse us, or we would snitch to our mother that he
was kissing strange girls. More importantly, Berney liked to make a
good impression on las voladas, the flirtatious young girls who hung
around him. He had to be generous with his younger siblings or appear to be a cheapskate. At home our mother often stressed that we
should not be candil de la calle, obscuridad de su casa. This dicho
meant one should not glow like a candle in public yet be a source of
darkness at home. Berney did not fail us. After we had finished with
him, Josey and I went in search of Ronnie.

At the bazaars Ronnie and her friends were surrounded by half
the male population of Pacoima. Ronnie was generous to a fault and
liked nothing better than to share her hard-earned money with her
younger siblings. She could be counted on to slip nickels and dimes
into my dress pocket. We waited until she was with friends, then in
our most winning voices and smiles, asked,

"Ronnie, Josey wants to know if . . ."

"Liar, she's the one who . . ."

"Hummm, I take it you're asking for . . ."

"Just a dime."

"How about a quarter?"

"Gosh! Thanks Ronnie. Come on Josey, let's go find . . ." If we
timed it right, we would have money the whole night. While Virgie
and Concha worked on their siblings, Josey and I begged nickels
from Doña Luisa, Berney, and Ronnie. This was great sport, almost
as much fun as watching the pachucos, dressed "to the nines," riding
by in low-slung cars with loud pipes, looking for a fight.

Now and then a fight did break out during the bazaars. Father
Mueller was careful not to antagonize the zoot-suiters, many of
whom were parishoners who only wanted to look tough to impress
the "chicks." One hot September night, however, he got fed up with
the fights that erupted in the alley; he felt they gave the bazaars a
bad name. He walked into the alley, flanked by Don Crispín and
Don Rojelio, and told the chucos to leave or he would call the cops.
The pachucos and their leader, a guy called "el Brains," tried to
jump Father Mueller, but Don Crispy interfered. They left vowing
to "get him."

The following Wednesday, on a dark, windy night, the Stella Maris

Club met. Once finished with business, we prepared to leave. We bowed our heads in prayer and waited to be blessed by our pastor. Just then a car full of pachucos rode by, "Brains" in the lead. As they approached the rectory, the car slowed down and a voice called out: "Orale, Mickey!"

I cringed with embarrassment and fear at what was coming; I knew our pastor was in for it. But Father Mueller had lived in a Texas barrio for years and was tougher than I thought. When once more the car, its pipes screaming in the night, approached the rectory, he jumped up, put out the lights, opened the hall door and ran out to the street. As the toughs went by, he shouted: "Orale cabrones." He then came inside; the meeting was resumed. Father Mueller said not a word more, but his ears, now a deep red, betrayed him.

When word got around that Father Mueller had challenged the pachucos, kids on Hoyt Street treated him with great respect. But out of carshot they still called him "el Padre Mickey."

Las Vistas

Although Pacoima was twenty-odd miles from Los Angeles and close to San Fernando, a town with three movie theaters, I rarely went to the movies. I accompanied my sisters when they shopped in town, but not to the movies. They liked to go on a Saturday night, when anyone who counted would show up. But the show was too expensive for large families such as ours. I had to be content with films shown at school, most of which were old, cracked, and boring, and the black-and-white movies screened at the church hall.

I attended las vistas, as the church-sponsored movies were called, with Doña Luisa, who although she was as poor as a churchmouse, paid my way. The movies were part of the parish activities organized by Father Mueller. He disapproved of gambling, so he did not organize bingo games. Nor was he fond of church-sponsored dances; he claimed that young people danced much too close, which led to "occasions of sin." The movies he showed were considered a harmless and proper way to bring people together, and they generated money for the school fund. For me they were great fun.

The movies were held on Sunday evenings, right after the rosary. Following benediction Father Mueller reminded all parishoners about the show that was to benefit the parish. He never gave the movie title, but mumbled something about a new, wonderful movie with leading Hollywood actors. He feared that people might recognize the title of some ancient movie. Folks in the neighborhood attended the movies out of respect and also because there was nothing else to do on Sunday evenings.

My mother, who constantly reminded us to speak proper Spanish, called the movies las películas. Doña Caridad hated words that might indicate she was uncultured and insisted that the correct word for motion pictures was *el cine*. Depending on how well they spoke el inglés, my friends liked to say they were going to el "chow." I called the movies *las vistas*, out of loyalty to Doña Luisa, who used words said to be muy rancheras.

At first I attended the church movies with a group, or with Doña Luisa. Trina refused to join us, saying they were too dull for her taste; she was a teenager. She and her friend Sally preferred the San Fernando movies. They played Frank Sinatra records on Sally's chipped record-player (you could hear the music all the way to Hoyt Street) and pretended to swoon. They experimented with "slow dancing," a style popular in the Los Angeles dancehalls, which allowed couples to hold each other close and to slide back and forth in time to the sultry music. Now and then the girls jitterbugged, twirling away for hours, until they fell to the floor from exhaustion. Once they had rested, back they went to dancing the very latest and most "hip" steps.

When she saw me changing my dress for las vistas, Trina would just snicker. "I wouldn't be caught at them old movies. It's not hep!"

"I like em."

"That's cause you're a square."

She tossed back her page boy, arched her eyebrows (just like Joan Crawford), then locked herself in the bathroom to check her makeup. In time las vistas were identified with los santuchos, the overly religious, and kids like me.

The movies were mostly westerns—old westerns, in black and white. Father Mueller drove to "Los," as we called Los Angeles, to pick up the films and assorted reels. He never explained why western movies were all he got; I figured he knew a cowboy. But since that was all he ever came up with, that's what we saw. In spite of his efforts and enthusiasm, it was difficult to mask our disappointment with the old movies.

Among my favorite western heroes were Hopalong Cassidy and Roy Rogers. El Cassidy, as Doña Luisa called him, was sort of pure. He wore a dark cowboy shirt with a fancy design and a white cowboy hat. Not only was he the "good guy," who neither swore nor started a fight, but he never kissed women! He held their hands, gazed into their blue eyes, then smiled, tipped his white hat, and rode off into the sunset. He left behind some pretty and puzzled women.

El Cassidy fought the "bad guys": Mexican bandits in torn shirts, with huge mustaches and shifty eyes. Their filthy, matted hair hung across their sweaty faces. He fought Indians too, men with swarthy complexions and sweaty bodies, who wore buckskin and feathers, and who wielded tomahawks and shot bloody arrows in battle. El Cassidy saved the ranch from the banker, the cattle from the cattle rustlers, the townspeople from the outlaws, and fair maidens from Indians.

El Roy Rogers was cute and much younger than Hopalong. His slanted eyes crinkled when he smiled, which was often, and his straight hair escaped from under his cowboy hat to land on his wide brow. He was slender, not as husky as el Cassidy, but in his high-heeled boots, astride a horse, Roy Rogers looked strong, even mighty. His partner was Dale Evans, a pretty woman who wore western clothes and rode a frisky horse. Like el Cassidy, Roy Rogers treated women like sisters; he never looked at Dale Evans with lovesick eyes.

Roy Rogers lived somewhere in the West, where he fought Indians and bandidos. Whenever he whistled, his horse Trigger would trot to him, then off they would ride. Other than look pretty on her horse, Dale Evans never did much.

Before the movie began, Father Mueller and the Holy Name Society members, who were in charge of the event and felt terribly important, dusted the folding chairs stored in back of the hall, then lined them up in neat rows, leaving a narrow space to the right. The stage curtains were pulled apart; the movie screen came down. Sodas were laid out in tubs filled with chipped ice, oil for popcorn was heated, and boxes of assorted candy were stacked inside the kitchen.

When el chow was scheduled, rosary ended promptly at seven thirty. I found it miraculous that Father Mueller ended prayers so soon on a movie Sunday. He never dared to skip a Mystery, but prayed at a fast clip; often he skipped the Litany of the Saints, thinking no one would notice. As soon as he had blessed the congregation, he bolted into the sacristy to change his skirt. While Don Crispín locked the church and snuffed out the candles, our pastor dashed into the church hall to prepare for las vistas. Within minutes people began filtering in. Some still clutched holy beads; women with scarves over their hair quickly took them off, stuffed them in a pocket, and looked around for a seat.

"Did the chow start yet?"

"Todavía no."

"Is he chowing el Cassidy?"

"Neh, es el Roy Rogers."

The hall kitchen teemed with activity. People went in and out, arms laden with boxed candy and Cracker Jacks, everyone's favorite treat. Others sorted the candy: Milk Duds, Baby Ruths, and Milky Ways, which sold for five cents, por un cinco. At the front counter (actually a half door that swung open), young girls kept busy measuring oil and popcorn into the popcorn maker. In the stretches when they weren't performing this loathsome chore, they pried open the caps on strawberry and orange sodas and made change. Eyes bright and expectant, they elbowed each other, vying for position, as behind them the popcorn machine spat out white fluffy chivitas and the church hall filled with the delicious smell of hot popcorn.

I wanted to help sell popcorn, but the teenage girls, all of whom acted superior, monopolized the counter. They licked their red lips, fluffed their dark hair, and told me to sit down. As soon as the boys lined up, they acted sweet and passive, fluttering their eyelids in perfect rhythm. They flirted outrageously, elbowing each other in the ribs, while pretending to sell el esquite.

"May I help you?"

"You chure can."

"Don't act smart! Whadda ya want, popcorn or . . ."

"He wants a kiss!"

"I'm gonna tell Father . . ."

My primary job at las vistas was to translate the movies for Doña Luisa and her friends. While they understood what was taking place, many things in the show escaped them. It was up to me to fill them in on what had or was about to occur. In return for this, Doña Luisa and the Trinidads (all but Doña Caridad, who was stingy), would give me money to spend. I would have preferred to be with my friend Elena, near the boys, but sat with Doña Luisa out of loyalty.

I sat in the middle, between Doña Luisa and Doña Magda, who sat next to Doña Cari. Doña Clarissa rarely went to the movies, saying her eyes were too weak. Once el rosario let out, the ladies staked the third row for themselves and their reluctant interpreter.

As soon as the movie started, I immediately began to translate. In an effort to impress the señoras and earn a nod of approval from Doña Caridad, I would search my mind for the most appropriate and similar Spanish words to reflect the action taking place, then whispered them to the women, all of whom sighed with relief. Often I became flustered at my lack of Spanish, and took too long to respond.

"Que está pasando?" Doña Cari had to know what was happening.

"Nada."

I paused when appropriate; when the action picked up, I too accelerated. I tried not to lag behind, and in an effort to see everything, would practically fall off my seat. I hated to lose sight of the action, and I feared mixing up the "good guys" with the "bad guys."

El Cassidy rarely spoke. He merely grunted, tipped his hat to the ladies, then dug his silver spurs into his horse and rode off. El Roy Rogers spoke only to Trigger or Dale Evans. Mostly he smiled a lot, his eyes squinting in the sun. His movies all ended on the same note. He would whistle to Trigger, jump into the leather saddle, then ride off, leaving behind swirls of dust.

At times the movies were too long, the plot too predictable. I would tire of my job and yearn to sit in front with Elena. By now I had spent the money given me by Doña Luisa and the Trinidads. As the show dragged on, I fidgeted in my seat, edging toward Elena. Once I had collected más cincos, I sought ways to escape from the boring job of translating an old cowboy movie. One usually worked.

"Qué están diciendo?" Doña Magda would hiss, her breath hot on my face, eager to know what the actors had said.

"Que la va a matar."

"No es posible!" Doña Caridad screeched, about to fall off her seat. Even when flustered she spoke in precise, proper Spanish. In the darkened hall her myopic eyes searched for mine; her chins quivered in agitation. She leaned across Doña Magda, her eyes probing mine. "It's not possible," she hissed in Spanish, then covered her eyes with a linen hankie she kept in her pocket. Doña Cari would not accept that El Cassidy, who had just saved the pretty girl from the bandits, was planning to kill her.

"Sí. He's gonna kill her just the same." I pulled at the hem of my dress, then crossed my arms in front of my chest, daring her not to believe.

Doña Luisa (who always knew when I was fibbing), was not about to feed me to the lions. In a voice hoarse from yelling at me, she volunteered her opinion. "*Hmmm, puede ser.* It could be," she lied, her dark eyes glued to the movie screen.

I remained unruffled, my fist tight around the nickels I had earned, as I pushed my way toward Elena. Around me the thoroughly confused women sat in wonder at this sudden turn of events. They squabbled, each wanting to believe only what they had seen on the white screen, until told to "hush" by those sitting in back.

I joined Elena, who had saved my seat, knowing how resourceful I could be. She welcomed me with a knowing grin. I stuffed myself with the popcorn and Milk Duds bought with my earnings, then giggled at the cute boys sitting next to me.

On the way home, the Trinidads discussed the movie, el Cassidy, and the translation that did not fit the action. I pretended not to hear and moved away from the prying eyes of Doña Caridad, the sour breath of Doña Magda. The heated discussion was led by Doña Caridad, who even in the dark had a commanding presence, and easily intimidated Doña Magdalena. As she picked her way between the many rocks on Hoyt Street, she voiced her concern about her idol, el Cassidy.

"Ay, Dios mío!" Her chest rose and fell in agitation. Doña Caridad would not give up on the aging, white-haired cowboy.

"El Cassidy would not do a thing like that," hissed Doña Magda, knowing that this is what Doña Cari wanted to hear. She pulled her rebozo around her head, then shuffled on down the street.

"Pues, yo sí," said Doña Luisa, throwing caution to the winds. She yanked me by the arm, then propelled me toward home.

"Hmmm, pos hoy en día no hay respeto," concluded Doña Cari, adjusting her wool shawl around her ample shoulders. "Today there is no respect." This ended the argument.

At times I felt guilty about the translation and the nickels, especially when the señoras began to bicker among themselves. My guilt would last until the following Sunday, when once more I might recite an original version of an old western.

Rose

Her name was Rose. Not Rosa, Rosie, or Rosita, but Rose, like the flower with the scent all its own.

I first heard about Rose on the day of my confirmation rehearsal, when my godmother-to-be, Tiburcia, or Toby as I called her, did not show up, and I was forced to walk up the church aisle alone. Later that evening when Toby came by to explain her absence, I refused to greet her, angry as I was. She told my mother she had been shopping for velos, confirmation veils, and was detained when she stopped off to deliver a veil to a girl named Rose, whom she was also going to sponsor at *her* confirmation. Rose lived in San Fernando and was about my age.

I was curious to learn more about this girl, this Rose. It angered me to know that I had to share my godmother. I asked first! It wasn't fair! Then Toby explained that she had made arrangements for Rose to be confirmed with my class. Rose had missed her confirmation because of illness; this was her only opportunity to receive the sacrament. This explanation pacified me for a time, but I was still resentful of this intruder.

I began to wonder if Rose was pretty and slim. Smart, even. I was chubby, and although I was growing like a weed, I hated my thick arms and round nalgas. I had no way of knowing what Rose looked like and was not about to ask Toby to show me her picture. Secretly I hoped that Rose was fat and ugly.

Toby was my sister Elizabet's best friend. She was in and out of our house often, so that when it came time for me to select a confirmation madrina, I quickly pounced on her. She immediately said "yes," and gave me a hearty squeeze. She then promised to buy me a pretty veil from the best store in town and a white prayer book with my name on it. I practically jumped up and down, delirious with happiness.

Toby was most stylish. She dressed like the lawyer's secretary that she was: in smart suits and tailored blouses. I've selected the right person, I thought. It was certain that Toby would select a confirmation veil that was unique and expensive! When once more she spoke of Rose, I no longer felt angry. I was absorbed in trying to memorize my confirmation prayers, the Latin responses, the correct method of kneeling before a bishop, and experimenting with ways to straighten my curly hair.

The week before my confirmation was one of intense activity. I washed my hair at least four times. I rolled it both in rags and in the aluminum curlers borrowed from Concha, who sneaked the curlers from her older sister. Elizabet took me to Penney's in San Fernando to shop for confirmation clothes: white socks, a white slip, and a pretty white dotted-swiss dress (size 12 Chubby). Try as I might, I could not steer them toward my favorite shoe store and the fancy white shoes in the window. When we left for home, I knew I would have to wear my school oxfords—and hate it.

The night before mi confirmación, I scrubbed my knees extra hard with the pumice stone kept by the bathtub. I scrubbed until they bled, but they still looked dark brown. I put vaseline on my eyebrows and eyelashes, praying they would grow overnight, then rubbed some on my red knees, hoping it might bleach them. I hardly slept that night; I lay awake thinking of the ceremony to come, of the bishop whom I should address as "Excellency," and of my dress, veil, and prayer book. Now and then I thought of Rose, the girl with whom I would share my godmother.

Confirmation day dawned bright and clear. The April sun was never so bright, the air so clear. The church bells tolled the hour as we lined up for the ceremony. My knees ached from the scabs now forming. My head reeled from the tight curlers. My dress was too tight. I had lied to the salesclerk at Penny's and had refused to try on a size 14 Chubby, fearful of having my friends find out my dress size. I now tried to hold in my stomach, then loosened the belt and white pearl buttons near the waist and took a deep breath. I wanted to look like St. Teresa of Avila, known as the Little Flower. I felt pious, holy, and fat.

The sleeves that encircled my round arms cut into my flesh. The pretty lace, stretched thin, no longer flounced in the morning breeze. My socks felt tight around my ankles. I began to perspire, anxious for His Excellency's arrival. Just then I looked up to see Toby; with her walked a tall, white-veiled girl.

Toby was dressed in a polka-dot dress with a short peplum. She wore a cluster of red cherries on her shoulder and spotless white gloves on her small hands. On her shapely feet were black-and-white spectator pumps with a small bow. She looked stunning. I felt proud to have her as my godmother and quickly put my hand through hers. It was then I remembered the girl who stood next to her. Rose.

Toby introduced us. Rose said "hello" in a shy, soft voice, then moved closer to Toby. In that instant I saw how lovely she was. Her skin was a light almond; her cheeks a soft pink. Her large brown eyes were the color of caramel candy; her pink mouth a moist rosebud. Her straight hair hung almost to her waist! I hated her!

What held my attention however, was her confirmation veil. It was identical to mine! I stared and stared at the veil, hoping to see a ribbon or flower that was different. I soon gave up. I wore the same veil as another "candidate for confirmation," as the Sisters had labeled us. I was furious and wanted to snatch the veil off my head and sling it at Toby, but just then the procession started.

When the organ began to peal "Asperges Me," the entrance hymn reserved for a bishop's visit, we quickly secured our veils, pulled up our socks, and made sure our sponsors were nearby. The older girls dabbed rouge from the catechists on their already flushed cheeks. I froze in line, too angry to move, aware of the figure that moved next to me. It was her, that Rose.

She took her place beside me, then turned and smiled. I stood mesmerized, not daring to breathe; the look she gave me was one of love, affection. I felt my eyes smart with angry tears. I didn't want to like her! My hands itched to fling my prayer book and rosary beads at her. I stood and twisted my veil, trying to ignore this girl who smiled so sweetly at me.

I felt awkward; my dress was tight and hot. Next to me stood the tall girl whose white dress skimmed over her slight body. The bodice of *her* confirmation dress had tiny tucks and two rows of lace; a pink rosette was pinned to her waist. Her nylon socks had a lacy top and her patent leather shoes, gleaming white in the sun, had a small heel! I stared at my oxfords and cotton socks, which although new, had plain tops, then turned and glared at Toby, who was behind us. I now hated her, too. I was sorry I had asked her to be my madrina. I thought of tripping her, but changed my mind; every time I turned around, my eyes met those of Rose. Eyes of caramel brown, full of affection and goodwill. Eyes that bore neither envy nor malice. Eyes that said "I want to be your friend."

When finally the march began, Rose turned to me; I reluctantly turned to her. She reached out and took my hand. She gently squeezed it; I squeezed back. She smiled at me; I grinned at her. Then hand in hand, we walked up the church aisle as behind us Toby beamed with pride.

Las Camisas Blancas

From the age of twelve or so, of the five girls in our family, I alone ironed best the white dress shirts worn by my older brother Berney.

Berney was fussy about his clothes. He changed tee shirts twice a day, which kept my mother and Doña Luisa busy, but they seemed not to mind the heavy workload imposed by Berney's fetish for crisp white shirts. Mexican mothers in the barrio took pride in how they clothed la familia, especially the eldest, and often the favorite, son.

During the late 1940s, Berney dressed in the most current styles. He took great care with his dress clothes and preferred shirts with French cuffs and pin-striped suits from a store in Los Angeles. The suit jackets had wide shoulder pads that made Berney look huskier than he was; the pants, with a moderate drape, hung snug on his slender waist. He wore black shoes and socks that never slid down his skinny ankles.

Unlike my father's shirts, Berney's dress shirts were washed, starched, and ironed to perfection. If a shirt appeared scorched, had a wrinkled collar, or smelled funny, fastidious Berney would turn up his nose and refuse to wear it until my mother or Doña Luisa (who liked nothing better than to please my lanky brother), had rewashed it.

When my mother and Doña Luisa did the family laundry on Monday mornings, Berney's white shirts were set aside to be washed separately from those of my father and other brothers. First the shirts were boiled in Purex bleach, scrubbed until snowy white, then rinsed several times in cool water. In the final rinse my mother added a piece of bluing, which was sold in squares like chocolate candy.

Doña Luisa then hung the camisas to dry on the clothesline. The white shirts dancing on the line made a pretty picture, their long arms flapping in the wind.

While the shirts dried, my mother called Josey and me inside the kitchen.

"No juegen junto las camisas," she scolded, warning us to stay clear of the white shirts. The dirt raised when we kicked a ball might stick to the shirts, she explained in her moderate voice, and then they would have to be rewashed and restarched. Since Berney was so special, Josey and I readily obeyed. We played in the street until Doña Luisa brought the shirts indoors, then ran around the clothesline and the woodpile at will.

My mother took pride in how she cooked the blue starch for Berney's dress shirts. She first boiled water in a blue enamel pot. Then she took a cup of starch, mixed it in cold water until the lumps dissolved, then added the liquid to the pot. She stirred the starch with short, brisk movements of her trusty wooden spoon, to make sure that no lumps formed. Once the starch bubbled, my mother stirred it until it was the right consistency, dumped it into a pan inside the sink, then cooled it down with tepid water.

After checking Berney's shirts for dust, my mother dipped them into the starch, making sure the sleeves did not touch the kitchen counter. She swished them around until they were evenly coated, wrung them out, then hung them back on the clothesline. When the shirts were dry again, she laid them on the kitchen table (which had been scrubbed clean), then lightly sprinkled them with tap water. I was allowed to sprinkle the stiff shirts, provided I didn't soak them— or back to the clothesline they went. The shirts were then spread out on the kitchen table with the collar points even, and the sleeves were folded along the front placket. After that they rolled the shirts into a tight ball and put them in a clean funda, a pillowcase, until they were ironed. Most of the time Doña Luisa elbowed me out of the kitchen, anxious to be in charge of the shirts belonging to "el padre," as she called Berney.

Berney's white shirts were at first my older sisters' obligation. But by the time I was eleven or so, I was taller than all four of them; they said I looked older and should share the adult chores. I was put in charge of sweeping the kitchen, assured that only I knew how to get the dirt from the corners. They flattered me about the way I raked leaves, then surrendered the yard broom with a smile.

I raked the leaves in neat rows, inching the rake along the fence, pressing down on the loose dirt. I gathered the aromatic eucalyptus leaves that filled the yard in one giant sweep. When leaves tossed by the wind fell where I had already swept, I raked it over, racing against the elements. I bundled las ojas, carried them to the trash, then hosed down the yard, satisfied with my work. When my siblings saw how neat I could be, they insisted that I iron las camisas.

I liked to iron (unsightly wrinkles were always annoying to me) and to wear clothes still warm from the iron, calientes de la plancha. I even took pride in getting things ready. Up until the time my father wired our house for electricity, and even afterward, I used the flatirons heated the old-fashioned way. I learned to smooth out handkerchiefs on Doña Luisa's planchas, which drew heat from her wood stove. The electric iron that Elizabet bought was too light and cumbersome, but the flatirons fit my small and eager hands.

I hated using a dirty iron, so first I cleaned it with Old Dutch cleanser, to make sure the bottom was free of dirt and rust. I rubbed paraffin on the iron bottom or slid it on wax paper, to ensure that it would glide smoothly over the cotton material, then I would test to see if it was ready. I wet my finger with saliva, then touched the iron with a flick of my hand. If it hissed, the iron was ready.

While I waited for the iron to heat, I reswept the kitchen and ran the mop back and forth across my work area, fearing a shirt sleeve might fall to the floor, then took out the ironing board from the hall closet.

The wooden board was covered with old sheets (which I hated). The thought of laying white shirts on a yellowed pad was utterly repulsive to me. I wanted the ironing board to be immaculate, so I searched in my mother's trunk for an old white sheet, tore it into wide strips, and then wound these around the pad. I secured the sheets with large safety pins from my mother's sewing box. Now I was ready.

I first ironed a small section of the shirttail to test the iron's heat, then did the inside of the shirt. I ironed the French seams twice, then went on to the shirt collar, breathing in the fragrance of el almidón.

I flipped the shirt over and smoothed the inside of the collar, taking care to begin at the tip and iron up. Berney was most particular that his shirt collars be wrinkle-free.

Next I ironed the yoke, inside and out, then the sides and back. The cuffs were last, and were also ironed from the bottom up. I hated the thick and bulky French cuffs; they took forever to iron! If I wasn't careful, I tended to scorch them; then they smelled like burnt cloth. Ughhhh!

Working with the flatirons was tedious, but also fun. I liked to get all the heat from an iron before it cooled; I raced with it! My hands like wings, I flew back and forth over the spotless white shirts, my face bathed in a fragrant mist of starch. Often I timed myself, but because I didn't own a wristwatch, I would sing songs instead. I sang a three-verse song as I ironed a camisa at a fast clip. Then I would pick up the pace and the beat, determined to finish the next shirt after two verses.

When a shirt was done, I gave it a quick once-over to get rid of any remaining wrinkles, then hung my masterpiece on a wire hanger. I was very systematic and hardly varied from my routine. I had had a good teacher.

When I was about ten, without anyone knowing I had been using Doña Luisa's flatirons for ages, Nora offered to teach me how to iron "correctly." I followed her into the kitchen, then watched as she pulled back her hair from her fair brow, removed the pretty bracelets from her slender arms, then swished her hands back and forth in soapy water. She tested the iron, smoothed the ironing pad, and began.

Nora had delicate hands with long, tapered fingers. To watch her iron was a treat. Her hands flew across the ironing board with the speed of lightning. She lifted the iron just in time, then, in one smooth motion, slipped it inside sleeves and across hems. I yearned to iron just like Nora; if I ironed like she did, maybe in time I could even look like she did!

One summer day I volunteered to iron las camisas blancas. I rose early, bolted down my oatmeal and toast, and went to work. I ironed seven of Berney's white shirts, each more perfect than the rest. The day was hot; I was tired and sick of the smell of starch. I hung the shirts on wire hangers and was about to put the ironing board away when my mother came into the kitchen and commented on my work. I don't recall her exact words, but she criticized my effort somehow. I was hurt, very hurt.

I must have been very angry, too! In one giant sweep I gathered up the shirts, kicked open the kitchen door, ran out into the backyard, threw the shirts on the ground, and began to trample them in the dirt. My sisters ran out, as did Doña Luisa. They stared at the snowy white shirts on the ground, as I stood there crying, scared and humiliated.

My mother came out of the house, picked up the shirts (with the help of Doña Luisa, who always appeared during a crisis), dusted them off and took them back inside. She said not a word, nor did she even glance over to where I stood. I stayed outside near the trusty walnut tree, our dog Duke at my side, until dark. I felt scared and terribly ashamed. I was relieved to be called in for supper.

At the dinner table no one spoke of las camisas blancas; not even Josey mentioned the dusty shirts in the closet. I felt awful for having lost my temper; I regretted my rash behavior. Although I had acted out of anger, I had been disrespectful to my mother, a thing not allowed in our family. I ate in silence, trying to avoid the look of disappointment in Nora's eyes.

The guilt and shame lasted for a long, long time. Even today I feel ashamed of those infamous camisas blancas.

Hide-and-Seek

As the years passed, I made friends with the older kids on Hoyt Street, such as Celly, who was all of fourteen, and Rebecca, who while her mother worked, stayed with her abuelita. I got to stay out late and take part in grown-up games. Bored with Josey's tattling and his Frankenstein bike, I welcomed the change. On hot summer evenings I took off to play a las escondidas.

Although my favorite game was kickball, the game of hide-and-seek was more of a challenge. In anticipation of what lay ahead, I searched my head and assorted backyards to find donde esconderme. All too often I ended up in a familiar area that included Doña Luisa's yard. Younger kids like Josey were scared stiff of the dark; they were the first to be found, and often stomped home, angry and indignant at being caught. They were followed by the girls, who tended to give away their hiding places by giggling aloud. Among my friends, Virgie and Concha were the least adventuresome, being content with the same, predictable spot. I hated their lack of enthusiasm as much as I hated being among the last to find a hiding place.

"The boys got the best places."

"It ain't fair!"

"Shhhh. Someone's coming."

Mundo and Beto were fast on their feet, so they were able to take their time hiding from the rest. They first scoured the immediate neighborhood, then ran in and out of our backyard, hoping that a new hiding place would materialize. They were not too fussy about hiding behind cactus plants, but their undying wish was that, if only my brothers hadn't locked up a jalopy, they could crawl into it to hide.

One summer night I was "it." Mundo ran into our yard, wanting to scare Nancy, whom he secretly liked, but she ran from him. Near the woodpile he pulled a gunnysack over his head, then ran around in a circle, calling out to her. "Ooooowww, Nancy, I'm gonna get you." He failed to notice where his feet were taking him. Near the goat pen he stumbled and fell headfirst into a pile of fresh turds.

"Shit!"

"Shhhh."

Mundo yanked off el saco, slung it toward the fence, then slid underneath two old tires. He held his breath. I circled the yard and was about to give up when I smelled cagada coming from behind the tires. I reached over and touched Mundo's shoe, now smeared with goat turds. Then I dashed "home" to the pepper tree, Mundo hot on my heels. I counted him out, then ran to the faucet to wash my hands.

Often the boys refused to take the game seriously. They felt they were playing with "babies," kids without imagination or stamina, girls who would just as soon scrunch down behind a bush, put their hands over their eyes, and pray no one would find them. For boys like Mundo, playing hide and seek with chavalas was neither a challenge nor fun, but only an interlude between more interesting, rougher games.

Dressed in long pants and sturdy shoes, the boys were experts at hiding on the roofs of houses, behind wide fences, and inside gloomy sheds. Long legs flying, they would leap from one yard to the next, just like the green grasshoppers that in the summer jumped between my father's tomato plants. During the day the boys on our street were not the least bit nervous about stomping on a black widow spider or a cockroach. When at las escondidas, they went wild. In and out of yards they dashed, colliding with clotheslines full of freshly laundered clothes, timid girls at their heels, dogs barking furiously. I envied the boys their energy, their boldness, and their ability to find a hiding place in a dark corner that even in early evening was difficult to spot.

The most fun games were played on summer evenings. I felt free to climb walls and scale fences in the dark, knowing no one could see my homemade calzones trimmed in rickrack. Although my dress belt might come loose or a button unexpectedly pop, if I tried I could always outplay the less ingenious boys.

One time while playing hide-and-seek, Nancy got her dress caught in a tree branch. She made a big fuss; all the boys came running. While Mundo flipped her dress higher and higher, as though to loosen it, Nancy blushed and giggled. When finally her dress was freed, most of the boys had seen her lace-trimmed underwear.

"Did ya see Nancy's calzones?"

"Yeah! She sure don't care!"

"About what?"

"Showing her . . ."

As a warm-up to the more serious version, we would begin playing hide-and-seek in the early evening, with one of the young kids as "it." But they often tested my patience. Slow to count and even slower to find us, the little kids took forever to get started. But the wait gave the older kids a chance to try out one hiding spot, discard it, and then, without being detected, tear off to find another.

"Psssst, Beto, help me con la tina."

"You don't fit in a tub."

"Sez who?"

The pepper tree in front of our house was "home," the safe place for those who could outsmart and outrun "it." We rarely chose sides, but merely waited to see who wanted to be "it." Once "it" was ready, face pressed to the tree, off we ran to hide, scampering between thorny cactus, pampered rose bushes, and the rusty washtubs stored in backyards. We bumped into cars, collided with loose rocks, and stepped over tender chiles in our quest for a hiding place.

"Five, ten, fifteen, twenty."

For some kids, especially Bernabé, nicknamed "el Brains," counting numbers in sequence was a challenge. "Brains" was slow-witted and lousy at arithmetic; he tended to get the numbers mixed up.

"Five, ten, fifteen, twenty; five, ten, fifteen, thirty." He repeated the same number over and over, until Mundo ran past shouting: "Twenty-five, thirty, *pendejo!*"

Once the count was finished, there was dead silence. Not a leaf rustled; not a dog barked. By now kids were either behind a bush, up a tree, or hiding under a tub.

The boys, being the most daring, often hid behind my father's lumber pile, in the eucalyptus trees near the alley, or up on a low roof. While there they would jostle each other in play and slide to the ground, to be quickly put out.

One time a friend of Norbert's named Peter asked to play with us. We were impressed; older boys rarely wanted to be around us. "You can hide in my yard too," he said, pointing to the pepper trees that grew alongside his house. Mundo nodded in agreement; Beto followed suit. As they talked Mundo strained to see into Peter's yard, which teemed with yonque: rusty bedsprings, old mattresses, a dismantled washing machine, and a faded couch.

Concha and I whopped with joy! Certain we now had a wider choice of hiding places, we smiled at Peter. No longer would we have to fight over the few available spots in our backyard, nor revert to Doña Luisa's shrubs, most of which by now only came to our waists.

That night, while Concha counted in a slow, low voice, I ran off toward the alley, my dress flying in the evening breeze. I could barely make out the forms that darted here and there, but knew they had to be Beto or Mundo. Determined not to retreat to the safety of my own backyard, I dashed from one yard to the next, trying not to stumble in the dark. I had almost given up when I remembered Peter's offer; I whirled around, hitched up my dress, and off I went toward where Peter lived.

I jumped over the chicken-wire fence and stumbled across the unfamiliar yard, trying to see in the dark. Suddenly I heard someone call my name; I recognized Peter's voice. "Up here," he whispered, his voice low, insistent. "Dey can't find ya here."

I looked up to where Peter and two boys sat on the roof that connected his house to their garage. Crouched low, they hid between the low branches of a pepper tree full of red berries. Grateful for such luck, I scrambled up the low roof, jumped onto a branch, and made my way over to Peter.

Peter was almost fourteen, a stocky fellow with pimples on his face. He had a flat nose and dark brown eyes fringed with short eyelashes. He dressed in tight Levis and white T-shirts. Now and then he and a cousin drove an old jalopy back and forth along Hoyt Street. Although we rarely spoke, I accepted him as a friend of my brother's.

I grabbed Peter's husky arm, then edged close to the roof, as the soft berries fell to the ground. When I recognized Mundo and Beto next to him, I took a deep breath and smiled at them in the dark. As he pulled me across the roof, Peter's strong arms encircled my waist and lightly brushed against my chest. The smell of berries filled the air. I moved away from him, crossed my legs, pulled down my dress, and peered around. I could see very little beyond the branches that brushed against my face. Below me rowdy kids ran to and fro, looking for a place to hide from Concha.

"It's scary up here," I said to no one in particular.

"Girls ain't nuthin but sissies," grumbled Mundo, as he flipped berries down to the ground.

"Not me," I assured him, with a toss of my head.

Mundo grew impatient with Concha and with how slowly the game was progressing. He crouched on the roof, yanked at his belt, then jumped off, followed by Beto, who first secured his suspenders, adjusted his beanie, then slid down the tree and dropped to the ground in one giant leap.

Peter and I were left on the roof. He began to whistle. I felt his hot breath on my neck; his sweaty arm brushed against my dress. "No te asustes," he murmured, as his arm slipped around my neck. "Don't be scared."

While I was afraid of the dark and of falling off an unfamiliar roof, I was more afraid of Peter, now pressing closer and closer. This must be how older kids play, I decided, so don't start acting like a crybaby. I said nothing. Peter bent his head closer; his thick hair brushed my hot cheek. I could barely see his eyes; his sour breath mingled with the smell of the berries.

I moved away, brushing at the tree branches, sick of the smell I associated with sling shots and Josey, anxious to get away from Peter, now whistling an unfamiliar tune. I slid, then pushed myself toward the tree trunk. Suddenly I realized I had moved too far; my legs were now dangling from the roof. A warm breeze crept up my dress. I was petrified!

I inched back against the roof; my legs scraped against the rough asbestos. I rubbed my knees and was beginning to feel safe, when I felt Peter's hand slide under my dress. I sat still, my breath coming in gasps. I didn't know what to do! If I moved forward, I would fall off the roof; but if I didn't make an effort to jump, Peter would think I wanted to play dirty. Just then I recognized Beto's shiny beanie, studded with bottlecaps, beneath us. "Come on, Peter," Beto shouted, "the game's over."

Peter moved across the roof, then slid down the tree trunk; his dark head brushed my face. I followed close behind, trying to see in the dark, as my arms gripped the unfamiliar pepper tree. I placed my right foot on a stump, a tronco that protruded from the tree, then pushed off. With my free hand I pulled at a branch, hanging on for dear life, then slowly worked my way down. I was almost to the ground when I slipped and tore my dress.

"Owwwww." I tried to muffle my shout, as I fell to the ground. My dress ruffle had caught on a low branch and had completely torn off. My dress is ruined, I sobbed; I'm gonna get it. I hobbled toward home.

Once on safe ground, I dried my eyes, then looked for Concha and Beto, but they were nowhere to be seen. Neither was Mundo. I went toward the light in our kitchen, relieved to be in a familiar surrounding, away from the dark and the strange ways of older boys. I locked myself in the bathroom, scrubbed my grimy knees, washed the smell of pepper berries from my hands, then took my mother's sewing basket and with shaky fingers, tacked the ruffle back onto my dress. Once inside Doña Luisa's house, I put on my nightgown and jumped into her lumpy bed. I snuggled close, mumbled a prayer to my Guardian Angel and then, exhausted by the evening's events, fell asleep.

I developed an intense dislike for Peter, who I felt had betrayed my trust. He first had offered me a hiding place then tried to play cochinadas, as kids on Hoyt Street called dirty games. I was tempted to tell Norbert, but didn't. After that I rarely played with the older kids.

La Nancy

The year I was eleven, my best friend was la Nancy. Unlike Concha and Virgie, girls my age who giggled and acted silly, Nancy, at twelve, was quite sophisticated. She walked with a slight swing of her skinny hips and tilted her head to the left when talking to boys. Often she halfway closed her eyes, wanting to look like the movie stars who were supposed to have "bedroom eyes." She licked her lips to make them glisten and plucked her eyebrows into a wide arch.

I yearned to be like Nancy; at home I locked myself in the bathroom to imitate her. I put out the lights to create "an atmosphere" (as in the movies), then stood in front of the mirror to tilt my head and close my eyes halfway. I pushed my hair back, just like Nancy did, then strained to see the effect. When I was unable to see anything in the dark room, I quit doing it. But every chance I had, I studied Nancy.

Nancy was almost as tall as I, with light brown hair, light skin, a pert nose, and eyes already caked with Maybelline. She no longer wore her hair in braids, but piled it atop her head in what was called an "upsweep." She took makeup from her sister, then ran to find me and Concha. We would tear off to sit underneath a pepper tree, as Nancy, her dark eyes glowing with excitement, rubbed our olive cheeks a warm rosy color and slathered us with Evening in Paris perfume.

"Do I look older?"

"Not yet. Here, try the magenta lipstick."

"I like how the powder smells. Did you buy it at . . ."

"Neh, I took it."

As she painted our lips, Nancy told us about her boyfriends and who she planned to marry once we graduated from Pacoima Elementary.

Nancy was the first of my friends to wear a bra. The tiny size 32AA bra that hung over her skinny chest sold for $1.99 and was the smallest one available. It was bought for her by her sister. Nancy, however, didn't mind that the brassiere did not fit correctly; she was concerned only with the lace "cups." She constantly pulled at the straps, making sure we knew she now wore a bra.

She also wore rayon panties bought at the Five & Dime. I thought them ugly and cheap-looking, but Nancy liked them because they came in all colors: lavender, pink, and her favorite, black. I was jealous of her underwear. All I had to wear were cotton underpants and the white undershirts that stretched across my flat chest.

Nancy thought she was "so big" because she had an Anglo name, one associated with blond hair and blue eyes. Her real name, I knew was Natcha, but her older sisters had Anglicized it so that she was now called Nancy.

During summer Nancy hated to attend both catechism and church, saying they were boring and took up too much time. She rarely showed up at the Stella Maris Club, saying she had to help wash the supper dishes. She often missed school, too, saying the teachers were dumb, stupid even, and she knew more than they did. This I believed, for Nancy was the most advanced of my friends. Certainly she knew more about boys and kissing than Concha did.

She also knew how to French-kiss, or so she hinted to Concha, who immediately told me. French kissing was something that we never saw in the movies, but I knew this kind of thing could get a girl in trouble. I once heard Trina and her friends, all older and wiser than me, talk about a girl who had "gotten in trouble."

"Miranda thinks she's P.G."

"How come?

" 'Cause Bennie gave her a French kiss."

When I repeated this to Nancy, she bent over laughing. When she had regained her composure, she tilted her head to the left and said that it was all a lie, because nobody in France had died from kissing. She tried to teach Concha and me, along with some other girls from Hoyt Street, how to kiss properly

"We need a boy."

"We can ask Mundo."

"Ugggghh."

"How about Sandy?"

"Neh. Tiene miedo. I asked him, but he ran off."

Nancy knew where babies came from, but refused to tell anyone. She alluded to "things" that boys and girls did underneath the pepper trees and in the back row of the San Fernando theatre. When asked for details, Nancy pulled at her bra, swung her skinny hips, and with a wicked grin, stalked home.

Whenever a new boy came to Pacoima Elementary, Nancy was the first to spot him. She then took it upon herself to decide whether or not he was cute. She circled him, her pointy chest sticking way out, then tilted her head to observe him better. We slouched against the chain link fence that bordered the playground, until she joined us. With baited breath we waited to see what pronouncements would spew from Nancy's bright red mouth.

"He's cute, but . . ."

"But what?

"He smells of sobacos."

Having smelly armpits was one of the worse things that could befall a boy. Stinky feet were acceptable, as was bad breath and greasy hair. But the smell of sobacos was terribly offensive and meant that a kid was poor, backward even, and never took a bath except at Christmas. At school when I was assigned to sit next to someone who reeked of sweaty armpits, I would quickly ask to be moved.

In the seventh grade Nancy, who still read and wrote at the fifth-grade level, claimed to be receiving love letters from a boy in San Fernando named Ramón. He lived in a nice house with a wide sidewalk and a pretty lawn, and "sat" with her at the movies. During school recess one day she called us over.

"I got a love letter from Ramon."

"Another one?"

"No stupid, that was from Jimmy."

Nancy knew how to fight, too, and often beat up on the boys who teased her about her skinny legs. All of them were scared of her except for Mundo, who was meaner than she was; given the chance, he would kick anyone who "asked for it." However, she was loyal to the kids that lived on Hoyt Street, and during an argument could be counted on to take my side. In return I had to treat her to candy at the corner store. It was good to have Nancy as a friend.

During the summer Nancy and I attended all the church bazaars held at Guardian Angel Church. We not only went on Saturday nights but also on Sundays, when the prizes were raffled off. We helped the older girls make boutonnieres of fresh flowers that were sold, usually to men and boys, for a dime each. Nancy and I were considered too young to do the "fun" part: sauntering around the boys at the fiesta with a box of carnations in our hands and an eager smile on our lips. The older girls, all experts at flirting, had this job. They would sidle up to an unsuspecting boy, pin a botón on his chest, then smirk as he fidgeted for change. When a guy was really cute, the girls pinned not one but two carnations on his jacket.

"How are you, Bartolo?"

"Uhh . . ."

"That will be fifty cents, please!"

"Keep the change, girls!"

The boutonniers were of red and white carnations and crespón, a fragile fern. They were kept in a zinc tub filled with water at the back of the church hall, away from the flow of traffic and bothersome kids.

One Sunday night Nancy and I, being the best of friends and inseparable (for at least those two weeks), were preparing to fix the carnations. Nancy wore a red jumper and a red-and-white polka-dot blouse. She reeked of Evening in Paris. Right before we began, she went into the bathroom to paint her mouth. I gaped at her glowing lips and at her pretty outfit, one I had never seen before. We worked quickly, aware that the girls would be angry if we kept them waiting.

I was busy swishing water off the carnations, taking care not to spot my newly shined shoes. Engrossed in cutting the stems from the flowers, I glanced up after awhile to see Nancy near the door, talking to an older man. I paid little attention; people often entered the fiesta through the church hall, then went out a side door and on to the booths.

Nancy began to trim the flowers, her brown eyes full of excitement. Her face was flushed a deep pink. She tossed her hair back, licked her lips, and kept looking out the door. She then walked over to me, pushed back my thick hair, and whispered:

"I know how we can make twenty-five cents!"

"How?"

"See that man over there? The one . . ."

". . . you were talking to?"

"Yeah. He'll give us some money if . . ."

At that time twenty-five cents was a lot of money. At the jamaica, most things cost either a nickel or a dime. A quarter at the Penny Pitch would go a long way, it might even earn me a prize.

"Yes, I want to earn twenty-five cents."

Nancy took my hand; we went outside. I could smell Evening in Paris. It was dark; the streetlight flickered as if it were about to go out. The street was completely empty. The tall shrubs behind the church hall appeared menacing. Nancy in the lead, we turned the corner, then stopped.

"What are we waitin for?" I hissed, eager to return to the flowers. In my haste I had walked off with a red carnation; I was afraid it would lose its freshness.

"Wait here." She took a deep breath, looked around for oncoming cars, and said: "If you let him see under your dress, he'll give ya twenty-five cents . . . and if you let him touch *it,* he'll give ya fifty cents!"

What she was saying didn't make sense. I turned to leave, but Nancy pulled me back. In my confusion I didn't see the dark figure emerging from the shadows, until he got close. I gasped in surprise at the familiar figure of el Señor José, a respected church member and friend of my father's. He hesitated then stepped back into the shadows, as Nancy went up to him.

"Aquí estamos," she said, her dark eyes bright. "Here we are."

He glared at Nancy, mumbled something inaudible, then walked off toward Hoyt Street, his heavy tread echoing in the dark night. We lingered near the shrubs as Don José disappeared. I was trying to understand what had happened, when an angry Nancy turned to me.

"You spoiled it," she hissed. "Now he won't give me any more money. I hate you! You're not my best friend anymore." She stomped off, leaving a wake of French perfume behind her. I was left holding the wet carnation. It was some time before I understood that the "friend" Nancy said would give us money had recognized me and bolted. I was so shocked I could barely make the botones after that. I never told my mother or anyone else about that incident. I thought of telling our new pastor, who was understanding of younger kids, but was too ashamed. After that night I hardly saw Nancy. I did, however, see Don José, but he avoided my glance. I began to fear him. During Sunday mass, when he came by with the collection baskets, I cringed when he drew near. Later, when I was allowed to sell the boutonnieres to the men and boys, I never approached him, but avoided him for the rest of my life.

My Boyfriend Lupe

I don't remember who wrote first, he to me or I to him. But I think it might have been me, since I liked to write. I was about twelve when I began to write love letters to Lupe.

His name was really Guadalupe, which I hated worse than Lupe. Both were girl's names, and although not uncommon en un hombre, kids on Hoyt Street made fun of funny Mexican names like Narciso, Crispín, Agapito, and José María. The thought of a grown-up man named Joseph Mary kept us in stitches for hours.

I don't remember now who told me that Lupe liked me, but I was thrilled to learn that he did; because even though people said I was cute, I was chubby. Very chubby. I feared I would never be slim and eligible for a boyfriend. I equated slim bodies with novios. In the movies the slender girl always got her man. My sisters assured me I only had "baby fat," but I feared I would never outgrow it. It was gratifying to find out Lupe liked me, even though I was una gordita.

Lupe was short, stocky, and sweet. His hair fell across his wide forehead in thick curls. His light brown eyes peeked out from between thick eyelashes. His teeth were white and even; his breath smelled sweet from the spearmint gum he always carried in his pocket.

We met at the jamaicas, the church bazaars held in summer. We never made a date to meet at these functions, but merely spotted each other, then sat near a booth to talk. Mostly I went to the bazaars with Concha and Virgie, but now and then Nancy joined us. She would wait until dark, then saunter over, her skinny hips undulating, her skirt pulled above her knees.

Lupe always had spending money, money his doting mother (who called him Lupito when no one was around) gave him. He was generous and shared snowcones, cotton candy and warm sodas with me. When he offered me hot, buttered popcorn and I ate the entire bag without thinking, I felt I should buy *him* something, but Lupe shyly refused. He felt it only right that a boy pay for everything.

On Hoyt Street there were certain rules of behavior that boys and girls were supposed to observe, even kids not yet teenagers. If a boy let a girl treat him to "el chow," he was not acting like a man. If a woman picked up a date in her car, he was made fun of for weeks. Worse, if a girl was seen walking past a boy's house more than once, folks said she was muy adelantada, too forward, and would come to no good.

There was little my friends and I could do at the jamaicas without arousing suspicion. We giggled and chased boys, then went our separate ways. I was content to walk with Lupe, looking at the fish in their tiny bowls, and to listen to the músicos upon the stage. When it got dark Lupe held my hand, but only if his mother wasn't watching.

Lupe came from a musical family. His older brother played the accordion, an instrument I associated with Italians and circus monkeys. His solemn sister, Esperanza, played both piano and violin. His mother, a sour-faced woman who wore dark serge dresses, sang in the church choir, as did Lupe and I. There was only one problem: his mother didn't like me.

Lupe's mother, Doña Pomposa, was of medium height, with a slender body. She rarely smiled, and certainly not at me. Each Sunday, flanked by her daughter and sons, all dressed in their Sunday best, they walked to mass. They came by way of Pierce Street and arrived as the last bell was ringing.

In the choir Doña Pomposa stood next to the sopranos, her daughter alongside her. Her voice was not that of a true soprano, yet she refused to sing with those of us who were pushed to one side because we were altos. From the time she arrived, huffing and puffing, until mass was over, Doña Pomposa would glare at me. During communion when Lupe and I, flushed from singing the Mass of the Angels, sneaked to the front of the choir loft to wave at our friends below, she almost had apoplexy. She tried to keep him next to her, too. But Lupe and I sang the same part and range (we were both altos). She had no choice but to let him stand next to me.

Lupe and I shared the same music, too. Although all the choir members had their own copies of the Saint Gregory Missal, we often sang from sheet music distributed prior to the mass. Lupe was in charge of our music. He first scanned it, then pressed close. We sang on cue and made good music together.

The summer I was twelve, I knew it was almost time for me to have my first kiss. I would lie awake nights thinking about it, wondering if it might be the way it was in the movies or in the books I sneaked from Nora. Would his mouth feel soft? Wet? What if my teeth got locked in his?

One thing really bothered me: where did the noses go? What if we bumped noses? In the movies when a girl kissed a boy, theirs slipped right into place. They parted with her lipstick intact and his moustache still in place. I yearned to practice with someone, but Josey was my brother. I snuggled up to Duke, but he licked my face. I decided to ask Nancy, who knew everything there was to know about kissing. And I made up my mind that Lupe would give me my first kiss.

One night during a jamaica, Lupe asked me to meet him by the back entrance to the church hall, near the bushes. He took a friend and I took a friend. Our friends waited near the door, while Lupe and I talked. He acted shy, different from how he was in the choir. He stood looking down at his feet. I stood looking at him looking at his feet.

We talked awhile, then he put his arm around me. Just at that moment a car went by; he quickly pulled away. He reached over to hold my hand, but suddenly Father Mueller walked out to the street. Our friends whispered, "Jiggers!" We waited until he went inside again and his footsteps no longer echoed through the hall. Finally I could stand it no longer. When Lupe tentatively reached for me, I grabbed him by the shoulders and smacked him on the lips. We smashed noses.

Poor Lupe. He could barely speak from the shock. He rubbed his nose, pushed back the hair on his damp forehead, then waited to see what was next. I wiped my mouth, remembering what Concha had said, and adjusted my hair barrette, satisfied that I had been properly kissed. Our sentries whistled; it was time to go.

The next day I wrote him a letter. Whether in gratitude or in the first flush of "puppy love," I don't know. Perhaps I wanted to document the kiss.

Dear Lupe
I think you are cute.
Do you want to be my boyfriend?
Yes [ ]   No [ ]
Love and xxxxxx

Lupe's mother got hold of the letter. She gave it to Doña Luisa, who handed me the incriminating paper, a dark frown on her face.

"No tiene vergüenza!" Her dark eyes bored into me as she said I had no shame. Chasing after boys was to her a serious matter.

"No fue nada." I assured her it was nothing at all.

"Hmmmm."

Doña Luisa was hurt and embarrassed. She hated having anyone think badly of me, especially someone like Doña Pomposa, who talked only to God. She walked off to tend to the chickens, as I clutched the love note in my sweaty hand, grateful she had not given it to my mother!

Later she told me that Doña Pomposa had issued a warning, too: I'd better not bother her son again, or else. For a time I didn't. And then it was pointless, because that summer I shot up to my present height of five feet five inches, and left poor Lupe behind at four feet eleven. The romance was clearly over, but I still saw him in church. And his mother still glared at me.

That year I learned to read music quite well. I memorized the Mass of the Blessed Virgin Mary, which was terribly demanding and difficult to sing. The older choir members found this piece especially challenging; they had to read ahead and breathe without an apparent break. But I loved it! Especially when Lupe's mother began to gasp for air. I would smile sweetly at her as I sang "Kyrie Eleison" three times without breathing once. She would just glare some more.

Marta la Güera

Marta, nicknamed "la güera," was married to Don Roque, called Rocky by everyone but my father, his compadre. She was slender, of medium height, with fair skin, light brown eyes, a straight nose, and eyebrows that arched above her sad eyes. Her hair was worn in a limp pageboy; her skin was like fresh buttermilk. From her tiny ears dangled gold earrings in the form of a cross.

Marta rarely raised her voice at anyone, nor argued with her loud husband and obnoxious kids, all of whom towered over her. She rarely talked with anyone outside her family, nor did she belong to church clubs. When I met her on the street, she would smile politely, her eyes darting back and forth, then she would scurry off, her dress swishing below her slender knees.

Often I visited with Marta's daughters, Asuncion and Adelina, both of whom went to a private Catholic school and rarely played with the rowdies on Hoyt Street. Asuncion, or Chona, was small and frail; she resembled her mother except for the eyes. Adelina, called Lina, was short and tough like Rocky, whose stocky body she had inherited. She cussed a blue streak, relishing the Spanish words learned from her father. Mostly I was friends with Lina, who was my age.

Marta and her family lived three blocks away, in a large house with a picture window and furniture bought in Los Angeles. A maroon horsehair sofa sat in the living room; next to it was a glass coffee table. On one wall stood a china cabinet with glass doors, which held Rocky's whiskey glasses and assorted candy dishes. To the side were what in the better stores were called "occasional chairs," covered in a maroon-and-green flowered print. In the dining room sat an elegant mahogany table with eight chairs covered in red velvet. On the polished table there were crocheted doilies, edged in purple. These were starched stiff and resembled large fans. In the center of each doily was a fruit or flower arrangement.

The large house had a number of rooms. Each girl had her own bedroom. Asunción's was next to the bathroom; Lina's was toward the back. I thought Lina's bedroom the prettiest of the two, although both had twin beds and a dresser set. At each window in Lina's room hung pink dotted-swiss curtains, held back with ties of pink gros-grain ribbon like that I used on my hair. Next to Lina's bed was a table, and on it was a ceramic lamp etched with a man and woman wearing silks and lace. The two looked like George and Martha Washington, except for the powdered wigs.

Lina's bed was covered by a pretty taffeta bedspread. Fluffy pillows shaped like hearts, squares, and circles nestled against each other. Each pillow was of pink satin covered with a white crocheted design, made by her grandmother, I knew. I thought Lina's family was terribly rich! Not only did they have a fine house, but each girl had her own bed. At home three of my sisters had to share a bed!

Marta and Rocky were very sociable. Although Marta appeared not to have close friends, the couple hosted parties throughout the year: bautismos, birthdays, and wedding showers. Since Rocky was from Texas, each summer he hired a man to dig a pit in the backyard for la barbacoa. He would haul an old oil drum to the backyard, cut it in half, fill it with brasitas, then cook huge chunks of meat on it.

One time when the family gave a birthday party for Rocky, my parents, although older than their friends, were invited. I was not included, but I went along anyway. Lina, spoiled rotten and at eleven already bigger than her mother, insisted that I be there.

"If she don't come, I'll break the . . ."

"Ay dios mío, how can you talk that way to your mother!"

"Like this, see! Con la boca."

During the party, while Lina served us enchiladas, rice and beans, potato salad, and Kool Aid, I walked through the pretty house. I ran my hand over the smooth velvet cushions in the living room, fingered the glass ashtrays on the coffee table, then went into the bathroom and locked the door.

I tiptoed on the maroon tile to inspect the white tub and enclosed

shower that shone bright even in the dim light. I fingered the fancy
faucets, nearly burning my hands with the hot water that gushed
from the one marked C, then pulled the handle on the toilet tank and
flushed el toledo, as we called it. It made a quiet noise. Our toilet,
installed by my father when he remodeled our bathroom, had a tank
suspended over the commode with a handle and chain that released
what I called "Niagara Falls." Often I kept my head sideways when
I was sitting on the seat, just in case the tank fell and drowned me.

That night while the adults talked, Lina and I sneaked into her
parents' bedroom.

"Close the door."

"I did, see?"

"Lock it!"

Lina first closed the curtains, then turned on a lamp. From her
mother's closet, she brought out an assortment of dresses, jackets,
and coats, including one made of "wallaby," a fake fur that was then
quite popular. Lina let me try on the coat, while she struggled into
a red coat called a Chesterfield; then we both stood in front of the
mirror. I looked like a fat bear; Lina like a red refrigerator.

Undaunted, we inspected her mother's size 5 ½ shoe collection,
none of which fit, except on our hands. Some shoes had shiny buckles
and tiny straps of fine leather. A pair of black platform shoes also lay
on the closet floor. These were identical to those worn by my sister
Nora. To the side were slippers called "mules," with pink pom-poms,
like those worn by glamorous women in the movies.

Exhausted from fingering all the pretty things, we took a short
break. While I folded and put away Marta's clothes, Lina sneaked
into the kitchen. When she came back her round arms were loaded
with an array of goodies: pie, cakes, and empanaditas. While we
gobbled the treats, Lina pulled out a narrow drawer from the maple
dresser next to the wall. Inside on a velvet pad lay her mother's
jewelry: pins, earrings, a rhinestone necklace, a string of matching
pearls, a charm bracelet, and a jade ring surrounded by tiny dia-
monds. Against the soft velvet the jewels glowed as if alive.

Lina then explained that each time her parents fought, Rocky (as
she called her father) would lose his temper and hit la güera. The
next day he would vow never to do it again. A contrite Rocky would

climb into his shiny Buick and drive to the best store in San Fernando, where he had a standing account, to buy his wife a small trinket.

Rocky offered his wife the jewelry in exchange for the forgiveness she always granted him. The ruby earrings, Lina explained, picking her nose, were bought when Rocky punched la güera and cracked two of her ribs. The silver bracelet was given her after Rocky, furious at his wife for smiling at the butcher, twisted Marta's wrist until it cracked. Although she wore a cast for a time, that was now her favorite pulsera, Lina said, giggling all the while.

"And these?" I held a pair of earrings up to the light.

They were diamond earrings. The tiny droplets of clear, glistening crystals, Lina told me, were presented to Marta after Rocky, in a rage, smashed her against the china cabinet and fractured her collarbone.

Lina was not the least bit ashamed to talk about her parents, nor was she afraid of being overheard. No tenía vergüenza! Many times, while waiting for her to come out to play, I would hear her screaming at her amá.

"You better buy me that dress, or else . . ."

"Ay mija! It's not your size."

"Buy it anyway, or . . ."

From a distance she sounded just like her father.

That night we sat cross-legged on the fluffy pink lace-edged bedspread that covered la güera's bed like frosting on a cake. I munched on a cookie as Lina sifted through her mother's jewelry, recounting its history. "The opal ring is from Mexico," Lina said, brushing cake crumbs on the pink bedspread. "Rocky went to Texas to visit mis tíos. They got drunk, then went across the border to a whorehouse in Matamoros. Rocky came home with something called syphilis and the ring. He gave her the ring first, then el sífilis. She gots real sick and had to go to a doctor in Los Angeles. El doctor wanted to examine him, but Rocky said no."

"Gosh! And then what happened?"

"Rocky called my mother a whore. He said she gots sick from doing bad things while he was in Texas. He hit her real hard, until my granma called el Padre Juanito."

"These are from Japan." Lina held a string of matching pearls against the lamp, then slowly hung them on my neck. They were heavy; I could bearly keep my head up. I looked at myself in the mirror, then gently removed the necklace and handed it to Lina.

"One day Rocky came home drunk. He was angry 'cause his truck broke down and the mechanic cheated him. He caught my mama in the kitchen, then chased her to the bedroom and smacked her; he broke her nose. Rocky felt real bad. Then the doctor threatened to report him! After he paid the doctor, in cash, he bought the pearls. The next day we got dressed up and went to visit mi mamá at the hospital. She had a private room, so I got to sit on her bed. Right before we got there, Rocky stopped to buy flowers, you know, at the place on the corner. They cost ten dollars. Rocky felt bad! He bought me and Asunción small bouquets, too. Chona threw hers in the garbage. She hates Rocky."

"Do you?"

"Neh. Besides, she asked for it."

Lina stifled a yawn, then got up and put the pearls back in their velvet bed. I followed her out of the room and into the kitchen, where we gorged on vanilla ice cream.

Marta, it seems, was not immediately aware of the pearls' perfection and beauty; her swollen nose and eyes, ringed with purple bruises, were covered with gauze. But in time she wore them. They were added to the collection of pins and earrings in the drawer.

Soon after that Rocky gave his wife a black laquered jewelry box lined with red velvet. One large enough to hold her growing jewelry collection.

The Movies at Sanfer

Watching movies was my favorite pastime. I rarely missed the old westerns with predictable plots and aging cowboys shown at the church hall, but like most of my friends, I preferred the popular movies show in the theaters.

By the time I was in eighth grade and getting ready to graduate from Pacoima Elementary, I was allowed to attend the movies in "town," as my sisters referred to San Fernando. I went with Concha and Virgie. Immediately after Sunday mass, stopping only to toss my hat on the hall table and to hound my parents for money, I would tear off to meet my friends. We met in front of Concha's house, next to the shady trees that flanked the gate.

"Where's Concha?"

"She's in the toilet."

"We're gonna be late!"

"Yeah, but she'll make it in her pants."

I checked my purse for change, smoothed my hair, and wanting to feel grown up, hitched up my skirt, praying that neither my mother nor Doña Luisa were near a window. Virgie, more impatient than I, knocked at Concha's door until she came out. We inspected each other until we were satisfied with how we looked, then walked at a rapid pace toward the bus stop on the corner of Van Nuys Boulevard and San Fernando Road. We plunked in a dime, then settled down for the ride to town, anxious to be en el chow.

On Sundays, busses were filled to the top with kids going to movie matinees. Everyone liked best to ride in the back. The seat there was wide and easily held four or five rowdies. This was also a favorite place for kids going steady; it allowed them to sit close. Each time the bus swerved, they would cling to each other and giggle with delight.

When it came time to choose a seat, I had to decide who I wanted to be next to, Concha or Virgie. Concha was sort of sensitive and often reminded me that she and I had been friends before Virgie moved to Hoyt Street. She tended to forget the many times she had ignored me while talking to Beto Torres. If the back seat was full, I scouted around for someone I knew, then thumped myself next to them, leaving my two friends to fend for themselves. This way, I told myself, they won't get mad and leave me stranded behind, like Nancy did

Nancy went to the show more than anyone else on Hoyt Street. She chaperoned her older sister on Friday nights and accompanied her mother to the Mexican movies at the San Fernando Theater on Tuesdays. These were mostly in black and white, with actors like Jorge Negrete, María Felix, and a funny man called El Piporo, who told jokes and got in everyone's way. Now and then they featured movies "straight from Mexico City," with hippy women in skimpy costumes and blonde hair. All the important women, I noticed had light hair; the servants were all indias. Their long braids dangled down their thick backs as they walked three paces behind their blue-eyed mistresses. Unlike me, Nancy did not translate movies for her mother. Her job was to keep her parents supplied with treats: esquite, and sodas from the tiny snack bar in the lobby.

I liked the Mexican movies. Not only were they in a different language, but all the leading men could sing. Often while chasing each other on sweaty horses, they would pull to the side and break into song. It fascinated me that the sound of violins and trumpets would fill the screen; where, I wondered, were the músicos hiding? I scanned the rocks and bushes, but could never locate el violín.

María Felix was considered to be the most important female movie star of the Mexican cinema. Her expressive face was dominated by high cheekbones; her dark eyes were framed by eyebrows that resembled black wings. When she was agitated, which was often, her right eyebrow dramatically twitched up and down. She wore her hair in a long bush, and when angry at her boyfriend, tossed it behind her shoulder. Now and then she wore feathers in her hair. They fluttered around her dark eyes like rare birds.

María Felix wore tight dresses with huge shoulder pads and draped skirts that skimmed her full hips. On her shapley feet she wore ankle-strap shoes with platform heels. Often I confused her with Joan

Crawford (she too wore jackets with huge shoulders), except that Joan spoke English. It amazed me that most Mexican movie stars sang, danced, and cried on cue. American actors were only good at one thing—either they danced or sang. Few did both.

Mexican-Americans were not welcome in all the theatres. Although no one tried to keep us out, we knew where we were welcome and where we were not. We exchanged stories of the many times we were made to feel unwelcome at a movie house. Concha told of the time her sister and her date were told to move to the Mexican section. Others told of how when they laughed aloud, the Anglo ushers stuck a flashlight in their faces:

"Hey you, not so loud!"

"We wasn't doing nuthin'."

"Shut up or we'll kick you out."

The older boys sat upstairs, where they could smoke if they wanted. Young couples liked to be in the back, where they could "neck" until intermission. When the lights went on, the girls would dash to the bathroom to fix their lipstick, wanting the other girls to know they had been kissing. They would dab at mouths with toilet paper, slap on another layer of lipistiqui, then scurry back to their dates, ready for more kisses.

Mundo and other rowdies like him sat upstairs, where they were undetectable to the frenzied ushers. From there they threw gum and popcorn at the girls below. Once Mundo threw a wad of gum and hit Nancy.

"*Baboso*," she screamed. She looked up and saw Mundo duck. Without a word to her date, a skinny boy named Fausto, she stalked up the stairs, yanked Mundo by the shirt collar, and smacked him across the ear.

"Toma!"

With a toss of her dark head, Nancy stalked back to her seat, as Mundo's buddies jeered and smacked Mundo on the back.

"Ya gonna let a girl hit you?"

"She ain't touched me!"

"Oh yeah? What she do, kiss ya?"

Of the three movie places in town, we were made to feel welcome only at the San Fernando Theater, next door to Thrifty Drugs. It was like most others, except that it was shabbier, with worn carpeting in the lobby and seats held together with electrical tape. At the entrance was a small booth that dispensed snacks; behind it was a wide mirror where we could see who was walking in. Two narrow doors with red velvet drapes swung open each time someone went through; they led to the seats below. The girls bathroom had two toilets, both of which leaked. One of the seats was cracked in the middle. If I wasn't careful, I tended to get my behind caught in the crack.

A wide mirror lined an entire wall of the girls bathroom; an aluminum shelf below could hold makeup and assorted hairpins. The line to the girls bathroom was always long; I often missed the best part of a movie. Right before el chow began, the girl's bathroom was a beehive of activity.

"Gimme the comb."

"Hurry up, the chow is startin'."

"I gotta pee . . ."

Across town was the Rennie Theater. Larger, with a wide lobby carpeted in rich maroon and two snack bars, this place was off limits to the chicanada, the Mexican-Americans, of Pacoima and "Sanfer." It catered mostly to Anglos. Not until after World War II did Mexican-Americans become socially acceptable at local movie houses and restaurants. Men from the barrio, it became known, were also wounded and killed while fighting for their country, the good old USA. It was unpatriotic to turn away nonwhites in uniform, especially those with medals and Purple Hearts pinned to their chests.

And so we were made welcome and allowed to sit in any section of the theaters: in the loges, as the upstairs was called, or smack in the front, where the picture appeared to come out at us. By this time however, we had already chosen to attend the San Fernando Theater, where the owner was friendly and made us feel most welcome.

Mort was Jewish and tolerant of other minorities. His was the only theatre that allowed Negroes in, too, although there were less of them than of us. Mort was also a good businessman and made sure the snack bar was fully stocked. He was among the first to hire Mexican kids as ushers, and he rarely called the cops on the pachucos. For the Mexican-Americans of "Pacas" and "Sanfer," the fun place on Sunday afternoons was the San Fernando Theater, on Brand Street.

The "draw" for the Sunday matinees were the weekly serials. Kids from Pacoima took the long bus ride, then stood in line under the hot sun, eager to learn the latest escapades of the blond heroine of *The Perils of Pauline* and of the curvaceous girl called "Nyoka of the Jungle." Even then the serials were ancient; the women wore clothes seen only in museums.

The boys, however, cared not a whit if a movie was old. What held their interest were the buxom women with sultry eyes and pouting lips. They adored la Nyoka, and each time she appeared in a skimpy outfit, they would whistle and stomp their feet.

"Owwweeee."

"Whatta fine chick!"

"*Que nalgotas.*"

The women's hairdos too, were dated, similar to styles worn by the "flappers" of the 1920s. Their makeup often looked coarse and heavy. Up close their tiny mouths were painted wide and full. They looked grotesque. Their eyes were ringed by black circles; their pencil-thin eyebrows appeared to melt.

In each episode Pauline and la Nyoka were caught up in hair-raising adventures that had me gasping for air and clinging to the edge of my seat. Each episode was better than the last, with Nyoka (whom I preferred), lying on the edge of a deep abyss, blond hair in disarray, her blue eyes wide with fear. Pauline wore a tiara on her head. She was chased by monsters who spewed smoke from their huge nostrils. The women fought back with spears and rocks, but lost out in the end. Each serial ended with Pauline and Nyoka on the brink of death, waiting to be rescued by a handsome hero.

My friends and I especially liked the heroes, most of whom were also blond, with blue eyes and wide, powerful chests. Some wore breastplates that shimmered in the light. They resembled the Roman soldiers in our catechism books who had killed Christ. In one especially exciting episode, la Pauline was being chased by a horde of Huns led by a dark-haired man who wore heavy bracelets on his arms and anklets on his legs. He wore a short tunic with a design near the bottom, similar to a skirt, that showed off his muscular legs. On his feet he wore Roman sandals with leather thongs. When he finally caught up with Pauline, rather than break her neck, he took her in his arms and off they rode into the sunset.

When Nyoka's dress blew in the wind and exposed her shapely legs, Mundo whistled and clapped his hands. He poked fun at Pauline's headpiece and runny makeup, and cheered for the sweaty men that chased after her. He sided with the hairy monsters that were after Nyoka, too, encouraging them to catch her. I hated to sit near Mundo; each time he acted smart, I yearned to smack him across the mouth. When the words "to be continued" finally flashed on the screen, I would sink back in my seat, exhausted and exhilarated.

As we left the theater, and all the way to the bus stop, we talked of the coming episodes and of our plans to return to the San Fernando Theater the following Sunday.

Other than Nancy, few of the girls who lived on Hoyt Street dated or went steady. But by the time I was twelve, my friends and I would make arrangements to sit with someone we liked at the movies. Nancy, who was one year older and twenty years wiser, was very picky about who she sat with. Not until we were at the theater door did she decide whom to honor with her presence.

"Nancy, Nancy, you wanna sit with me?"

"Gosh Nancy, you sure look pretty! I'm in row ten!"

"You're too good to sit with him, Nancy."

Nancy first looked a boy over, checking to see if he wore nice clothes and new shoes. She would then open wide her brown eyes and with a toss of her dark hair, smile at the Chosen One. Always determined not to spend her own money, she would act coy when her "date" insisted on paying her way. Once she had decided, Nancy would put her skinny arm through the lucky fellow's, and off they would go. She knew enough to sit near the gang, since if she went upstairs to the loges, she might end up being kissed and more. Nancy was smart.

One year George S., or "Chochis," as his mother called him, asked me to go with him to a matinee. I wasn't too thrilled; Chochis was un gordito. The fact that I too was chubby was of no consequence to me. I mean, we didn't both have to be gordinflones! At first I told him I had promised Virgie and Concha I'd sit with them, but when I saw his downcast eyes and pouting mouth, I changed my mind; I told him to meet me in the theater lobby. I dreaded having my friends see me with fat George! But when he whispered "I wanna pay your way," I forgot my embarrassment and quickly joined him in line.

It was fun to sit with George; he ate all during the movie. He loaded up beforehand, his chunky arms laden with sodas, popcorn, and candy. During intermission he waddled down the aisle to buy more dulces. Just before the movie ended, he shoved his way to the lobby once more to stuff his pants pockets with chocolates. To be with him was to partake in a continuous feed. Food was happiness for Chochis and for me.

There was a certain security in being with him. He was content to stuff himself during the movie and to leave me alone. He would plunge his hands into a popcorn bag, tearing it in the process, then bring his buttery paws to his wide mouth, stuff it with popcorn, and chomp away. When finished with the popcorn, he wiped his hands on his pants, then from a shirt pocket he slipped Milk Duds and Milky Ways into my eager hands.

Chochis was so busy eating he never had time to get fresh with me; all he ever did was put his arm around me. One arm on my shoulder, the other buried in a big bag of buttered popcorn. While the other girls were kept busy fighting off los frescos, I munched my way contentedly through the movie, mesmerized by the antics of Pauline and Nyoka, secure with an array of my favorite candies.

Sometimes the movies included leftover news of World War II. Black-and-white scenes of battles, soldiers, and tanks flashed on the screen: the fighting men of the USA! These newsreels were boring. My friends and I thought the war was over or at least about to end, what with Hitler dead and the Japanese daily committing hari-kari. The war news was like another movie, part of the entertainment offered to youngsters on a Sunday afternoon.

One time during intermission, they showed a short propaganda movie. It included a funny jingle that the audience was urged to sing:

> *Stinky Jap, off the map,*
> *Benito's jaw, oh, ho, ho.*

We sang several verses, all funny and clever. I stopped eating just enough to sing along. We sang and sang; the theater rocked with shouts of laughter and jeers.

But it felt wrong to be making fun of olive-skinned Japanese and swarthy Italians. *We* were neither blond nor blue-eyed, but brown.

Morenos, trigueños, prietos, not white enough to be accepted in the Rennie Theater, yet encouraged to laugh at others who, like our Mexican ancestors, had fought and lost a war against this country. People who to this day were mocked and called "dirty Mexicans."

I was grateful that this "short" was not screened again. My parents were not racist; neither was I. Mort, I think, disliked the film, too. Or perhaps he thought it old, dated, and in poor taste. In any event, he never showed it again.

El Faite

When in Pacoima Elementary I was well liked. I wasn't quite a teacher's pet, as I talked too much, but I was able to get along with most kids. My good friends were Elvira, an *A* student with whom I competed for gold stars, and Fat Lupe, a spoiled girl who was generous with candy. Both girls lived on Mercer Street. But Concha was still the one to whom I told all my secrets.

Our room in eighth grade was Room 8A. Across the hall was Room 8B. Here were found a group of girls, "toughies," who cussed at teachers, fought among themselves, and formed, if not a gang, a clique. During recess, while the teachers refereed games, they would trip unsuspecting students and yank smaller girls by the hair. When they were caught fighting or were hauled off to the office, the rowdies, voices raised high, would insist that they were only teasing, daring the harassed teacher to say otherwise.

"Angie says you kicked her on purpose!"

"Yeah, and who else?"

When they couldn't scare girls their own age, they would pick on younger kids by ripping up their school papers and demanding that they hand over their lunch money. I often thought that they only wanted attention from the teachers—and the older boys.

None of the girls lived on Hoyt Street nor in the immediate neighborhood. These overripe girls, some of whom were very, very pretty, were not the least bit interested in school; some had been put back a grade or two. Each morning, long past the final bell, they would saunter into class, lips pasted with lipstick and eyes coated thick with mascara that on rainy days ran down their cheeks. They spent the school day chewing bubble gum, filing their painted nails, and trying to look grown-up. They liked nothing better than to intimidate the substitutes assigned to their room, usually frail-looking women who were never again seen at our school.

Mrs. Paynes taught in Room 8B. She was a mousy-looking woman with thin, wispy hair, pale grey eyes, and bad breath. She trembled when challenged by the older students and practically fainted when called to the principal's office. Each day from 8:20 A.M. to 3:00 P.M., she endured the tauntings of the "toughies."

"Gotta pain, Mrs. Payne?"

"Rain, pain, en la vieja Mrs. Payne."

She rarely complained to the principal about her rowdy students, all of whom were taller than she. It was said that she not only feared repercussions from the big kids, but was also afraid of having the principal think she could not control her class.

Mrs. Goodsome, our principal, was a kind, elderly woman; we felt lucky to have her at Pacoima Elementary. When school officials were screening applicants for her position, it was said, they had turned down women with advanced degrees and outstanding letters of recommendation, wanting someone who they felt understood Mexican-American culture and our educational needs. They lured Mrs. Goodsome, then an assistant principal at a Van Nuys school, not with promises of money, but by describing the importance of education to Mexican-American children. She readily accepted.

Among her many talents, Mrs. Goodsome had a way of building students' self-esteem. She complimented us on our pretty Spanish names, and tried to pronounce each one correctly.

"Gwadaloopee?"

"Lupe."

"Secundina?"

"My amá calls me Suki."

She asked after our parents by name, said she was pleased to be our principal, and on warm, sunny days, sauntered out to the playground to watch us play ball. During Christmas the holiday program included Spanish songs such as "Noche de Paz," as well as traditional carols sung in English. Our principal kept in touch with the public-health nurse who worked out of the San Fernando Clinic and periodically visited our town, especially before each school term began. She felt it her duty to ensure that all school-aged kids, especially those about to enter kindergarten, were vaccinated.

Mrs. Goodsome knew most of the families on Hoyt Street. She encouraged kids to stay in school and tried to convince parents to keep their children there.

"Senïor Lopez, Juan is such a good student. Is there any way he can remain here while you're in Mexico?"

"No es posible."

"Will he still attend school?"

"Hmmm."

When an errant student was called to her office, she would scold him by name, threaten to send home a note written in both Spanish and English, or she would use the belt. Some students, knowing full well their parents could barely read, accepted the note; still others opted for a swat, knowing that the principal had delicate, veiny hands that could barely hold el cinto. Mrs. Goodsome rarely swatted girls. In a thin, quavering voice, one she rarely used, she would ask a girl to do her best, then send her back to class.

Students sent to the principal's office were made to sit outside the glass door, usually scared stiff of this lady, who never raised her voice. We knew she kept a wooden ruler, used to rap knuckles, atop her desk. Few kids talked back to Mrs. Goodsome; none dared to hit her back, but once out of sight, boys like Mundo would stick their tongues out at her. My parents felt that students who did not respect their own parents would not obey teachers either. They cautioned us to respect our teachers at all times and especially to respect Mrs. Goodsome.

One day in the office I saw Chita walk into Mrs. Goodsome's office, a note clutched in her hand. She gave it to the principal, then sat to wait. Although I lingered in the hallway, I was unable to hear a thing; later I learned that Mrs. Goodsome had asked Chita to be office monitor for her room! For mousey Mrs. Paynes! I found this hard to believe; most teachers chose their office monitor from the top students.

"I'm the monitor now, get it?"

"Yeah!"

In the following weeks Chita arrived early to school, unrecognizable in regular clothes. Gone was the tough stance, the tight skirts, and sweaters. Things went well for about a week.

One day I was in the girls' bathroom, when I looked up to see

Chita slap Fat Lupe. Fat Lupe began to cry; her flat nose started to bleed. I wet a paper towel, handed it to Lupe, then dared to look up.

"Whatcha lookin at?"

"You're gonna get in trouble."

"Yeah? You gonna tell on me?"

The following day Fat Lupe's father drove up to our school in a shiny Buick. He parked right in front of the school, jumped across the side gate, then marched into the principal's office. He berated Mrs. Goodsome for allowing a bully to hurt his precious child. Mrs. Goodsome, her face flushed a deep pink, offered an apology. She then sent for Chita, who could not be found. When by the next week Chita had not shown up, a new room monitor took her place.

Chita was short, stocky, and tough. She had a pug nose with freckles across it and reddish hair. All six members of her family looked alike, with the same frizzy hair and hazel eyes. Her family was part Irish, folks said, because of their fair skin and last name, but Chita was actually María Jovita and spoke Spanish like we did. She lived in a clapboard house near the railroad tracks, with pink wisteria vines hiding the front door. Toward the back was the usual cactus grove.

Chita and her friends were just hanging around until eighth-grade graduation, bored with books they could not read and school assignments that never made sense. They hated teachers and school rules and wanted nothing more than to quit school and get a job.

Few of them went on to high school. In most large families, certainly those on Hoyt Street, there was little money set aside for education. What's more, boys were encouraged to go on to high school, while it was generally thought that girls would not need a diploma to change diapers. Girls were often forced to drop out of school to help at home or to harvest crops. They would leave in the heat of summer, never to return to la escuela. In such cases Mrs. Goodsome, eyes full of understanding, would sign the necessary forms, then usher the girl to the door.

Once I was sent to deliver a note to Room 8B. I knocked and knocked, then nearly fell backwards when Lily, a roly-poly girl, finally opened the door. The room was dark, the shades at half-mast. At her desk Mrs. Paynes read aloud from a history book. Toward the rear sat Chita and her cousin Della, painting their nails from a tiny bottle balanced between two schoolbooks. Chita looked up, snickered, then continued to paint magenta polish on her nails. I handed the note to Mrs. Paynes and had started to walk out, when something hit my head. A stubby pencil, like that used by kindergartners, lay near my feet. My face turned red; my ears tingled. With trembling hands I picked up the pencil and laid it on the chalktray. Mrs. Payne, myopic eyes glued to the page, never looked up. I felt a twinge of fear, but once in my room I managed to return to my schoolwork. When later that week I heard that Chita was planning to "get me," my terror knew no bounds.

I don't recall who first told me that she was after me, but I think it might have been Mundo, who liked nothing better than a good "faite." At first I thought it was a joke. A bad joke. Although we were not good friends, Chita sometimes said "Hi" to me at the grocery store. But at recess my best friend Concha ran over to whisper "Chita's gonna get you"; I began to take it seriously. I begged Concha not to tell Mrs. Blynders, our teacher. I tried to act normal, but my stomach was in a tight knot, my ears alert for the recess bell. My fear of Chita overwhelmed me; I couldn't even play kickball.

There was no reason for Chita wanting to "get me." But none was needed. The fear I felt was immediate, urgent, and almost ran down my legs. I tried not to show how scared I was as we filed back to the classroom. In the bathroom I wet paper towels, then held them to my sweaty brow.

I feared violence. I didn't know how to fight! I had only fought with Josey, who neither scratched nor pulled hair. I had never seen my sisters slap each other. Not even Berney, who for years had chased me across the yard, dared to lay a hand on me. I often hit my brother's punching bag, but even that I did without enthusiasm.

During lunch Chita had passed by me three times, taunting me with a fist. Nostrils flared, brown eyes blazing, she sought my eyes, but I refused the challenge. I didn't want to be known as a "stoolie," but neither did I want to be beaten up. I kept silent and ate my lunch.

When the final bell rang at the end of the school day, I lingered in the girls' bathroom, hiding in the stall. I flushed and reflushed the toilet, hoping Chita would tire of waiting and go home. Finally I collected my books and my courage, walked silently along the empty corridor, then bolted out the school gate for home. I was about to cross the alley behind Virgie's house, when I looked up to see Chita and her friends waiting near the corner.

In a panic I looked for a way to avoid her and get home in one piece, but other than to backtrack around Virgie's house and cross the alley, there was none. But that route was even more dangerous; Chita could reach the alley and cut me off. I took a deep breath, then walked toward her, books tight against my trembling chest, praying that someone would come to my aid.

Unbeknownst to me, Josey had run home to tell our mother that I was fighting in the street, which was about the worst thing a girl could do at that time. As I walked toward the smirking Chita, I looked up to see my mother coming from the other direction, Josey hot on her heels, as Virgie and Concha walked out to the street. In her right hand my mother carried una escoba, a broom. She slowly walked toward us, her round face flushed. Chita and her friends saw her approach and moved aside, all the while taunting me with their dark eyes.

I stood frozen, not knowing what to expect, as Chita moved back from the deadly circle. I saw my mother come closer and closer. When she stood in front of me, she slowly raised high the broom. Not at them, but at me! As the broom came down, my hand shot out to ward off the blow; my books went flying. The broom turned in midair and struck my mother in the face.

"Ay! Me pegaste," exclaimed my mother, her hand to her cheek.

"Gosh! She hit her own mother," gasped Virgie.

"That's a mortal sin," cried Concha, looking at me with frightened eyes. She glanced at my mother, then looked down at her feet, ashamed to have witnessed something so vile.

"Jesús, María, y José," cried Doña Remedios from her front porch, hands clasped together as if in prayer, "se te va secar la mano! Your hand is going to shrivel up!" (On Hoyt Street folks said that if a child dared to hit a parent, his or her hand would shrivel up as a form of punishment.) I looked up at Doña Remedios, then at my hand, which was beginning to tingle.

I stood smack in the middle of the street, fighting back tears. My mother rubbed the welt on her cheek, smoothed her apron, then turned and walked home, Josey at her side. Chita and her friends tapped their feet on the dirt path. Bored with waiting, they walked off to the corner store where the boys congregated. Only the broom and I remained, with Doña Remedios squinting at me from her porch.

I picked up the broom and dusted my books off. My heart was pounding as I walked home; my feet dragged on the dirt. The broom appeared to weigh a ton.

Soon everyone in our family and on Hoyt Street knew that I had been en un faite. And worse, that I had hit my mother with the broom. As we set the table for dinner, my sisters avoided my eyes; even Josey was subdued. Duke rubbed against me and licked my hands. When I was done in the kitchen, I sat near the walnut tree where Doña Luisa found me.

"How could you hit your mother," she wailed, dark eyes full of despair. "Pero cómo?"

"I didn't do it on purpose," I stammered, my eyes to the ground. "No fue de adrede."

"Bueno, ask God not to shrivel your hand," she instructed, then went indoors, her apron flapping.

Later that evening Doña Luisa once more came to my rescue. She waited for my father to drive up, then once he had parked the truck, gave him her version of el faite. At dinnertime I did not eat with the family; I walked home with Doña Luisa to eat cinnamon toast. And although I no longer slept over with our adopted grandmother, I stayed the night, secure in the lumpy bed that dipped in the middle.

I cried myself to sleep. I had had a trying day, first with Chita, and then with the broom. My hand felt dry and stiff. God was punishing me for having hit my mother. Within weeks, I knew, my entire arm could just fall off!

Only Doña Luisa consoled me. "Ya duérmase, she whispered, as she put out the kerosene lamp and checked under the bed for the bacinilla.

That night I began to grow up. I felt older, wiser, and in some ways, bitter. I had felt fear where I had felt trust, among girls I had known all my life. I felt rage at Josey for having snitched to my mother and for having left me alone to face the broom. I felt betrayed by a God who would punish me for accidentally hitting my mother. I began to hate the dichos, the Mexican folk sayings that served to keep us in line by frightening us with their scary predictions. I did not look forward to the grown-up world. My hand, however, remained whole.

The May Day Festival

My last year at Pacoima Elementary, Mrs. Betty Blynders came to teach at our school. She was promptly assigned to our class of rowdy "seniors" in Room 8A. This was the best time of our lives, or so our teachers emphasized. While some kids were planning to drop out of school, many more planned to go on to high school. Once our winter class graduated in January, we would leave behind our secure world and kind principal. We were determined to make our last year in elementary school one worth remembering. When we were told that we would have a new teacher to guide us through the last semesters, we felt almost blessed.

"Gosh, a new teesher."

"I wanted Mrs. Paddington."

"She teaches second grade, stuped."

"But she's so nice."

Mrs. Blynders was tall, with a slim body that belied her thirty-odd years. She wore bright, flowered dresses that swirled around her trim ankles and were a marked contrast to the drab clothes the other teachers wore. The pretty clothes, rich chestnut hair, blue-green eyes, and flashing smile made her special to us. I thought of her as not unlike a fairy-tale princess, not because she was comely, but because she was kind and appeared to like us. Each morning she waltzed into Room 8A, smiling as she opened windows, erased blackboards, and arranged the papers on her desk. From the first we adored her; within a week we became her willing slaves.

Mrs. Blynders had a lovely singing voice; high and clear, not quite a soprano, but almost. Soon after the semester began, she organized a choir of eighth-grade girls.

One sunny day we marched to the auditorium, where the piano

was located, to audition for the choir. Mrs. Blynders told us we could sing as a group, or each girl could sing a favorite song, one she knew the words to. We lined up next to the piano where our enthusiastic teacher sat, fingers poised, ready to accompany us.

School songs such as "My Country, 'Tis of Thee" and "America the Beautiful" we knew by heart. Yet we each longed to impress our new teacher with a song that was different, special. We formed a huddle.

"I wanna sing 'My Country, 'Tis of Thee,'" insisted Concha, as she leaned against the old mahogany piano.

"I know most of the words to "O Susanna," said Virgie, looking anxiously toward the door.

"I wish it was recess," sighed Elvira, a shy girl whose voice barely rose above a whisper. "I hate to sing."

When we failed to agree on any one song, we decided that each girl should sing the song she knew best. We pushed Concha forward and stood back to listen. Concha smoothed her dress, adjusted her barrettes, then took a deep breath and began to sing:

"Columbus, the jam of the ocean . . ."

"Excuse me Conception, uhhh Concha," interrupted Mrs. Blynders, "but are you singing 'Hail Columbia'?"

"Yes, ma'am."

"But isn't that 'Columbia, the *gem* of the ocean'?"

"That's what I said. The jam," answered Concha with a toss of her head.

"Oh, I see. Well, that's fine. Next," said our embarrassed teacher, as she thumbed through the music on the piano stand.

Gloria Solís was next. She was tall and thin, with big buck teeth. Mundo, who had names for everyone, called her "la Bugs Bunny," but never in front of teachers. She shuffled to the front, scratched her nose, pushed back her straight hair, then in a soft, whispy voice began to sing "America the Beautiful" as she stared at her feet.

"Thank you, Gloriiiia," chirped Mrs. Blynders looking quite pleased. "Next."

"I'm next," announced Fat Lupe, as she shoved her way to the front. This unpleasant and spoiled girl liked to give orders. This day she wore a starched pinafore over a pink cotton dress, thick wool socks that came to her fat knees, and a pink velvet ribbon on her dark braids. As she went past me, she removed a wad of bubble gum from her mouth and stuck it under a seat. Once stationed to the left of the piano, Fat Lupe began to sing:

> *A la huerta, vamos a la huerta,*
> *A la huerta, chante fumaré.*

Mrs. Blynders looked puzzled. She finally removed her foot from the pedal and asked the surprised Lupe: "Are you singing 'Alouette'?"

"No, I'm singing "A la Huerta," Lupe answered, looking slightly offended.

"Are you sure?"

"That's what the song is," volunteered Nancy and Rosie from the back of the room.

"Well it sounds like 'Alouette,'" insisted Mrs. Blynders. "It's French, you know."

"Well this one's Mexican," answered Concha smugly. "We sing it when we go to the nuts."

"To the nuts?"

"Yes'm, when we pick nuts, uhh, walnuts. 'La huerta' means the trees, I think."

"Oh, but of course! Well, that was very, very nice!"

While Lupe sang, I began to clear my throat. I felt nervous, my hands clammy. I wanted to sing something different, but could not decide what. I feared making a mistake or, worse, having a frog in my throat. Finally Lupe finished and took her seat, a smug grin on her face. I immediately stood up, adjusted my plaid skirt, pulled in my stomach, and walked toward the piano. Mrs. Blynders hit middle C, then waited. I took a deep breath and began to sing the "Kyrie" from the Mass of the Blessed Virgin Mary, an intricate, moving piece. I had learned this hymn to perfection in the church choir. It was one of my favorites, not because it was in Latin (a language I barely understood), but because of its melody.

> *Ky-i-i-i-ri-i-e, E-e-e-e-le-i-son,*
> *Criste-e-e-eh, Ele-e-i-son . . .*

Mrs. Blynders tried to follow along. Her slender hands plunked out the F chord, then hit B-flat, but nothing sounded right. She looked up at me as if for a signal, then finally gave up and listened. Fat Lupe had a puzzled look on her face; it was clear that she neither knew nor cared about what I sang. Nancy and Concha tried not to laugh; I tried not to miss a beat. I sang for myself and for our teacher. When I was finished, I took a seat next to Concha, my face hot and flushed. "Well, fancy that," said our music teacher. "Fancy that!"

The choir met every Wednesday, right after lunch. At first Mrs. Blynders allowed us to sing naturally. We had an ear for music, she informed us, and almost perfect pitch. She seemed quite pleased. As was the custom in most Mexican families, one or more members played the guitar and sang. In our family everyone sang except the dogs. My father and Norbert played guitar; Berney liked the harmonica, as did Tudi, Concha's brother. And Elvira's living room boasted a mahogany piano played by an elderly aunt.

But Mrs. Blynders wanted us, her star pupils, to learn to sing the proper way. Forehead creased in concentration, she flipped through old music books, humming each song to herself, testing to see if it was worthy of our musical talents. She insisted that we pay attention to the signature note and to learn the words said to be Italian, but which sounded Spanish: *allegretto, forte,* and *crescendo.* But for the first few weeks, we sang as we always had.

The day came when Mrs. Blynders, impatient with our progress, asked to see Mrs. Goodsome.

"The music books are falling apart and . . ."

"The other teachers haven't complained."

"But if only they could . . ."

"Very well. I'll see what I can do."

And then one fine day the books *We Sing* were delivered to our eager teacher, who immediately passed them out. The thick books full of new songs, musical notes, and brief lessons were our pride and joy. I quickly wrote my name inside the cover; at home I covered it with the paper from a grocery bag. *We Sing* was illustrated with numerous drawings and many, many lines and black musical notes that appeared to have Mickey Mouse ears. We memorized the different notes, which was easy; reading them was another thing. Mrs.

Blynders explained that notes were like money; each worth so many points, or pennies, then sat back to see what we came up with.

She first played a song, one bar at a time. Our voices soft and low, we followed along until it sounded perfect. When a complete line was memorized, we moved on to the next. She then split us into two groups: the "highs" sang soprano, or melody; the "lows" sang harmony, or what our parents called "segunda." Among my favorite songs was "The Scissors Grinder," sung in a round:

> *Poor scissors grinder,*
> *Poor scissors grinder,*
> *Artichokes, apples, bananas so sweet,*
> *All that they want to eat.*

Clever as we were, and eager to tease our new teacher, we improvised on the song:

> *Poor Mrs. Blynders,*
> *Poor Mrs. Blynders . . .*

She smiled and kept on playing, her blue-green eyes merry.

We later learned "The White Dove," which was sung in both English and Spanish. That too became a favorite.

> *Noche oscura, nada veo*
> *Solo llevo mi farol*
> *Por tus puertas, voy pasando*
> *Y cantando con amor*
>
> *Mas voy cantando, con ansia plena*
> *Quién compra mis tostaditas?*
> *Tortillas buenas . . .*

Our beloved teacher had ordered music books that included songs about Mexican life, in a language we were otherwise told not to use when in school. The choir's popularity grew; we were asked to sing at school assemblies and holiday programs. As I sang, my heart swelled with pride and love: pride for my school and love for our new teacher, who had in such a short time given us so much. When she later spoke of organizing a school festival, my esteem knew no bounds.

Early that spring Mrs. Blynders spoke about having a May Day Festival at our school, similar to those at schools where she had formerly taught. The program, she emphasized, would include songs, dances, and speeches. Once again she met with Mrs. Goodsome, who agreed to consider this new and exciting proposal. When a few weeks later Mrs. Blynders announced that permission had been granted for our school to celebrate May Day, our class was in a dither.

She rapped her desk for attention, stood tall, then asked for our undivided attention. Only Fat Lupe, who twitched in her seat, kept talking. The May Day Festival, she stressed, would include all grade levels. Kindergarten and lower-grade students would sing. The older students would help plan the program, select songs, and decorate the maypole. More importantly, all eighth-grade girls could, if they chose, enter the contest for Queen of the May. To us girls this was the most exciting news. A Queen contest! Wow!

And, Mrs. Blynders continued, all participants would get to wear long dresses and a crown of "garlands" (as she called flowers) in their hair. The eighth-grade boys would be asked to vote for their favorite girl to reign as queen. Upon hearing this, Concha said she had to go to the bathroom, then scurried out the door. Fat Lupe ran after her, needing water to quench a sudden thirst. This was by far the most exciting thing to happen at our school since the janitor set fire to a broom closet.

All the eighth-grade girls entered the contest; each of us yearned to be Queen of the May. In the following week, girls who lived on Hoyt Street were extra friendly with the neighborhood boys, even those they disliked. Jesús was seen walking home with two girls. During recess Nancy traded comic books with Mundo, while Fat Lupe sent Chito a note asking for his vote, and enclosed two shiny quarters. Not to be outdone, Virgie broke open her piggy bank to buy Milk Duds for Sandy. Only Concha was certain of Beto's vote; he alone proclaimed his vote far in advance.

All of the teachers, including Mrs. Blynders, then selected the boys

and girls who would participate in the maypole dance. I was thrilled
to be chosen and went to tell Concha my good news.

"I'm gonna be in the maypole dance."

"I am too, I think."

"And Virgie too! Gosh, we're all gonna get to dance."

During the next week those selected for the dance were excused
from regular recess to practice el baile. First the tetherball pole was
moved to the front lawn, then we were put through our paces. We
practiced to an imaginary beat and pulled at imaginary ribbons. We
swirled, turned, and pranced as Mrs. Blynders counted out: "and a
one, two, turn, three, bow. And a one, two, three, turn, and back to
your place."

The voting for the Queen of the May took place on the Monday
before the festival. Soon after lunch all the eighth-grade boys were
summoned to the auditorium, handed a slip of paper, and told to
write on it their choice for queen.

"Make sure to vote, uhhhh, write one name only," the teacher
cautioned, as she handed out pencils.

"How do ya spell Dominga?" asked a short boy, chewing on a
pencil stub.

While the boys voted, we tried to appear uninterested in the commotion near the auditorium. But within minutes Nancy swore she
had a stomachache; when sent to the nurse's office, she walked past
the group of boys, all of whom looked the other way. Concha was
given permission to return a book to the office, saying it was for
Mrs. Goodsome. I asked to go to the bathroom, then circled the
auditorium, but all I saw was the janitor weilding a broom.

All the next day the boys acted superior; even Sandy (whom everyone liked) snickered aloud during recess. They were using this occasion to get back at girls who had in the past been nasty to them.
Mundo said his vote went to his favorite movie star, la Lana Turner.
Willy Lopez cast his vote for Lassie, the dog from the movie, while
Petey said he had voted for Flicka, or whoever helped him with long
division.

The days dragged on; I could barely concentrate on my schoolwork. By Thursday most of the girls were back to their old ways: acting smart with the boys they disliked. On Friday morning right after

recess, the votes were counted. We waited for the general announcement, which was to be made by the principal on the front lawn.

At exactly three o'clock, Mrs. Goodsome, dressed in a light gray dress, walked out to the front of the main building. She instructed Mr. Putty, the janitor, to adjust the microphone, then stepped forward, holding a piece of paper in her hand. When she was unable to read the name, she looked around for her glasses, then realized she had left them in her office. While her secretary ran back for them, we waited in the hot sun, anxious to know who had been chosen queen. At long last she announced the winner: Magdalena, or Maggie, as she was usually called, was declared Queen of the May.

Maggie was a quiet, serious girl. Too quiet, I thought, but very, very pretty. And sweet. She was neither as tall as I nor as smart as Elvira, but the boys liked her. Even Chita and her cousin Della, who disliked anyone who found favor with teachers, said nothing when Maggie's name was announced. We crowded around the queen.

"Congratulations Magdalena!"

"I knew it was gonna be you!"

"Ya gonna wear a formal, Magdalena?"

I felt jealous and resentful, as did most of my friends, none of whom had slept for days. When my name was announced as one of two runners-up, I decided it was not a bad thing to be a princess.

Mrs. Blynders had described for us the May Day Festival at her last school and how the girls who participated in the maypole dance or were part of the queen's court were supposed to wear formal dresses. As the day for the festival approached, our happiness turned to panic. None of us owned a formal! While some girls still clung to their confirmation dresses, they no longer fit. And as Nancy said, who wants to wear a church dress to the festival? Not me! Nor Concha. Our panic, however, was short-lived, as most of our older sisters had, at one time or another, been either bridesmaids or brides. Surely a dress hanging idle in a closet could be lent to a younger sister? And so we plotted and begged.

Concha announced she would wear her sister Celina's white eyelet wedding dress (without the train and sleeves). Virgie sewed un olán, a ruffle, onto a pink peasant skirt that skimmed the floor. Nancy hinted of a trip to a Los Angeles bridal shop that specialized in long dresses, while shy Elvira said her mother would make her a red dress.

I was thrilled to discover I fit into Nora's cornflower-blue formal, a dress she had worn as a bridesmaid. It had a square neckline, puff sleeves, a fitted bodice, and a ruffle at the bottom. With it Nora had worn a large picture hat (what 1940s bridesmaids always wore) with a wide band and a velvet flower. I slipped on the dress, reduced the neckline with safety pins, then, stumbling over my large feet, I ran across the street to show Concha and Virgie, el Duque trailing behind.

"Gosh, you look so tall!"

"I know, but it's all we got."

Problems with the dress neck and hem persisted. Out came my mother's sewing basket. First I hiked up the waist, but the dress bunched up in the middle and made me look fat. The neck, cut in a deep square, was too wide and kept falling off my shoulders. Although I had used seguros while trying on the dress, I was not about to use safety pins for the May Day festival. Even among school-kids, that was considered muy ranchero. Finally I decided I could do one of two things: hike up the hem and sew darts on the bodice, or wear falsies and high heels! When no one offered to buy me high heels or agreed to let me borrow an old pair, I brought out the sewing basket and began to sew darts.

All the girls wanted to look grown-up. After all, we were about to graduate to high school. We aren't babies anymore, we argued, determined to look at least sixteen. The May Day Festival was the place to experiment. Not only with high heels and Maybelline, but with a bra, stockings, and a new hairdo.

More than anything, I was dying to wear a bra. A First Bra! Not all of us needed one; most girls were just developing, but this important event demanded we look our best. Glamorous! Still, for some well-developed girls, such as Lupe, wearing a bra was essential. Lupe hated recess and having to play baseball, because her breasts bobbed up and down when she ran. Once again Concha and I sought out our older sisters.

"Nora, do you have an old, uhhhh . . ."

"A what?

"You know, one of those things you wear on top?"

"A brassiere?"

"No, a bra."

Concha's sister gave Concha a faded pink bra that was hanging on the line. I waited until Nora was gone, then rummaged in her bottom drawer until I discovered an ivory lace bra that had seen better days. I quickly tried it on. It fit around my back, but flopped in front. I knew of ways to remedy that, however, and appear (as the movie magazines suggested) curvaceous. I ran to call Concha. We locked ourselves in the bathroom and stuffed Kleenex inside our bras. We used an entire box, but could not make both sides appear even.

"It itches."

"Put some more in the left one."

"They look too pointy. Squash em down like this, see?"

"Sí."

Tired of the whole thing, Concha and I dropped the box of Kleenex to concentrate on our hair.

By the eighth grade, we had grown tired of wearing checkered dresses and ribbons in our hair. We wanted to be glamorous, like the movie stars. While I yearned to be like Nora, on May Day I wanted my hair to look different, elegant, unlike Nora's hair, which fell straight and listless about her face. The black hair that sprang from my head like Moses's burning bush, drove me to despair.

The upcoming festival drove us crazy, especially when it came to hairdos. On Hoyt Street many girls still wore braids, trensas, to school. Others wore Shirley Temple curls and barrettes bought at the five and dime. But the eighth graders at Pacoima Elementary all wanted new hairdos for this occasion. Among older women (anyone over twenty-one), stiff ringlets, "upsweeps," and pompadours were the rage. Younger girls wore pageboys that flipped up and down when they walked. Trina and her teenage friends borrowed from both older and younger hair styles; they wore both ringlets and pageboys. But for schoolkids, there was little we could do with our hair, other than wear the dreaded Buster Brown bangs or experiment with wave set and bobby pins.

Days before the festival, in an effort to change how she looked, Concha ran to the Pacoima General Store to buy wire curlers. Nancy saturated her dark hair with the green slime called wave set, used by our sisters to keep their hair in place. Chita's sister, said to be una pachuca, lightened her hair with peroxide and henna.

Frantic with worry, I brushed my hair with a wire hairbrush usually used on Duke. I had first scrubbed the brush clean, then ran it through my hair. If Duke's curly pelt can be trained, I vowed, so can my hair. I wanted to wear my hair in a pageboy, as did Trina, who thought she was so big. And I swore not to let Elizabet talk me into Shirley Temple curls on that special day. They were much too childish!

We in the queen's court agreed to wear flowers in our hair at the May Day Festival. Ribbons and barrettes were for everyday; hats and veils for church. Flowers, though, were special and could be had from our own yards. Although I would have liked gardenias and orchids, I was limited to the daisies in our backyard; if I moved fast, I could snitch a posy from my mother's rosebush.

From the first I hinted about needing new shoes—white sandals or ankle straps—but no one paid any attention to me. When Nora was out, I ran into her room and squeezed my foot into her narrow shoes, but I couldn't walk in them. When it was clear that I would wear old shoes, I lowered the dress hem so that it swept the floor. The blue dress was sure to be long enough to hide my zapatos.

At last it was May Day! Overhead the California sky was blue and clear, except for fluffy white clouds flitting across the sky. I rose early, washed, then dressed. I brushed my hair until the tight curls, wound the night before, fell in deep waves. I locked myself in the bathroom, where I spread a layer of Pond's cream on my cheeks, then rubbed Tangee Peach lipstick on my cheeks as rouge. I slid my brother's hair pomade from a shelf and smoothed some on my eyelashes; I had read that this would make them long and luscious, almost like those of María Felix. Satisfied with how I looked (for the time being), I ran outdoors to where my mother's roses bloomed, still wet from the morning dew. I cut off the rose buds and picked some yellow daisies, then wound them with ribbon. These I set aside to wear as a corsage. I then twisted larger roses, ferns, and leaves to form a crown (after checking for thorns). Satisfied with my handiwork, I dashed indoors and once again locked myself in the bathroom.

I stood facing the bathroom mirror. I turned from one side to the other, trying to find my "best side" (as suggested in the movie magazines). I placed the crown of flowers on the curls that now sprang back with a vengeance. I poured wave set on my sweaty hands, spread it on my hair, and pressed down, but the stubborn curls refused to lie down. In desperation I clamped bobby-pins (snuck from Trina's drawer) onto my head, then split my crown of flowers into two bunches, one for each side. I secured them with long hairpins (taken from Elizabet's purse). At long last I felt ready, but as I went out the door, I tripped on my long dress. Down came the flowers. I began to cry, frustrated and angry with how my morning was going. Just then Ronnie (who was to accompany my mother to the festival) came to my rescue; expertly she attached the flowers to my hair. I gobbled some hot oatmeal and with a bite of toast still in my mouth, rushed out the door. I walked to school, the flounce on my blue dress flapping against my polished shoes.

I approached Pacoima Elementary school from el llano, the open field overgrown with moss-green grass. I took care not to stumble on rocks, but edged my way impatiently toward Van Nuys Boulevard, and on to Norris Street, anxious to get to class. Even from afar I sensed the excitement; the entire school was in an uproar. Kids dressed in their Sunday best ran every which way. Girls in long dresses and high-heeled shoes tottered to class. Although the last bell had already rung, everyone, including a frantic janitor, was still near the front gate. I joined my friends, eager to compare dresses, hairdos, and rouge.

At the far end of the yard stood Queen Magdalena, by far the prettiest girl present. She wore a mauve velvet dress with a sweetheart neckline and short sleeves. Down the bodice front was a row of tiny black bows. Her brown hair fell to her shoulders in waves; her brown eyes, devoid of Maybelline, shone with happiness. I strained to see what shoes Maggie was wearing.

Chita was unrecognizable. Her hair shone a bright copper, her hazle-brown eyes were thick with mascara; her full lips glistened with magenta lipstick. On her head she wore a small tiara. I hated her! Around her stood a circle of boys, waiting to try on the tiara, which I was certain had come from the five and dime.

"Hi 'Red,' Uhhhh, Chita."

"Gosh, you look como la Rita Hayworth!"

"Yeah?"

"Neh, como la Hedy Lamarr."

When the teacher took attendance, no one was absent! "Hooray for our class!" we cheered. We went through the motions of reading and working on fractions, itching for the bell to release us for the day's festivities.

The program went off without a hitch. Mrs. Goodsome welcomed the parents, among them my mother, Doña Luisa, and Ronnie, who, as always, looked very pretty. She wore a crisp black-and-white dress with a short peplum. On her head was a black straw hat with a cabbage rose that, on this glorious May afternoon, looked almost real. Alongside Ronnie, the other women, including my mother, looked elderly, dressed in their one good dress.

We stood for the "Pledge of Allegiance." The opening bars of "The Stars and Stripes Forever," played at all school functions on the dilapidated record player (set out earlier by Mr. Putty), filled the air. First the lower grades (kindergarten through third) performed a dance. They went around in circles to what sounded like "Three Blind Mice." They were followed by the girl's choir, led by Mrs. Blynders; we sang "The White Dove" and "The Scissors Grinder." Finally it was time for the crowning of the queen.

Sandy was the lucky boy selected to crown Queen Maggie. Of all the eighth-grade boys, he had the best manners. It was assumed that he would not botch up the job of crowning la reina. As an altar boy, Sandy had yet to drop a chalice or the sacred host. He too was dressed in his best clothes: a long-sleeved white shirt and dark pants. After another short speech from the principal, Sandy took the crown of "garlands" (made by Mrs. Blynders) and with a bow, placed it on Queen Magdalena's head. He then took his seat, his face flushed and happy. The crowd, with Mundo in the lead (unrecognizable in a new shirt and short hair), applauded. I clapped for Queen Maggie —and for Sandy.

The maypole dance followed. During the program I had stood with the queen's court, but once the music for the dance began, I prepared to do as instructed earlier: walk down the steps to the dancers below. I was anxious to join Concha and Virgie and others of my classmates, each of whom looked like royalty in their long dresses. But the hateful Chita was lying in wait.

From the moment the program began, Chita had begun to act tough. She pushed Fat Lupe off her seat and gave Nancy the finger: toma! Chita was neither a finalist in the queen contest, nor had she been selected to perform the maypole dance. She now sat near the dance area, resentful of the crowd that smiled at us while snapping Brownie cameras.

When the music began, I hitched up my dress, secured my flowers, then walked carefully down the steps toward the dancers, smiling at my friends, mother, and sister. As I moved toward the circle of dancers, Chita stuck out her foot and tripped me. I began to fall; the ruffle of my dress pulled taut and I could feel the flowers sliding off my head. I swerved but managed to stay on my feet; my bouquet fell to the ground. Just then Mr. Putty, busy adjusting the record player, turned and caught me. The music began once more, with Mr. Putty alert for mishaps. I quickly took my place, my face flushed with shame and embarrassment. Then I lost myself in the dance, trying to remember when to dip and when to loop the colored streamer over another dancer's head. This took concentration; Chita was soon forgotten.

We danced gloriously, gracefully swaying and dipping to the tune of the maypole dance. We neither missed a step nor a turn. In our pastel dresses and fresh flowers, we smiled at our siblings and parents. The colored streamers obeyed our command as we dipped and wove to make a braid, which we then uncoiled, all the while skipping and dancing around the flowered maypole. From her throne Queen Magdalena smiled at her subjects; from their chairs, our families and friends smiled their approval. In the front row, Mrs. Blynders called out: "And a one, two, three, turn."

Soon it was over. Mrs. Goodsome thanked our parents for having attended, Queen Maggie gave up her throne, and Mr. Putty dismantled the tetherball maypole. I lingered to gather the wilted flowers, then once more hitched up my pretty but cumbersome dress and left for home.

I walked home with Ronnie, who had remained to ensure that Chita would not trip me again. The day that had begun anxiously ended perfectly. That warm, wonderful day of the Pacoima Elementary May Day Festival.

It

I remember well my twelfth birthday, a cold Sunday in January. The icy wind that blew through the pepper trees and bedroom window had kept me awake most of the night. I felt sick; my head ached, my stomach hurt.

The day before, when we were dismissed from el catecismo, Virgie, Concha, and I rushed back to Don Jesús's store, anxious to sample los dulces, the Mexican candy only he sold. Virgie quickly found what she wanted: jelly beans, gumdrops, and cacahuates, peanuts in the shell, sold in tiny bags. Concha bought two pieces of calabasa, sweet pumpkin jelled into squares. I walked around the store, my shoes scraping against the wooden floor, but couldn't decide what it was I wanted. The pan I loved so much appeared dry, unappetizing. I wanted something different from the usual candy that stuck to the roof of my mouth and clung to my teeth, but all I saw were shelves of arroz, leche de bote, and dusty cans of Campbell's soup. I fingered ripe tomatoes and crispy green chiles nestled in crates near the entrance, and was about to pinch grapes from a tray, when I spotted the patas de cochi, pink pigs' feet swimming in a jar. The patas, including the hooves, were kept in a wide jar next to the cash register; their wrinkled skin shimmered in the brine. Pigs' feet, kids on Hoyt Street said, were a favorite of the winos who hung around the alley behind the store. Still they *were* different.

I turned the jar around as the piggy feet slapped against the glass, and pondered. Did I really want a pata? Should I spend my nickels on wino food? Hungry for something and eager to get home to my chores, I asked Virgie for my share of our bottle money, selected the biggest pata, paid, then ran out of the store. We walked back along the dusty path next to Doña Chonita's house. As I gnawed on the gristly skin, I smiled at Virgie, whose mouth was smeared with chocolate.

I pretended that the pig's foot was delicious, determined not to gag on the vinegar. Once at home I changed clothes, then went about my Saturday chores: washing out my underwear and cleaning the dining room chairs, both of which I hated. When I had finished with the loathsome jobs, I pulled back the cotton spread on my bed and lay down in the bedroom I shared with Trina.

I felt sick. My stomach was making funny noises. I could taste the vinegar, la pata. I began to moan and groan as I rubbed my stomach. Trina, busy plucking her eyebrows, became alarmed at my cries and ran to fetch Elizabet. The two of them stood in the hallway, dark heads pressed close, whispering in low, muted voices.

"Her stomach hurts . . ."

"Hmmm, well, she *is* twelve."

Elizabet went into the bathroom, then returned with a purple box, which she silently slid under my bed. She then filled the hot-water bottle from the kitchen faucet and gave it to me to press against my tender middle. She tiptoed out of the room, then softly closed the door. I lay in bed, pale and wan, waiting for It.

It seemed I had been waiting for It for so long! At least since the summer before, when Nancy got It and acted even more superior. Upon hearing Nancy's news, I moped around the house for days, feeling terribly juvenile and left out. Later that year, when Virgie, a smug look on her round face, announced she was now a señorita, I became even more depressed. It just wasn't fair! Morning, noon, and night, I checked my calzones, frantic to see signs of It. I was sorely disappointed not to find even a trace.

I still wore camisetas, undershirts that I couldn't wait to replace with lacy bras. I also hated the cotton slips with the tiny tucks in the front that looked so childish, infantile really. My itching breasts were beginning to push against my dresses. My clothes are all wrong, I grumbled to my mother, refusing to wear the prissy dresses with white collar and cuffs from the previous year. When Trina wasn't looking, I would squeeze into her clothes, feeling terribly grown-up; until the day when I burst the zipper of her favorite skirt. Determined to update my wardrobe, I took my mother's sewing basket and hid in the bathroom to hike up the hem of my favorite skirt. All in preparation for It.

I had a mustache, which I hated. I had hairy legs that I was not allowed to shave. Sometimes I could almost smell my sobacos, a smell I attributed to the scraggly armpit hairs I had recently sprouted. The long black hairs visible on my arms appeared longer each day; at times I wound them around a pencil. And hated it. I resorted to wearing long-sleeved dresses even on hot days. And hated that, too.

My curly, black hair was unmanageable; it surrounded my face like a dark juniper bush. On wet and rainy days it got frizzier and frizzier, so that it resembled Brillo Pads. But I detested the Shirley Temple curls that earlier were my trademark and refused to wear the common trensas that I associated with elementary kids. On school days an amused Elizabet secured my unruly hair with shiny barrettes bought in town, saying I looked fine. But once I was out the door, I yanked them off, stuck them in my pocket, then slipped a handful of bobby pins into place.

One March day while Mundo, Concha, and I were playing kickball, we needed a fourth player.

"Can Virgie come out?"

"No."

"Por qué?"

"Ummm, she's sort of sick . . ."

Virgie, I was told, could not play for at least three days; I immediately knew why. So did Mundo and Concha. Virgie had It! Later in our game I fell and scraped my knee; I stopped the blood with the hem of my dress, then ran home. When my mother saw the stains on my dress, she told me to go wait for her in the bathroom. Her face held a look of respect. Clearly she thought I had It.

When she realized I had only cut my knee, however, she scolded me por andar en la calle and for ruining a good dress. Doña Luisa, never too far from a crisis, cautioned me not to run around too much. "No es good for you," she said, her eyes troubled, "no es good." She then walked me to her house, stoked the wooden stove, and fed me warm milk and bread. Satiated with cinnamon toast, I sat back to wait for It.

That evening, when it was my turn to wash the supper dishes, I began to moan.

"My stomach hurts. Me duele el estógamo."

"Estómago. And do you feel dizzy too?"

"Sí."

I was excused from clearing the table, washing dishes, and sweeping the kitchen floor. Told to lie down in my bedroom with the hot-water bottle, I did just that.

Then Concha got It. And Josie too, followed by Terry, who was only eleven! Only I was left. I, the tallest girl in our class, had not gotten It! And then it was June, July. Childhood games of hide-and-seek bored me, as did bike rides down Hoyt Street. I now preferred to spend the afternoon beneath a cool pirul, my favorite pepper tree, to embroider flowers and birds on bleached sacking. I sat with my legs primly crossed, the skirt of my dress pulled low. Just in case It creeped up on me.

I began to stuff Kleenex inside my underwear, just in case It caught me unawares, until one day, while running across el llano, I dropped a batch.

My mustache grew darker. I sneaked Pancake Number 2 from Nora, wet a sponge, then smeared it across the offensive black veil, but it still showed. I then sought out la Nancy, who knew everything.

"I hate my bigote."

"Well bleach it! Como yo."

I ran to the store, bought the necessary supplies, then locked myself in the bathroom. In a small bowl I mixed peroxide and white henna, making sure to use a wooden spoon. I slathered the smelly potion on my upper lip, then (while Josey pounded on the bathroom door) washed off the dried powder and stared into the mirror. I was dismayed to see no immediate results. Within days, however, my moustache turned first a brownish-red and then a bright yellow.

Each month my legs got hairier and hairier. I dared not wear summer shorts, but began to borrow Norbert's Levis, making sure not to roll them past my calf. When I could stand it no longer, I waited for Berney to leave, then shaved my legs with his trusty Gillette razor, making sure I had first secured the bathroom door. I then spent hours applying alcohol and adhesive tape to the many cuts that decorated my legs. All the while I longed for It.

More than anything, though, I hated my hair. Nancy now sported un permanente that was the envy of the girls on Hoyt Street. Not to be outdone, Concha had her hair cut in cute bangs. Desperate to be rid of the curl and having read that braiding kinky hair made it straight, I began to braid my hair at night. Each morning I fought to be first in the bathroom. With mounting excitement I would unbraid my thick trensa, but my hair sprang out around my face like a dark bush again.

When school started in September of my twelfth year, I was sent to the nurse for a routine checkup. I was weighed and measured; my eyes, ears and throat checked, and my reflexes measured with a tap on the knee. The nurse then read my chart and asked if I had experienced any changes since school let out. It was disappointing to have nothing to report. Check!

And then a new girl came to our school. Her name was Barbara. I hated her because she had an American name, two dimples, and had already started It! I now hated anyone with dimples, too. I began to sleep with a pinto bean attached with surgical tape to each cheek, confident that in time I, too, would have dimples. When I swallowed a bean in my sleep and nearly gagged, I decided that dimples were not all that important. Certainly not as important as It.

During Christmas I stuffed myself with my mother's sugar tamales. I ate so much masa I got a stomach ache. Once more I was put to bed with the trusty water bottle. And then it was January again. I would soon be all of thirteen. A teenager! A tall teenager who still had not gotten It! I began to cross off each day on a calendar hidden from Trina's prying eyes. I waited until evening to make an X across the date; just in case It arrived during the day.

As my birthday approached, I began to panic. I begged Elizabet to take me to the doctor in San Fernando. "Something is wrong," I wailed, "somethings wrong with me!" But Elizabet only smiled and went about her business. In my bedroom I kicked the purple box against the wall. It had not helped me at all!

I dared not miss mass; I was diligent in taking Holy Communion. But I avoided sitting next to viejitas said to be "barren," thinking I might catch their disease. I made sure not to eat meat on Fridays, certain that God in all His glory would reward this sacrifice. I prayed to all the female saints to intercede with the Virgin Mary on my behalf. "Saint Teresa of Avila, please send It. Santa Cecilia, help me get over It. All ye holy saints in Heaven, tell God I can't live without It."

I feared living out my life as an old maid, relegated to dusting church pews and caring for plaster saints. A vestir santos. I could never marry without It, that much was certain. Nor could I have children! Only when a girl had gotten It could she have babies, as everyone on Hoyt Street already knew. And so I waited for God to send me a sign of It.

My thirteenth birthday came and went. I now stood at five feet five inches in my bare feet. I was taller than my sisters and mother; I towered over Doña Luisa and most of my friends. My green winter coat came to above my knees; the waist of my red jumper rode above my midriff. My shoe size jumped from six to seven to eight. This made my older sisters, all of whom wore size five and six shoes, smirk with satisfaction.

And then one day, as if by magic, my arms lost their hairy look. My yellow mustache grew out; the dark veil no longer was visible. My legs grew long and lean, with less and less hair. I threw out las camisetas and was bought a cotton bra. When my mother wasn't looking, I hiked up my skirt hems, then opened up the slits on each side. I lavished Palmolive soap on my face, then followed with Ponds Cream, for that seven-day complexion wonder. My thick hair fell across my shoulders in a wavy pageboy.

I studied movie magazines in search of my face type: Oval? Square? Heart-shaped? I experimented with tweezers and wound up with two bloody, crooked lines, which I filled in with an eyebrow pencil snitched from Nora. I bought a cheap lipbrush and replaced Tangee Natural with Tangee Fire Red. I bought a red plastic belt (size 22 waist) for $1.99, and inherited, from a reluctant Trina, my first pair of high heels, on which I tottered to church each Sunday.

And then finally I got It! I was on my way to the store, about to climb the fence that led to the alley, when I detected signs of It on my beige culottes. I straddled the fence, not knowing whether to jump over or slide down, in a ladylike manner. My tomboy days were clearly over. I disengaged my legs, smoothed down my pants, and walked home feeling dizzy, elated. At last! At last I was a bonafide teenager! I itched to blurt out my news to Nancy, Virgie, and Concha, but told only Elizabet, who once more brought out the purple box.

That balmy night as I lay in bed, the hot-water bottle secure against my belly, I flipped through the booklet in the purple box. I think it was entitled "What Every Teenage Girl Should Know." I memorized everything about fallopians, ovaries, and twenty-eight-day cycles. I snuggled under the covers, sipped té de canela, cinammon tea, said to be good for It. I touched myself down there, just to make sure I still had It, then turned over and went to sleep.

About the Author

Mary Helen Ponce is the author of two novels, *Taking Control* and *The Wedding,* and has published extensively in this country and in Latin America. She received her Ph.D. in American Studies from the University of New Mexico. The mother of four, she currently teaches literature and creative writing at the University of California, Santa Barbara.